Casenote® Legal Briefs

PROPERTY

Keyed to Courses Using

Dukeminier, Krier, Alexander, Schill, and Strahilevitz's
Property

Eighth Edition and Concise Edition

Wolters Kluwer
Law & Business

This publication is designed to provide accurate and authoritative information in regard to the subject matter covered. It is sold with the understanding that the publisher is not engaged in rendering legal, accounting, or other professional services. If legal advice or other expert assistance is required, the services of a competent professional person should be sought.

SUSTAINABLE FORESTRY INITIATIVE Certified Sourcing
www.sfiprogram.org
SFI-00756

About Wolters Kluwer Law & Business

Wolters Kluwer Law & Business is a leading global provider of intelligent information and digital solutions for legal and business professionals in key specialty areas, and respected educational resources for professors and law students. Wolters Kluwer Law & Business connects legal and business professionals as well as those in the education market with timely, specialized authoritative content and information-enabled solutions to support success through productivity, accuracy and mobility.

Serving customers worldwide, Wolters Kluwer Law & Business products include those under the Aspen Publishers, CCH, Kluwer Law International, Loislaw, ftwilliam.com and MediRegs family of products.

CCH products have been a trusted resource since 1913, and are highly regarded resources for legal, securities, antitrust and trade regulation, government contracting, banking, pension, payroll, employment and labor, and healthcare reimbursement and compliance professionals.

Aspen Publishers products provide essential information to attorneys, business professionals and law students. Written by preeminent authorities, the product line offers analytical and practical information in a range of specialty practice areas from securities law and intellectual property to mergers and acquisitions and pension/benefits. Aspen's trusted legal education resources provide professors and students with high-quality, up-to-date and effective resources for successful instruction and study in all areas of the law.

Kluwer Law International products provide the global business community with reliable international legal information in English. Legal practitioners, corporate counsel and business executives around the world rely on Kluwer Law journals, looseleafs, books, and electronic products for comprehensive information in many areas of international legal practice.

Loislaw is a comprehensive online legal research product providing legal content to law firm practitioners of various specializations. Loislaw provides attorneys with the ability to quickly and efficiently find the necessary legal information they need, when and where they need it, by facilitating access to primary law as well as state-specific law, records, forms and treatises.

ftwilliam.com offers employee benefits professionals the highest quality plan documents (retirement, welfare and non-qualified) and government forms (5500/PBGC, 1099 and IRS) software at highly competitive prices.

MediRegs products provide integrated health care compliance content and software solutions for professionals in healthcare, higher education and life sciences, including professionals in accounting, law and consulting.

Wolters Kluwer Law & Business, a division of Wolters Kluwer, is head-quartered in New York. Wolters Kluwer is a market-leading global information services company focused on professionals.

Format for the Casenote® Legal Brief

Nature of Case: This section identifies the form of action (e.g., breach of contract, negligence, battery), the type of proceeding (e.g., demurrer, appeal from trial court's jury instructions), or the relief sought (e.g., damages, injunction, criminal sanctions).

Fact Summary: This is included to refresh your memory and can be used as a quick reminder of the facts.

Rule of Law: Summarizes the general principle of law that the case illustrates. It may be used for instant recall of the court's holding and for classroom discussion or home review.

Facts: This section contains all relevant facts of the case, including the contentions of the parties and the lower court holdings. It is written in a logical order to give the student a clear understanding of the case. The plaintiff and defendant are identified by their proper names throughout and are always labeled with a (P) or (D).

Palsgraf v. Long Island R.R. Co.

Injured bystander (P) v. Railroad company (D)

N.Y. Ct. App., 248 N.Y. 339, 162 N.E. 99 (1928).

NATURE OF CASE: Appeal from judgment affirming verdict for plaintiff seeking damages for personal injury.

FACT SUMMARY: Helen Palsgraf (P) was injured on R.R.'s (D) train platform when R.R.'s (D) guard helped a passenger aboard a moving train, causing his package to fall on the tracks. The package contained fireworks which exploded, creating a shock that tipped a scale onto Palsgraf (P).

🏛 RULE OF LAW
The risk reasonably to be perceived defines the duty to be obeyed.

FACTS: Helen Palsgraf (P) purchased a ticket to Rockaway Beach from R.R. (D) and was waiting on the train platform. As she waited, two men ran to catch a train that was pulling out from the platform. The first man jumped aboard, but the second man, who appeared as if he might fall, was helped aboard by the guard on the train who had kept the door open so they could jump aboard. A guard on the platform also helped by pushing him onto the train. The man was carrying a package wrapped in newspaper. In the process, the man dropped his package, which fell on the tracks. The package contained fireworks and exploded. The shock of the explosion was apparently of great enough strength to tip over some scales at the other end of the platform, which fell on Palsgraf (P) and injured her. A jury awarded her damages, and R.R. (D) appealed.

ISSUE: Does the risk reasonably to be perceived define the duty to be obeyed?

HOLDING AND DECISION: (Cardozo, C.J.) Yes. The risk reasonably to be perceived defines the duty to be obeyed. If there is no foreseeable hazard to the injured party as the result of a seemingly innocent act, the act does not become a tort because it happened to be a wrong as to another. If the wrong was not willful, the plaintiff must show that the act as to her had such great and apparent possibilities of danger as to entitle her to protection. Negligence in the abstract is not enough upon which to base liability. Negligence is a relative concept, evolving out of the common law doctrine of trespass on the case. To establish liability, the defendant must owe a legal duty of reasonable care to the injured party. A cause of action in tort will lie where harm, though unintended, could have been averted or avoided by observance of such a duty. The scope of the duty is limited by the range of danger that a reasonable person could foresee. In this case, there was nothing to suggest from the appearance of the parcel or otherwise that the parcel contained fireworks. The guard could not reasonably have had any warning of a threat to Palsgraf (P), and R.R. (D) therefore cannot be held liable. Judgment is reversed in favor of R.R. (D).

DISSENT: (Andrews, J.) The concept that there is no negligence unless R.R. (D) owes a legal duty to take care as to Palsgraf (P) herself is too narrow. Everyone owes to the world at large the duty of refraining from those acts that may unreasonably threaten the safety of others. If the guard's action was negligent as to those nearby, it was also negligent as to those outside what might be termed the "danger zone." For Palsgraf (P) to recover, R.R.'s (D) negligence must have been the proximate cause of her injury, a question of fact for the jury.

▶ ANALYSIS
The majority defined the limit of the defendant's liability in terms of the danger that a reasonable person in defendant's situation would have perceived. The dissent argued that the limitation should not be placed on liability, but rather on damages. Judge Andrews suggested that only injuries that would not have happened but for R.R.'s (D) negligence should be compensable. Both the majority and dissent recognized the policy-driven need to limit liability for negligent acts, seeking, in the words of Judge Andrews, to define a framework "that will be practical and in keeping with the general understanding of mankind." The Restatement (Second) of Torts has accepted Judge Cardozo's view.

Quicknotes
FORESEEABILITY A reasonable expectation that change is the probable result of certain acts or omissions.

NEGLIGENCE Conduct falling below the standard of care that a reasonable person would demonstrate under similar conditions.

PROXIMATE CAUSE The natural sequence of events without which an injury would not have been sustained.

Party ID: Quick identification of the relationship between the parties.

Concurrence/Dissent: All concurrences and dissents are briefed whenever they are included by the casebook editor.

Analysis: This last paragraph gives you a broad understanding of where the case "fits in" with other cases in the section of the book and with the entire course. It is a hornbook-style discussion indicating whether the case is a majority or minority opinion and comparing the principal case with other cases in the casebook. It may also provide analysis from restatements, uniform codes, and law review articles. The analysis will prove to be invaluable to classroom discussion.

Issue: The issue is a concise question that brings out the essence of the opinion as it relates to the section of the casebook in which the case appears. Both substantive and procedural issues are included if relevant to the decision.

Holding and Decision: This section offers a clear and in-depth discussion of the rule of the case and the court's rationale. It is written in easy-to-understand language and answers the issue presented by applying the law to the facts of the case. When relevant, it includes a thorough discussion of the exceptions to the case as listed by the court, any major cites to the other cases on point, and the names of the judges who wrote the decisions.

Quicknotes: Conveniently defines legal terms found in the case and summarizes the nature of any statutes, codes, or rules referred to in the text.

Wolters Kluwer Law & Business is proud to offer *Casenote® Legal Briefs*—continuing thirty years of publishing America's best-selling legal briefs.

Casenote® Legal Briefs are designed to help you save time when briefing assigned cases. Organized under convenient headings, they show you how to abstract the basic facts and holdings from the text of the actual opinions handed down by the courts. Used as part of a rigorous study regimen, they can help you spend more time analyzing and critiquing points of law than on copying bits and pieces of judicial opinions into your notebook or outline.

Casenote® Legal Briefs should never be used as a substitute for assigned casebook readings. They work best when read as a follow-up to reviewing the underlying opinions themselves. Students who try to avoid reading and digesting the judicial opinions in their casebooks or online sources will end up shortchanging themselves in the long run. The ability to absorb, critique, and restate the dynamic and complex elements of case law decisions is crucial to your success in law school and beyond. It cannot be developed vicariously.

Casenote® Legal Briefs represents but one of the many offerings in Legal Education's Study Aid Timeline, which includes:

- *Casenote® Legal Briefs*
- *Emanuel® Law Outlines*
- Emanuel® *Law in a Flash* Flash Cards
- Emanuel® *CrunchTime®* Series
- *Siegel's Essay and Multiple-Choice Questions and Answers Series*

Each of these series is designed to provide you with easy-to-understand explanations of complex points of law. Each volume offers guidance on the principles of legal analysis and, consulted regularly, will hone your ability to spot relevant issues. We have titles that will help you prepare for class, prepare for your exams, and enhance your general comprehension of the law along the way.

To find out more about Wolters Kluwer Law & Business' study aid publications, visit us online at *www.wolterskluwerlb.com* or email us at *legaledu@wolterskluwer.com*. We'll be happy to assist you.

How to Brief a Case

A. Decide on a Format and Stick to It

Structure is essential to a good brief. It enables you to arrange systematically the related parts that are scattered throughout most cases, thus making manageable and understandable what might otherwise seem to be an endless and unfathomable sea of information. There are, of course, an unlimited number of formats that can be utilized. However, it is best to find one that suits your needs and stick to it. Consistency breeds both efficiency and the security that when called upon you will know where to look in your brief for the information you are asked to give.

Any format, as long as it presents the essential elements of a case in an organized fashion, can be used. Experience, however, has led *Casenote* ® *Legal Briefs* to develop and utilize the following format because of its logical flow and universal applicability.

NATURE OF CASE: This is a brief statement of the legal character and procedural status of the case (e.g., "Appeal of a burglary conviction").

There are many different alternatives open to a litigant dissatisfied with a court ruling. The key to determining which one has been used is to discover *who is asking this court for what.*

This first entry in the brief should be kept as *short as possible.* Use the court's terminology if you understand it. But since jurisdictions vary as to the titles of pleadings, the best entry is the one that addresses who wants what in this proceeding, not the one that sounds most like the court's language.

RULE OF LAW: A statement of the general principle of law that the case illustrates (e.g., "An acceptance that varies any term of the offer is considered a rejection and counteroffer").

Determining the rule of law of a case is a procedure similar to determining the issue of the case. Avoid being fooled by red herrings; there may be a few rules of law mentioned in the case excerpt, but usually only one is *the* rule with which the casebook editor is concerned. The techniques used to locate the issue, described below, may also be utilized to find the rule of law. Generally, your best guide is simply the chapter heading. It is a clue to the point the casebook editor seeks to make and should be kept in mind when reading every case in the respective section.

FACTS: A synopsis of only the essential facts of the case, i.e., those bearing upon or leading up to the issue.

The facts entry should be a short statement of the events and transactions that led one party to initiate legal proceedings against another in the first place. While some cases conveniently state the salient facts at the beginning of the decision, in other instances they will have to be culled from hiding places throughout the text, even from concurring and dissenting opinions. Some of the "facts" will often be in dispute and should be so noted. Conflicting evidence may be briefly pointed up. "Hard" facts must be included. Both must be *relevant* in order to be listed in the facts entry. It is impossible to tell what is relevant until the entire case is read, as the ultimate determination of the rights and liabilities of the parties may turn on something buried deep in the opinion.

Generally, the facts entry should not be longer than three to five *short* sentences.

It is often helpful to identify the role played by a party in a given context. For example, in a construction contract case the identification of a party as the "contractor" or "builder" alleviates the need to tell that that party was the one who was supposed to have built the house.

It is always helpful, and a good general practice, to identify the "plaintiff" and the "defendant." This may seem elementary and uncomplicated, but, especially in view of the creative editing practiced by some casebook editors, it is sometimes a difficult or even impossible task. Bear in mind that the *party presently* seeking something from this court may not be the plaintiff, and that sometimes only the cross-claim of a defendant is treated in the excerpt. Confusing or misaligning the parties can ruin your analysis and understanding of the case.

ISSUE: A statement of the general legal question answered by or illustrated in the case. For clarity, the issue is best put in the form of a question capable of a "yes" or "no" answer. In reality, the issue is simply the Rule of Law put in the form of a question (e.g., "May an offer be accepted by performance?").

The major problem presented in discerning what is *the* issue in the case is that an opinion usually purports to raise and answer several questions. However, except for rare cases, only one such question is really the issue in the case. Collateral issues not necessary to the resolution of the matter in controversy are handled by the court by language known as *"obiter dictum"* or merely *"dictum."* While dicta may be included later in the brief, they have no place under the issue heading.

To find the issue, ask *who wants what* and then go on to ask *why did that party succeed or fail in getting it.* Once this is determined, the "why" should be turned into a question.

The complexity of the issues in the cases will vary, but in all cases a single-sentence question should sum up the issue. *In a few cases,* there will be two, or even more rarely, three issues of equal importance to the resolution of the case. Each should be expressed in a single-sentence question.

Since many issues are resolved by a court in coming to a final disposition of a case, the casebook editor will reproduce the portion of the opinion containing the issue or issues most relevant to the area of law under scrutiny. A noted law professor gave this advice: "Close the book; look at the title on the cover." Chances are, if it is Property, you need not concern yourself with whether, for example, the federal government's treatment of the plaintiff's land really raises a federal question sufficient to support jurisdiction on this ground in federal court.

The same rule applies to chapter headings designating sub-areas within the subjects. They tip you off as to what the text is designed to teach. The cases are arranged in a casebook to show a progression or development of the law, so that the preceding cases may also help.

It is also most important to remember to *read the notes and questions* at the end of a case to determine what the editors wanted you to have gleaned from it.

HOLDING AND DECISION: This section should succinctly explain the rationale of the court in arriving at its decision. In capsulizing the "reasoning" of the court, it should always include an application of the general rule or rules of law to the specific facts of the case. Hidden justifications come to light in this entry: the reasons for the state of the law, the public policies, the biases and prejudices, those considerations that influence the justices' thinking and, ultimately, the outcome of the case. At the end, there should be a short indication of the disposition or procedural resolution of the case (e.g., "Decision of the trial court for Mr. Smith (P) reversed").

The foregoing format is designed to help you "digest" the reams of case material with which you will be faced in your law school career. Once mastered by practice, it will place at your fingertips the information the authors of your casebooks have sought to impart to you in case-by-case illustration and analysis.

B. Be as Economical as Possible in Briefing Cases

Once armed with a format that encourages succinctness, it is as important to be economical with regard to the time spent on the actual reading of the case as it is to be economical in the writing of the brief itself. This does not mean "skimming" a case. Rather, it means reading the case with an "eye" trained to recognize into which "section" of your brief a particular passage or line fits and having a system for quickly and precisely marking the case so that the passages fitting any one particular part of

the brief can be easily identified and brought together in a concise and accurate manner when the brief is actually written.

It is of no use to simply repeat everything in the opinion of the court; record only enough information to trigger your recollection of what the court said. Nevertheless, an accurate statement of the "law of the case," i.e., the legal principle applied to the facts, is absolutely essential to class preparation and to learning the law under the case method.

To that end, it is important to develop a "shorthand" that you can use to make marginal notations. These notations will tell you at a glance in which section of the brief you will be placing that particular passage or portion of the opinion.

Some students prefer to underline all the salient portions of the opinion (with a pencil or colored underliner marker), making marginal notations as they go along. Others prefer the color-coded method of underlining, utilizing different colors of markers to underline the salient portions of the case, each separate color being used to represent a different section of the brief. For example, blue underlining could be used for passages relating to the rule of law, yellow for those relating to the issue, and green for those relating to the holding and decision, etc. While it has its advocates, the color-coded method can be confusing and time-consuming (all that time spent on changing colored markers). Furthermore, it can interfere with the continuity and concentration many students deem essential to the reading of a case for maximum comprehension. In the end, however, it is a matter of personal preference and style. Just remember, whatever method you use, underlining must be used sparingly or its value is lost.

If you take the marginal notation route, an efficient and easy method is to go along underlining the key portions of the case and placing in the margin alongside them the following "markers" to indicate where a particular passage or line "belongs" in the brief you will write:

N   (NATURE OF CASE)
RL   (RULE OF LAW)
I   (ISSUE)
HL   (HOLDING AND DECISION, relates to the RULE OF LAW behind the decision)
HR   (HOLDING AND DECISION, gives the RATIONALE or reasoning behind the decision)
HA   (HOLDING AND DECISION, applies the general principle(s) of law to the facts of the case to arrive at the decision)

Remember that a particular passage may well contain information necessary to more than one part of your brief, in which case you simply note that in the margin. If you are using the color-coded underlining method instead of marginal notation, simply make asterisks or checks in the margin next to the passage in question in the colors that indicate the additional sections of the brief where it might be utilized.

The economy of utilizing "shorthand" in marking cases for briefing can be maintained in the actual brief writing process itself by utilizing "law student shorthand" within the brief. There are many commonly used words and phrases for which abbreviations can be substituted in your briefs (and in your class notes also). You can develop abbreviations that are personal to you and which will save you a lot of time. A reference list of briefing abbreviations can be found on page x of this book.

C. Use Both the Briefing Process and the Brief as a Learning Tool

Now that you have a format and the tools for briefing cases efficiently, the most important thing is to make the time spent in briefing profitable to you and to make the most advantageous use of the briefs you create. Of course, the briefs are invaluable for classroom reference when you are called upon to explain or analyze a particular case. However, they are also useful in reviewing for exams. A quick glance at the fact summary should bring the case to mind, and a rereading of the rule of law should enable you to go over the underlying legal concept in your mind, how it was applied in that particular case, and how it might apply in other factual settings.

As to the value to be derived from engaging in the briefing process itself, there is an immediate benefit that arises from being forced to sift through the essential facts and reasoning from the court's opinion and to succinctly express them in your own words in your brief. The process ensures that you understand the case and the point that it illustrates, and that means you will be ready to absorb further analysis and information brought forth in class. It also ensures you will have something to say when called upon in class. The briefing process helps develop a mental agility for getting to the *gist* of a case and for identifying, expounding on, and applying the legal concepts and issues found there. The briefing process is the mental process on which you must rely in taking law school examinations; it is also the mental process upon which a lawyer relies in serving his clients and in making his living.

Abbreviations for Briefs

acceptance	acp	offer	O
affirmed	aff	offeree	OE
answer	ans	offeror	OR
assumption of risk	a/r	ordinance	ord
attorney	atty	pain and suffering	p/s
beyond a reasonable doubt	b/r/d	parol evidence	p/e
bona fide purchaser	BFP	plaintiff	P
breach of contract	br/k	prima facie	p/f
cause of action	c/a	probable cause	p/c
common law	c/l	proximate cause	px/c
Constitution	Con	real property	r/p
constitutional	con	reasonable doubt	r/d
contract	K	reasonable man	r/m
contributory negligence	c/n	rebuttable presumption	rb/p
cross	x	remanded	rem
cross-complaint	x/c	res ipsa loquitur	RIL
cross-examination	x/ex	respondeat superior	r/s
cruel and unusual punishment	c/u/p	Restatement	RS
defendant	D	reversed	rev
dismissed	dis	Rule Against Perpetuities	RAP
double jeopardy	d/j	search and seizure	s/s
due process	d/p	search warrant	s/w
equal protection	e/p	self-defense	s/d
equity	eq	specific performance	s/p
evidence	ev	statute	S
exclude	exc	statute of frauds	S/F
exclusionary rule	exc/r	statute of limitations	S/L
felony	f/n	summary judgment	s/j
freedom of speech	f/s	tenancy at will	t/w
good faith	g/f	tenancy in common	t/c
habeas corpus	h/c	tenant	t
hearsay	hr	third party	TP
husband	H	third party beneficiary	TPB
injunction	inj	transferred intent	TI
in loco parentis	ILP	unconscionable	uncon
inter vivos	I/v	unconstitutional	unconst
joint tenancy	j/t	undue influence	u/e
judgment	judgt	Uniform Commercial Code	UCC
jurisdiction	jur	unilateral	uni
last clear chance	LCC	vendee	VE
long-arm statute	LAS	vendor	VR
majority view	maj	versus	v
meeting of minds	MOM	void for vagueness	VFV
minority view	min	weight of authority	w/a
Miranda rule	Mir/r	weight of the evidence	w/e
Miranda warnings	Mir/w	wife	W
negligence	neg	with	w/
notice	ntc	within	w/i
nuisance	nus	without	w/o
obligation	ob	without prejudice	w/o/p
obscene	obs	wrongful death	wr/d

Table of Cases I

(If you are using the Eighth Edition of the casebook, use this Table of Cases. If you are using the Concise Edition, use Table of Cases II on page xiii.)

40 West 67th Street Corp. v. Pullman............ *143*

A Anderson v. City of Issaquah..................... *151*
Armory v. Delamirie................................. *28*

B Baker v. Weedon *43*
Bean v. Walker...................................... *99*
Berg v. Wiley.. *69*
Board of Education of Minneapolis v.
   Hughes *105*
Boomer v. Atlantic Cement Co. *118*
Broadway National Bank v. Adams................. *48*
Brown v. Lober *88*
Brown v. Voss *131*

C Chicago Board of Realtors, Inc. v. City
   of Chicago *73*
City of Edmonds, v. Oxford House, Inc. *157*
City of Ladue v. Gilleo *152*
Commonwealth v. Fremont Investment & Loan *95*

D Daniels v. Anderson *107*
Delfino v. Vealencis................................ *54*
Diamond v. Chakrabarty........................... *17*
Dolan v. City of Tigard............................ *176*

E Elkus v. Elkus *60*
Ernst v. Conditt *67*
Estancias Dallas Corp. v. Schultz *117*
Eyerman v. Mercantile Trust Co. *25*

F Feist Publications v. Rural Telephone Service *13*
Fisher v. Giuliani *154*
Frimberger v. Anzellotti *89*

G Garner v. Gerrish *65*
Ghen v. Rich.. *5*
Gruen v. Gruen *39*
Guillette v. Daly Dry Wall, Inc. *106*
Guru Nanak Sikh Society of Yuba City v.
   County of Sutter *153*

H Hadacheck v. Sebastian *163*
Hannah v. Peel..................................... *29*
Hannan v. Dusch *66*
Harms v. Sprague................................... *53*
Harper v. Paradise *109*
Harper & Row Publishers, Inc. v. Nation
   Enterprises..................................... *15*
Hawkins v. Mahoney *24*
Hickey v. Green..................................... *79*
Hilder v. St. Peter *72*
Holbrook v. Taylor *125*
Howard v. Kunto.................................... *36*

I Ink v. City of Canton................................ *46*
International News Service v. Associated Press..... *11*

J Johnson v. Davis.................................... *82*
Johnson v. M'Intosh *3*
Jones v. Lee *84*

K Keeble v. Hickeringill *6*
Kelo v. City of New London....................... *160*
Kendall v. Ernest Pestana, Inc. *68*
Koontz v. St. Johns River Water Management
   District *178*
Kutzin v. Pirnie *86*

L Lempke v. Dagenais................................ *83*
Lewis v. Superior Court............................ *108*
Licari v. Blackwelder.............................. *77*
Lick Mill Creek Apartments v. Chicago Title
   Insurance Co. *113*
Lohmeyer v. Bower................................. *80*
Loretto v. Teleprompter Manhattan CATV Corp. ... *162*
Lucas v. South Carolina Coastal Council *166*
Luthi v. Evans..................................... *102*

M Mahrenholz v. County Board of School Trustees ... *44*
Mannillo v. Gorski................................. *35*
Marriage of Graham, In re......................... *59*
Matthews v. Bay Head Improvement Association... *129*
McAvoy v. Medina *33*
Messersmith v. Smith............................. *104*
Miller v. Lutheran Conference & Camp
   Association..................................... *130*
Moore v. Regents of the University of California.... *21*
Morgan v. High Penn Oil Co. *116*
Mountain Brow Lodge No. 82, Independent
   Order of Odd Fellows v. Toscano *45*
Murphy v. Fin. Dev. Corp. *94*

N Nahrstedt v. Lakeside Village Condominium
   Association, Inc. *141*
Neponsit Property Owners' Association, Inc. v.
   Emigrant Industrial Savings Bank.............. *136*
Newman v. Bost.................................... *38*
Nollan v. California Coastal Commission.......... *175*

O O'Keeffe v. Snyder................................ *37*
Orr v. Byers.. *103*
Othen v. Rosier *128*

P PA Northwestern Distributors, Inc. v. Zoning
   Hearing Board *148*
Palazzolo v. Rhode Island........................ *168*
Penn Central Transportation Company v. City
   of New York.................................... *165*

Pennsylvania Coal Co. v. Mahon *164*
Pierson v. Post.. *4*
Pocono Springs Civic Association, Inc. v.
    MacKenzie....................................... *23*
Preseault v. United States *132*

R Rick v. West *140*
Riddle v. Harmon *52*
Rockafellor v. Gray.................................... *91*
Rosengrant v. Rosengrant............................ *93*

S Sanborn v. McLean.............................. *135*
Sawada v. Endo....................................... *58*
Shelley v. Kraemer................................... *138*
Sommer v. Kridel *70*
Southern Burlington County NAACP v. Township
    of Mount Laurel *158*
Spiller v. Mackereth *55*
Spur Industries, Inc. v. Del E. Webb
    Development Co. *119*
Stambovsky v. Ackley................................ *81*
State ex rel. Stoyanoff v. Berkeley................ *150*
Stop the Beach Renourishment, Inc. v. Florida
    Department of Environmental Protection *172*
Swartzbaugh v. Sampson........................... *56*

Sweeney v. Sweeney *92*
Symphony Space, Inc., The v. Pergola
    Properties, Inc. *49*

T Tahoe-Sierra Preservation Council, Inc. v. Tahoe
    Regional Planning Agency...................... *170*
Tulk v. Moxhay *133*

U U.S. Bank Natl. Assn. v. Ibanez *97*

V Van Sandt v. Royster *126*
Van Valkenburgh v. Lutz............................. *34*
Varnum v. Brien....................................... *61*
Village Commons, LLC v. Marion County
    Prosecutor's Office................................. *71*
Village of Belle Terre v. Boraas................... *156*
Village of Euclid v. Amber Realty Co. *146*

W Waldorff Insurance & Bonding, Inc. v. Eglin
    National Bank..................................... *110*
Walker Rogge, Inc. v. Chelsea Title &
    Guaranty Co. *111*
Western Land Co. v. Truskolaski *139*
White v. Brown *42*
White v. Samsung Electronics America, Inc. *19*
Willard v. First Church of Christ, Scientist......... *123*

Table of Cases II

(If you are using the Concise Edition, use this Table of Cases. If you are using the Eighth Edition, use Table of Cases I on pages xi.)

A Armory v. Delamirie 28

B Berg v. Wiley 69
Board of Education of Minneapolis v. Hughes 105
Boomer v. Atlantic Cement Co. 118
Brown v. Lober 88
Brown v. Voss 131

C City of Edmonds, v. Oxford House, Inc. 157
Commonwealth v. Fremont Investment & Loan 95

D Delfino v. Vealencis 54
Diamond v. Chakrabarty 17

E Ernst v. Conditt 67

F Feist Publications, Inc. v. Rural Telephone
Service Co. 13
Fulkerson v. Van Buren 30

G Gruen v. Gruen 39
Guillette v. Daly Dry Wall, Inc. 106

H Hannah v. Peel 29
Harms v. Sprague 53
Harper & Row Publishers, Inc. v. Nation
Enterprises 15
Hickey v. Green 79
Hilder v. St. Peter 72
Hollander v. World Mission Church of
Washington, D.C. 32
Howard v. Kunto 36

I International News Service v. Associated Press 11

J Jacque v. Steenberg Homes, Inc. 9
Johnson v. Davis 82
Johnson v. M'Intosh 3
Jones v. Lee 84

K Kajo Church Square, Inc. v. Walker 64
Keeble v. Hickeringill 6
Kelo v. City of New London 160
Kendall v. Ernest Pestana, Inc. 68
Kienzle v. Myers 124
Kutzin v. Pirnie 86

L Lewis v. Superior Court 108
Lick Mill Creek Apartments v. Chicago Title
Insurance Co. 113
Lohmeyer v. Bower 80
Loretto v. Teleprompter Manhattan
CATV Corp. 162
Lucas v. South Carolina Coastal Council 166
Luthi v. Evans 102

M Mahrenholz v. County Board of School Trustees ... 44

Martin Luther King, Jr. Center for Social Change,
Inc. v. American Heritage Products, Inc. 12
Messersmith v. Smith 104
Moore v. Regents of the University of California 21
Morgan v. High Penn Oil Co. 116
Murphy v. Fin. Dev. Corp. 94

N Nahrstedt v. Lakeside Village Condominium
Association, Inc. 141
Newman v. Bost 38

O O'Keeffe v. Snyder 37
Orr v. Byers 103
Othen v. Rosier 128

P PA Northwestern Distributors, Inc. v. Zoning
Hearing Board 148
Penn Central Transportation Company v. City
of New York 165
Pennsylvania Coal Co. v. Mahon 164
Pierson v. Post 4
Popov v. Hayashi 7
Preseault v. United States 132

Q Qualitex Co. v. Jacobson Products Co., Inc. 22

R River Heights Associates L.P. v. Batten 134

S Sawada v. Endo 58
Sommer v. Kridel 70
Southern Burlington County NAACP v.
Township of Mount Laurel 158
Spiller v. Mackereth 55
Stambovsky v. Ackley 81
State v. Shack 10
State ex rel. Stoyanoff v. Berkeley 150
Stop the Beach Renourishment, Inc. v. Florida
Department of Environmental Protection 172
Sweeney v. Sweeney 92

T Tulk v. Moxhay 133

U U.S. Bank Natl. Assn. v. Ibanez 97

V Van Sandt v. Royster 126
Varnum v. Brien 61
Village Commons, LLC v. Marion County
Prosecutor's Office 71
Village of Euclid v. Amber Realty Co. 146

W Waldorff Insurance & Bonding, Inc. v. Eglin
National Bank 110
Walker Rogge, Inc. v. Chelsea Title &
Guaranty Co. 111
White v. Brown 42
Willard v. First Church of Christ, Scientist 123

First in Time: Acquisition of Property by Discovery, Capture, and Creation

Quick Reference Rules of Law

PAGE

1. *Johnson v. M'Intosh.* The discovery of the Native American-occupied lands of this nation vested absolute title in the discoverers, and rendered the Native American inhabitants themselves incapable of transferring absolute title to others. 3

2. *Pierson v. Post.* Property in wild animals is only acquired by occupancy, and pursuit alone does not constitute occupancy or vest any right in the pursuer. 4

3. *Ghen v. Rich.* When all that is practicable in order to secure a wild animal is done, it becomes the property of the securer who has thus exercised sufficient personal control over the wild animal. 5

4. *Keeble v. Hickeringill.* Damages may be recovered for the intentional frightening of game off another's land. 6

5. *Popov v. Hayashi.* Where an actor undertakes significant but incomplete steps to achieve possession of a piece of abandoned personal property and the effort is interrupted by the unlawful acts of others, the actor has a legally cognizable pre-possessory interest in the property sufficient to support a claim of conversion. 7

6. *Jacque v. Steenberg Homes, Inc.* When nominal damages are awarded for an intentional trespass to land, punitive damages may also be awarded at the jury's discretion. 9

7. *State v. Shack.* Real property rights are not absolute; and "necessity, private or public, may justify entry upon the lands of another." 10

8. *International News Service v. Associated Press.* Publication for profit of news obtained from other news-gathering enterprises is a misappropriation of a property right. 11

9. *Martin Luther King, Jr. Center for Social Change, Inc. v. American Heritage Products, Inc.* Public figures have a right of publicity that survives the death of the figure, and thus is inheritable and devisable, the measure of damages for violation of which is the value of the appropriation to the user. 12

10. *Feist Publications, Inc. v. Rural Telephone Service Co.* To be copyrightable, a work must be original and possess at least some minimal degree of creativity. 13

11. *Harper & Row Publishers, Inc. v. Nation Enterprises.* The Copyright Act, Section 106, provides a copyright owner with the right to control the first public distribution of an authorized version of the work. 15

12. *Diamond v. Chakrabarty.* A mirco-organism that is not naturally occurring and is the product of manufacture is patentable subject matter. 17

13. *White v. Samsung Electronics America, Inc.* The right of publicity protects a celebrity's property interest in his or her identity from commercial exploitation, regardless of the method by which it is appropriated. 19

14. *Moore v. Regents of the University of California.* A person whose tissue is used for profitable research and development without his knowledge may not maintain a conversion action therefor. 21

15. *Qualitex Co. v. Jacobson Products Co., Inc.* Color alone may be registered as a trademark. 22

16. *Pocono Springs Civic Association, Inc. v. MacKenzie.* A landowner cannot abandon property to which he holds perfect title. 23

17. *Hawkins v. Mahoney.* Abandoned personal property may be appropriated by anyone with the intent to acquire title to the property, unless such property has been reclaimed by the former owner. 24

18. *Eyerman v. Mercantile Trust Co.* Because the taking of property by inheritance is not a natural right but one created by the state, the state may modify, add conditions, or prohibit testamentary orders or bequests if they are found to be against public policy. 25

Johnson v. M'Intosh

Successor to Indian title (P) v. Subsequent purchaser (D)

21 U.S. (8 Wheat.) 543 (1823).

NATURE OF CASE: Appeal in an action to determine title to land.

FACT SUMMARY: Johnson (P) claimed valid title to land granted him by the chiefs of certain Native American tribes.

🏛 RULE OF LAW
The discovery of the Native American-occupied lands of this nation vested absolute title in the discoverers, and rendered the Native American inhabitants themselves incapable of transferring absolute title to others.

FACTS: Johnson (P) claimed valid title to land by reason of two grants, purportedly made, in 1773 and 1775 respectively, by the chiefs of certain Native American tribes. The proofs showed that the chiefs executing the conveyances had the authority to do so, and that the tribes were in rightful possession of the lands they sold. Nevertheless, the trial court denied the power of the Native American to convey such lands since, although they had retained title to the land's occupancy, they nevertheless remained incapable of transferring absolute title to others. Johnson (P) appealed.

ISSUE: Do the Native American tribes have the power of conveying absolute title of their lands to others?

HOLDING AND DECISION: (Marshall, C.J.) No. The discovery of the Native American-occupied lands of this nation vested absolute title in the discoverers; and while the Native American inhabitants retained title of occupancy, they were nevertheless incapable of transferring absolute title to others. As the result, this title claimed by Johnson (P) cannot be recognized by the U.S. courts. The very history of America, from its discovery to the present, demonstrates this principle. For example, when the English discoverers first acquired territory on this continent, they assumed title to the lands despite their admitted possession by the natives. While still under Native American occupation, these lands and waters were conveyed to others by the English monarch. These extensive grants cannot be regarded as nullities. That this principle has been ever recognized is seen in the history of wars, negotiations, and treaties. In fact, all the nations of Europe who have acquired territory on this continent have recognized the principle. The validity of these titles has never been questioned by the courts. Finally, an absolute title cannot exist at the same time in different governments over the same land. It would be incompatible to vest absolute title in the Indians as a distinct nation and country. Therefore, they are regarded as merely occupants, to be protected while at peace but to be deemed incapable of transferring absolute title to others. Affirmed, with costs.

▶ ANALYSIS

As reflected in the case of *Tee-Hit-Ton Indians v. United States*, 348 U.S. 272 (1955), the courts have generally followed the principal case and denied Native American land titles. However, Congress has followed a fairly consistent policy of making voluntary payments to the Native Americans. See Cohen, "Original Indian Title," 32 *Minn. L. Rev.* 28 (1947). In his conclusion, Mr. Cohen said: "The notion that America was stolen from the Indians is one of the myths by which we Americans are prone to hide our real virtues and make our idealism look as hard-boiled as possible." The story, nevertheless, is not pleasant.

■■■

Quicknotes

ABSOLUTE TITLE Exclusive title to land.

RIGHT OF DOMINION Possessing both title and ownership of property and having total power over its distribution.

■■■

Pierson v. Post

Fox killer (D) v. Fox hunter (P)

N.Y. Sup. Ct., 3 Cai. R. 175, 2 Am. Dec. 264 (1805).

NATURE OF CASE: Action of trespass on the case.

FACT SUMMARY: Post (P) was hunting a fox. Pierson (D), knowing this, killed the fox and carried it off.

🏛 RULE OF LAW
Property in wild animals is only acquired by occupancy, and pursuit alone does not constitute occupancy or vest any right in the pursuer.

FACTS: Post (P) found a fox upon certain wild, uninhabited, unpossessed waste land. He and his dogs began hunting and pursuing the fox. Knowing that the fox was being hunted by Post (P) and within Post's (P) view, Pierson (D) killed the fox and carried it off.

ISSUE: Has a person in pursuit of a wild animal acquired such a right to or property in the wild animal as to sustain an action against a person who kills and carries away the animal, knowing of the former's pursuit?

HOLDING AND DECISION: (Tompkins, J.) No. Property in wild animals is acquired by occupancy only. Mere pursuit vests no right in the pursuer. One authority holds that actual bodily seizure is not always necessary to constitute possession of wild animals. The mortal wounding of an animal or the trapping or intercepting of animals so as to deprive them of their natural liberty will constitute occupancy. However, here, Post (P) only shows pursuit. Hence there was no occupancy or legal right vested in Post (P) and the fox became Pierson's (D) property when he killed and carried it off. The purpose of this rule is that if the pursuit of animals without wounding them or restricting their liberty were held to constitute a basis for an action against others for intercepting and killing the animals, "it would prove a fertile source of quarrels and litigation." Reversed.

DISSENT: (Livingston, J.) A new rule should be adopted: that property in wild animals may be acquired without bodily touch, provided the pursuer be in reach or have a reasonable prospect of taking the animals.

▌ ANALYSIS

The ownership of wild animals is in the state for the benefit of all her people. A private person cannot acquire exclusive rights to a wild animal except by taking and reducing it to actual possession in a lawful manner or by a grant from the government. After the animal has been lawfully subjected to control, the ownership becomes absolute as long as the restraint lasts. Mere ownership of the land that an animal happens to be on does not constitute such a reduction of possession as to give the landowner a property right in the animal, except as against a mere trespasser who goes on such land for the purpose of taking the animal.

■=■

Quicknotes

SEIZURE The removal of property from one's possession due to unlawful activity or in satisfaction of a judgment entered by the court.

TRESPASS ON THE CASE Action at common law in early England granting a remedy to a person who sustains injury to his person or property as a result of the defendant's conduct.

■=■

Ghen v. Rich

Whaling ship owner (P) v. Whale purchaser (D)

8 F. 159 (D. Mass. 1881).

NATURE OF CASE: Admiralty action to recover the value of a whale.

FACT SUMMARY: Rich (D) purchased a whale at auction from a man who found it washed up on the beach. The whale had been killed at sea by the crew of Ghen's (P) whaling ship which left Ghen's (P) identifying bomb-lance in the animal.

> 🏛 **RULE OF LAW**
> When all that is practicable in order to secure a wild animal is done, it becomes the property of the securer who has thus exercised sufficient personal control over the wild animal.

FACTS: Because of the problems involved in capturing whales for commercial use in nineteenth-century New England, a trade usage arose as follows: when the crew of a whaling ship killed a whale using its identifying bomb-lance, the ship's owner by custom was considered to be the owner of that whale. When the whale washed ashore, the finder could identify the owner by the bomb-lance and would send notice of the find to the whaling center, Provincetown, Massachusetts. The finder would be paid a reasonable salvage fee. In this case, Ellis, the finder, did not notify Provincetown, but sold the whale at auction where Rich (D) purchased it. Rich (D) removed the blubber, which he had processed into oil. Ghen (P) claimed to be the owner of the whale under the trade usage and sued Rich (D) for the value of the whale.

ISSUE: By the trade usage, was the whale placed under sufficient control by the capturing whaler so that it became his property?

HOLDING AND DECISION: (Nelson, J.) Yes. Ghen (P), through the use of the identifying bomb-lance, did all that was practicable in order to secure the whale. While local trade usages should not set aside maritime law, the custom can be enforced when it is embraced by an entire industry and has been utilized for a long time by everyone engaged in the trade. This particular trade usage was necessary to the survival of the whaling industry, for no one would engage in whaling if he could not be guaranteed the fruits of his labor. Decree for libellant.

▶ *ANALYSIS*

Under the common law rule, for a wild animal to be reduced to a possession, it must be placed under the control of the one making the capture. Here, two major considerations modified the application of the rule to the situation. First, all that was practicable to secure the whale was done. Second, the trade usage was industry-wide, necessary to the survival of the industry, and fair to all parties (including the whale's finder, who received a reasonable salvage fee). Note also that the rule here was not being applied to a sport such as hunting or fishing, but, instead, to an industry. Economic interests were certainly important in the holding of this case.

Quicknotes

BOMB-LANCE Device used by whaling ships in the nineteenth century to identify themselves as the owner of a captured whale.

MARITIME LAW That area of law pertaining to navigable waters.

SALVAGE FEE Charge incurred in the salvage of property.

TRADE USAGE A course of dealing or practice commonly used in a particular trade.

Keeble v. Hickeringill

Duck pond owner (P) v. Duck frightener (D)

Queen's Bench, 11 East 574, 103 Eng. Rep. 1127 (1707).

NATURE OF CASE: Action for interference with lawful use of land.

FACT SUMMARY: Keeble (P) contended Hickeringill (D) scared ducks away from his pond resulting in damage.

🏛 RULE OF LAW
Damages may be recovered for the intentional frightening of game off another's land.

FACTS: Keeble (P) owned land containing a duck pond. He loaded the pond with decoys to seduce game to come to the pond so that he could hunt. Hickeringill (D) discharged a shotgun near the pond, which induced the game to stay away. Keeble (P) sued and was granted recovery. Hickeringill (D) appealed, contending Keeble (P) had no title to the game, and thus no cause of action existed.

ISSUE: May recovery of damages be had for the frightening of wild game off one's property?

HOLDING AND DECISION: (Holt, C.J.) Yes. Damages may be recovered for the intentional frightening of wild game off another's land. Although no title to the game existed, Keeble (P) was using his land in a lawful manner. Thus Hickeringill (D) interfered with this lawful use and is liable in damages.

▶ ANALYSIS

Capture or control, in conjunction with being first in time, guides legal analysis of the ownership of wild animals. The present case represents somewhat of a departure from these rules, yet it is viewed as a natural and logical extension of them.

∎═∎

Quicknotes

INTERFERENCE WITH USE OF LAND An action to recover damages resulting from the wrongful interference with a party's property; otherwise, this is referred to as a trespass.

VIVARY A place where wild animals are kept.

∎═∎

Popov v. Hayashi

Baseball fan (P) v. Baseball fan (D)

Cal. Super. Ct., WL 31833731 (2002).

NATURE OF CASE: Action for conversion, trespass to chattels, injunctive relief and constructive trust.

FACT SUMMARY: Both Popov (P) and Hayashi (D) intended to establish and maintain control over a baseball that gave Barry Bonds his 73rd home run in 2001, but just as Popov (P) was getting it in his glove, a crowd engulfed him, and brought him to the ground. Hayashi (D), who was near Popov (P) and who also was brought to the ground by the crowd, found the ball and pocketed it. Popov (P) claimed he had established sufficient possession of the ball to gain title to it and brought suit to compel Hayashi (D) to return the ball to him.

🏛 **RULE OF LAW**
Where an actor undertakes significant but incomplete steps to achieve possession of a piece of abandoned personal property and the effort is interrupted by the unlawful acts of others, the actor has a legally cognizable pre-possessory interest in the property sufficient to support a claim of conversion.

FACTS: Barry Bonds, a professional baseball player, hit a record-setting 73rd home run on October 7, 2001. On that day, Popov (P) and Hayashi (D) and many others had positioned themselves in an area of the stadium where Bonds hit the greatest number of home runs in the hopes of catching a record-setting ball (so they brought their baseball gloves with them). The ball hit by Bonds initially landed in Popov's (P) glove, but it was not clear whether the ball was secure there, as Popov (P) may have lost his balance while reaching for the ball. However, even as the ball was going into his glove, a crowd engulfed him and he was tackled and brought to the ground, with people hitting and grabbing him. Hayashi (D), who had been near Popov (P), was also forced by the crowd to the ground, where he saw the ball. He pocketed it and revealed it only when a camera was trained on him, presumably because he wanted proof that he was the owner of the ball. Popov (P), seeing the ball, grabbed for it, believing it to be his, but Hayashi (D) refused to give it to him. Popov (P) then brought suit for conversion, trespass to chattels, injunctive relief, and constructive trust.

ISSUES: Where an actor undertakes significant but incomplete steps to achieve possession of a piece of abandoned personal property and the effort is interrupted by the unlawful acts of others, does the actor have a legally cognizable pre-possessory interest in the property sufficient to support a claim of conversion?

HOLDING AND DECISION: (McCarthy, J.) Yes. Where an actor undertakes significant but incomplete steps to achieve possession of a piece of abandoned personal property and the effort is interrupted by the unlawful acts of others, the actor has a legally cognizable pre-possessory interest in the property sufficient to support a claim of conversion. As an initial matter, there was no trespass to chattels—which requires injury to the chattel—because the ball itself was not damaged and because Popov (P) did not claim that Hayashi (D) interfered with his use and enjoyment of the ball. If there was a wrong at all, it was conversion, which is the wrongful exercise of dominion over the personal property of another. One, who has neither title nor possession nor any right to possession, may not assert a conversion claim. The key issue, therefore, is whether Popov (P) achieved possession or the right to it. "Possession," however, does not have one meaning; the meaning varies depending on the context in which it is used. Some guidelines, however, do exist, *e.g.*, that possession requires both physical control over an item and an intent to control it and exclude others from it. Here, Popov (P) clearly had the requisite intent, so the issue is whether he had exclusive dominion and control over the ball. Possession in this context is based on custom and what is physically possible. Here, "not only is it physically possible for a person to acquire unequivocal dominion and control of an abandoned baseball, but fans generally expect a claimant to have accomplished as much." Because Popov (P) did not establish by preponderance of the evidence that he would have retained control of the ball after all momentum ceased and after any incidental contact with other people or objects, he did not achieve full possession. This conclusion does not resolve the case, however, because Popov (P) was attacked illegally by the crowd, and because, therefore, it is unknown whether he would have retained control over the ball absent the crowd's actions. Because Popov (P) has a legally protected pre-possessory interest in the ball, he may advance a legitimate claim to the ball. Hayashi (D), too, was a victim of the crowd's illegal activity, but was able to extricate himself from the crowd. Although Hayashi (D) exercised complete dominion and control over the ball, the ball was encumbered by the qualified pre-possessory interest of Popov (P). Thus, awarding the ball to either of the two parties is unfair to the other. Both have a superior claim to the ball against all the world, but not against each other; they are equally entitled to the ball. Because the court sits in equity, it may devise an equitable solution to this problem. Here,

Continued on next page.

that solution is equitable division, whereby both Popov (P) and Hayashi (D) have an equal and undivided interest in the ball. Accordingly, Popov's (P) conversion claim is sustained only as to his equal and undivided interest.

▶ *ANALYSIS*

The parties agreed that before Bonds hit the ball, it belonged to Major League Baseball, but that at the time it was hit, it became intentionally abandoned property. Also, to effectuate its decision, the court ordered the sale of the ball, with the proceeds being equally split between the two men. The ball ultimately sold for $450,000—Hayashi (D) estimated that his share would only cover his legal fees.

■══■

Quicknotes

CONSTRUCTIVE TRUST A trust that arises by operation of law whereby the court imposes a trust upon property lawfully held by one party for the benefit of another, as a result of some wrongdoing by the party in possession so as to avoid unjust enrichment.

CONVERSION The act of depriving an owner of his property without permission or justification.

INJUNCTIVE RELIEF A court order issued as a remedy, requiring a person to do, or prohibiting that person from doing, a specific act.

POSSESSORY INTEREST The right to possess particular real property to the exclusion of others.

TRESPASS TO CHATTELS Action for damages sustained as a result of defendant's unlawful interference with plaintiff's personal property.

■══■

Jacque v. Steenberg Homes, Inc.

Property owner (P) v. Company (D)

Wis. Sup. Ct., 563 N.W.2d 154 (1997).

NATURE OF CASE: Suit for intentional trespass to land.

FACT SUMMARY: The Jacques (P) brought suit against Steenberg Homes, Inc. (Steenberg) (D) claiming intentional trespass to their land when Steenberg (D) plowed a path across their field, over their protests, in order to deliver a mobile home.

🏛 RULE OF LAW
When nominal damages are awarded for an intentional trespass to land, punitive damages may also be awarded at the jury's discretion.

FACTS: Steenberg Homes (Steenberg) (D) was delivering a mobile home. It found the easiest route of delivery was through the Jacques' (P) land. Despite the Jacques' (P) protests, Steenberg (D) plowed a path through the Jacques' (P) field. The Jacques (P) sued Steenberg (D) for intentional trespass. At trial, Steenberg (D) conceded intentional trespass but argued that punitive damages could not be awarded since no compensatory damages had been awarded. Though the jury awarded $1 in nominal damages and $100,000 in punitive damages, the circuit court set aside the punitive damages award. The court of appeals affirmed and the Jacques (P) appealed.

ISSUE: When nominal damages are awarded for an intentional trespass to land, may punitive damages also be awarded at the jury's discretion?

HOLDING AND DECISION: (Bablitch, J.) Yes. When nominal damages are awarded for an intentional trespass to land, punitive damages may also be awarded at the jury's discretion. Steenberg (D) argued that punitive damages could not be awarded by the jury without an award of compensatory damages as a matter of law. The Jacques (P) argued that the rationale supporting the compensatory damage award requirement is not applicable when the wrongful act is an intentional trespass to land. This court agrees. The rationale for the requirement is that if the individual cannot show actual harm, society has little interest in having the unlawful, but harmless, conduct deterred and punitive damages are inappropriate. The issue of whether nominal damages can support a punitive damage award in intentional trespass to land cases is one of first impression. This court has recognized that in certain circumstances of trespass, the actual harm is not the damage to the land, but the loss of the individual's right to exclude others from his property, and has implied that the loss of this right may be punished by a large damage award despite the lack of measurable harm. Thus, the compensatory damages requirement

should not apply when the tort supporting the award is intentional trespass to land. Next, we consider whether the $100,000 damage award was excessive. The court must consider three factors in determining whether a punitive damage award violates the Due Process Clause: (1) the degree of reprehensibility of the conduct; (2) the disparity between the harm suffered and the award; and (3) the difference between this remedy and the penalties authorized or imposed in comparable cases. Here the $100,000 award was not excessive. Steenberg's (D) intentional trespass demonstrated an indifference and reckless disregard for the law and for the rights of others. Moreover, such an award is necessary to deter similar conduct in the future. Reversed and remanded.

▶ ANALYSIS

The Supreme Court has recognized the interest of a landowner in the right to exclude others from his land as one of the essential property rights. The law recognizes that harm occurs in every trespass to land by the nominal damage award, whether or not actual damages are sustained. The potential harm resulting from intentional trespass to land, which if repeated might ripen into prescription or adverse possession, may result in the owner's loss of property rights. Moreover, society's interest in deterring wrongdoing supports the conclusion in this case as well.

■■■■

Quicknotes

COMPENSATORY DAMAGES Measure of damages necessary to compensate victim for actual injuries suffered.

PUNITIVE DAMAGES Damages exceeding the actual injury suffered for the purposes of punishment of the defendant, deterrence of the wrongful behavior or comfort to the plaintiff.

TRESPASS TO LAND Physical invasion of the plaintiff's property that is intended and caused by the defendant's conduct.

■■■■

State v. Shack

State (P) v. Attorney for migrant farmworkers (D)

N.J. Sup. Ct., 277 A.2d 369 (1971).

NATURE OF CASE: Appeal from a conviction of trespassing.

FACT SUMMARY: Tejeras (D) and Shack (D) entered upon private property, against the orders of the owner of that property, to aid migrant farmworkers employed and housed there.

🏛 RULE OF LAW
Real property rights are not absolute; and "necessity, private or public, may justify entry upon the lands of another."

FACTS: Tejeras (D) and Shack (D) worked with migrant farmworkers. Tejeras (D) was a field worker for the Farm Workers Division of the Southwest Citizens Organization for Poverty Elimination (SCOPE), a nonprofit corporation funded by the Office of Economic Opportunity that provided for the "health services of the migrant farm worker." Shack (D) was a staff attorney with the Farm Workers Division of Camden Regional Legal Services, Inc. (CRLS), also a nonprofit corporation funded by the Office of Economic Opportunity that provided (along with other services) legal advice for, and representation of, migrant farmworkers. Tejeras (D) and Shack (D), pursuant to their roles in SCOPE and CRLS, entered upon private property to aid migrant workers employed and housed there. When both Tejeras (D) and Shack (D) refused to leave the property at the owner's request, they were charged with trespassing under a New Jersey statute which provides that "any person who trespasses on any lands . . . after being forbidden so to trespass by the owner . . . is a disorderly person and shall be punished by a fine of not more than $50." After conviction for trespassing, Tejeras (D) and Shack (D) brought this appeal.

ISSUE: Does an owner of real property have the absolute right to exclude all others from that property?

HOLDING AND DECISION: (Weintraub, J.) No. Real property rights are not absolute; and "necessity, private or public, may justify entry upon the lands of another." This rule is based upon the basic rationale that "property rights serve human values. They are recognized to that end and are limited by it." Here, a central concern is the welfare of the migrant farmworkers—a highly disadvantaged segment of society. Migrant farmworkers, in general, are "outside of the mainstream of the communities in which they are housed and are unaware of their rights and opportunities, and of the services available to them." As such, here, the "necessity" of effective communication of legal rights and of providing medical services for the migrant farmworkers justifies entry upon the private property. Of course, the owner of such property has the right to pursue his farming activities without interference, but, here, there is no legitimate need for the owner to exclude those attempting to assist the migrant farmworkers. Furthermore, the migrant farmworker must be allowed to receive visitors of his choice, so long as there is no behavior harmful to others, and members of the press may not be denied access to any farmworker who wishes to see them. In any of these situations, since no possessory right of the farmer-employer-landowner has been invaded (i.e., since he has no right to exclude such persons), there can be no trespassing. Reversed and remanded.

▶ ANALYSIS

Generally, the right to exclusive possession is considered "the oldest, most widely recognized right of private property in land." This case, though, illustrates the central limitation on the right to possession or use of private property, i.e., it may not be used to harm others. Here, the exclusion of Tejeras (D) and Shack (D) was, therefore, invalid because it would harm a very disadvantaged segment of society (the farmworkers). Note, that under this principle, an owner of property, also, has no right to maintain a nuisance, to violate a building code, or to violate any "police power" laws (i.e., laws for the general public welfare).

Quicknotes

TRESPASS Unlawful interference with, or damage to, the real or personal property of another.

International News Service v. Associated Press

Wire service (D) v. Wire service (P)

248 U.S. 215 (1918).

NATURE OF CASE: Appeal from denial of injunctive relief.

FACT SUMMARY: Associated Press (AP) (P) sued to enjoin International News Service (INS) (D) from publishing as its own news stories obtained from early editions of AP (P) publications.

🏛 RULE OF LAW
Publication for profit of news obtained from other news-gathering enterprises is a misappropriation of a property right.

FACTS: AP (P) sued INS (D) for the latter's admitted use of AP (P) news stories in INS (D) publications. INS (D) would obtain advance publication of AP (P) news and would then use such in its newspapers. AP (P) contended it had a proprietary right to all news it gathered through the efforts of its contributors. INS (D) contended any such right terminated upon its first publication. The court of appeals issued AP (P) an injunction, and the United States Supreme Court granted a hearing.

ISSUE: Is the publication for profit of news obtained from other news-gathering enterprises a misappropriation of a property right?

HOLDING AND DECISION: (Pitney, J.) Yes. Publication for profit of news obtained from other news-gathering enterprises is a misappropriation of a property right. News itself is a collection of observable facts which obviously cannot be owned vis-á-vis by the public at large. The nonprofit communication of news, regardless of source, is endemic in a free society and involves no property right. However, when two competing news organizations are involved, each gaining their livelihood from beating the other's deadline, the use of such news, for profit, is a misappropriation of the other's product. As a result, injunctive relief is properly issued. Affirmed.

▶ ANALYSIS

Some commentators suggest this case as a prime example of the first in time–first in right principle of ownership. Some go so far as to argue it provides authority for the proposition that all things created, tangible or intangible, belong to the creator. This expands the reach of this case beyond news-gathering and into any area wherein exclusivity of design or idea is important. This would include everything from clothing design to computer programming.

Quicknotes

COPYRIGHT Refers to the exclusive rights granted to an artist pursuant to Article I, Section 8, clause 8 of the United States Constitution over the reproduction, display, performance, distribution, and adaptation of his work for a period prescribed by statute.

MISAPPROPRIATION The unlawful use of another's property or funds.

■=■

Martin Luther King, Jr. Center for Social Change, Inc. v. American Heritage Products, Inc.

Nonprofit organization (P) v. Manufacturer (D)

Ga. Sup. Ct., 296 S.E.2d 697 (1982).

NATURE OF CASE: Certified question from Eleventh Circuit Court of Appeals to Georgia Supreme Court.

FACT SUMMARY: Martin Luther King, Jr. Center for Social Change (P) sued Bolen (D) for the unauthorized development and marketing of a plastic bust of Dr. Martin Luther King, Jr.

🏛 RULE OF LAW
Public figures have a right of publicity that survives the death of the figure, and thus is inheritable and devisable, the measure of damages for violation of which is the value of the appropriation to the user.

FACTS: Bolen (D) is the sole proprietor of a business that manufactures and sells plastic products as funeral accessories. He developed the concept of marketing a plastic bust of Martin Luther King, Jr., and formed a company in order to sell them. Although Bolen (D) sought the endorsement of Martin Luther King, Jr. Center for Social Change (the Center) (P), it refused to endorse the product. He nevertheless pursued the idea, hiring persons to prepare the model and taking out advertising. The Center (P) filed suit demanding Bolen (D) cease and desist from further marketing and development of the bust. The Eleventh Circuit Court of Appeals certified the question to this Court of whether a right of publicity exists in the state of Georgia, and whether it is devisable and inheritable.

ISSUE: Do public figures have a right of publicity that survives the death of the figure, and thus is inheritable and devisable, the measure of damages for violation of which is the value of the appropriation to the user?

HOLDING AND DECISION: (Hill, J.) Yes. Public figures have a right of publicity that survives the death of the figure, and thus is inheritable and devisable, the measure of damages for violation of which is the value of the appropriation to the user. Similar to the right of privacy in private figures, a public figure has a right in the publicity value of his likeness, the rationale for which is the prevention of unjust enrichment. Private citizens as well as public ones have a right not to have their names and photographs used for financial gain of the user without their consent. Furthermore the right of publicity is inheritable and devisable, and as such furthers the purpose of rewarding and encouraging effort and creativity. There is no requirement that the owner of the right have commercially exploited it before his death for the right to survive.

CONCURRENCE: (Weltner, J.) This new right of publicity jeopardizes the right to freedom of speech.

▶ ANALYSIS

The right of publicity has been extended to also apply to imitations of public figures. Several California cases have held that where a well-known singer's voice is deliberately imitated in order to sell merchandise, misappropriation of the celebrity's likeness has occurred.

■━■

Quicknotes

FREEDOM OF SPEECH The right to express oneself without governmental restrictions on the content of that expression.

RIGHT OF PUBLICITY The right of a person to control the commercial exploitation of his name or likeness.

UNJUST ENRICHMENT The unlawful acquisition of money or property of another for which both law and equity require restitution to be made.

■━■

Feist Publications, Inc. v. Rural Telephone Service Co.

Publishing company (D) v. Phone book publisher (P)

499 U.S. 340 (1991).

NATURE OF CASE: Appeal from grant of summary judgment to plaintiff in suit for copyright infringement.

FACT SUMMARY: After Feist Publications, Inc. (Feist) (D) took 1,309 listings from Rural Telephone Service Co.'s (Rural's) (P) white pages when compiling Feist's (D) own white pages, Rural (P) filed suit for copyright infringement.

🏛 RULE OF LAW
To be copyrightable, a work must be original and possess at least some minimal degree of creativity.

FACTS: As a certified telephone service provided in northwest Kansas, Rural Telephone Service Co. (Rural) (P) published a typical telephone directory as a condition of its monopoly franchise. The white pages alphabetically listed the names, towns, and telephone numbers of Rural's (P) subscribers. Feist Publications, Inc. (Feist) (D) was a publishing company specializing in area-wide telephone directories. The Feist (D) directory that was the subject of this litigation contained 46,878 white pages' listings, compared to Rural's (P) approximately 7,700 listings. Feist (D) approached the 11 northwest Kansas telephone companies and offered to pay for the right to use their respective white pages listings. When only Rural (P) refused to license its listings, Feist (D) used them without Rural's (P) consent. A typical Feist (D) listing included each individual's street address, while most of Rural's (P) did not. Of the 46,878 listings in Feist's (D) 1983 directory, 1,309 of those listings were identical to listings in Rural's (P) white pages. Rural (P) sued for copyright infringement. The district court granted summary judgment to Rural (P), and the court of appeals affirmed. Feist (D) appealed.

ISSUE: To be copyrightable, must a work be original and possess at least some minimal degree of creativity?

HOLDING AND DECISION: (O'Connor, J.) Yes. To be copyrightable, a work must be original and possess at least some minimal degree of creativity. This case concerns the interaction of two well-established propositions. The first is that facts are not copyrightable; the other, that compilations of facts generally are. There is an undeniable tension between these two propositions. The key to resolving the tension lies in understanding why facts are not copyrightable. No one may claim originality as to facts because facts do not owe their origin to an act of authorship. Factual compilations, on the other hand, may possess the requisite originality. Compilations were expressly mentioned in the Copyright Acts of 1909 and 1976. Even a directory that contains absolutely no protectable written expression, only facts, meets the constitutional minimum for copyright protection if it features an original selection or arrangement. If the selection and arrangement are original, these elements of the work are eligible for copyright protection. No matter how original the format, though, the facts themselves do not become original through association. There is no doubt that Feist (D) took from the white pages of Rural's (P) directory a substantial amount of factual information. The question that remains is whether Rural (P) selected, coordinated, or arranged these uncopyrightable facts in an original way. It did not. Rural (P) simply took the data provided by its subscribers and listed it alphabetically by surname. There is nothing remotely creative about arranging names alphabetically in a white pages directory. Rural (P) expended sufficient effort to make the white pages directory useful, but insufficient creativity to make it original. Thus, because Rural's (P) white pages lack the requisite originality, Feist's (D) use of the listings cannot constitute infringement. Copyright rewards originality, not effort. Reversed.

▌ ANALYSIS

In the words of the Court, copyright ensures authors the right to their original expression, but encourages others to build freely upon the ideas and information conveyed by a work. This principle, known as the idea/expression or fact/expression dichotomy, applies to all works of authorship. As applied to a factual compilation, assuming the absence of original written expression, only the compiler's selection and arrangement may be protected; the raw facts may be copied at will. This is the means by which copyright advances the progress of science and art by encouraging creativity with the reward of exclusive rights for the original creation.

■■■■

Quicknotes

COPYRIGHT Refers to the exclusive rights granted to an artist pursuant to Article I, Section 8, clause 8 of the United States Constitution over the reproduction, display, performance, distribution, and adaptation of his work for a period prescribed by statute.

COPYRIGHT INFRINGEMENT A violation of one of the exclusive rights granted to an artist pursuant to Article I, Section 8, clause 8 of the United States Constitution over

Continued on next page.

the reproduction, display, performance, distribution, and adaptation of his work for a period prescribed by statute.

SUMMARY JUDGMENT Judgment rendered by a court in response to a motion made by one of the parties, claiming that the lack of a question of material fact in respect to an issue warrants disposition of the issue without consideration by the jury.

■≡■

Harper & Row Publishers, Inc. v. Nation Enterprises

Copyright holder (P) v. Alleged infringer (D)

471 U.S. 539 (1985).

NATURE OF CASE: Appeal from federal circuit court of appeals decision finding that a newspaper magazine's article using quotations from U.S. President Ford's unpublished memoirs qualified as a permissible fair use.

FACT SUMMARY: U.S. President Ford licensed a portion of his unpublished memoirs to Time Magazine for $25,000. Prior to publication, The Nation (D) magazine published an article using verbatim quotations from the unpublished manuscript.

🏛 RULE OF LAW
The Copyright Act, Section 106, provides a copyright owner with the right to control the first public distribution of an authorized version of the work.

FACTS: U.S. President Ford contracted with Harper & Row (P) to publish his memoirs. Before publication, pre-publication rights were licensed to Time Magazine for $25,000 to run a portion of the memoirs. Time Magazine would pay half of the amount in advance and the second half after publication of the article. Prior to publication, The Nation (D) magazine published a 2,250-word article using verbatim quotes from President Ford's memoirs. The author of the article admitted he had received a copy of the manuscript without permission or authorization from President Ford. Time Magazine cancelled its article and refused to pay the second half of the licensing fees. Harper & Row (P) brought a copyright infringement suit against The Nation (D) in federal district court. The lower court found in favor of Harper & Row (P). A federal circuit court of appeals reversed, finding that The Nation's (D) use of the quotations from the memoirs was a permissible example of fair use. The United States Supreme Court granted Harper & Row's (P) application for further review.

ISSUE: Does § 106 of the Copyright Act provide a copyright owner with the right to control the first public distribution of an authorized version of the work?

HOLDING AND DECISION: (O'Connor, J.) Yes. § 106 of the Copyright Act provides a copyright owner with the right to control the first public distribution of an authorized version of the work. While this right is subject to the fair use provision of § 107, the fair use analysis is always tailored to the specific case. The nature of the interest at stake is highly relevant to the determination of fair use. Here, the unpublished nature of the memoirs, though not determinative, tends to negate the defense of fair use. The author's control of first distribution

is significant for his personal interest in the work as well as his property interest in exploiting possible prepublication interests, such as the opportunity offered by Time Magazine in this case. In addition, the First Amendment does not protect The Nation (D). A broad application of the fair use doctrine should not destroy copyright protections of public figures. Turning to the fair use analysis, there are four factors that are relevant to the analysis: (1) the purpose and character of the use; (2) the nature of the copyrighted work; (3) the substantiality of the portion use in relation to the copyrighted work as a whole; and (4) the effect on the market of the copyrighted work. First, the use is reporting for a for-profit news magazine. While The Nation (D) argues the use is for reporting and not necessarily to drive up sales of the magazine, the inquiry here is whether the user's exploitation of the material was done so without paying the customary cost for licensing or publication fees. Clearly The Nation (D) sought to "scoop" Time Magazine, thus destroying President Ford's right to control the first publication. Turning to the nature of the work, it is an unpublished historical narrative. The Nation (D) did not use just isolated phrases from the memoirs, but rather full passages verbatim from the work. This use exceeds the recognized need to disseminate only facts. Similarly, regarding the amount of work used by the alleged infringer, the district court found that The Nation's (D) article used passages that form the "heart of the book." Fourth, regarding the infringement's effect on the market, Time Magazine's decision not to run its article and not to pay the additional $12,500 is evidence that The Nation's (D) article clearly affected the market for the memoirs. Based on all of these factors, The Nation's (D) use of the article does not qualify for protection from the fair use doctrine. Reversed.

▶ ANALYSIS

Fair use often provides a good defense for authors of factual accounts. However, it was the unpublished nature of the work and the illicit manner in which The Nation (D) received the manuscript that were fatal to the defense of fair use. The right of first publication is significant but it is just one part of the overall fair use analysis.

■=▬=■

Quicknotes

COPYRIGHT ACT Copyright Act of 1976 extends copyright protection to "original works of authorship fixed in any

Continued on next page.

tangible medium of expression, now known or later developed, from which they can be perceived, reproduced, or otherwise communicated, either directly or with the aid of a machine or device." 17 U.S.C. § 102.

FAIR USE An affirmative defense to a claim of copyright infringement providing an exception from the copyright owner's exclusive rights in a work for the purposes of criticism, comment, news reporting, teaching, scholarship or research.

■═══■

Diamond v. Chakrabarty

Acting commissioner of patents and trademarks (P) v. Microbiologist (D)

447 U.S. 303 (1980).

NATURE OF CASE: Certiorari review of patentability of living organisms.

FACT SUMMARY: Chakrabarty (D) discovered a bacterium that can break down multiple components of crude oil. He filed a patent claim on the bacterium itself. The patent examiner rejected his claim. Chakrabarty (D) appealed the decision to the Patent Office Board of Appeals, and the Board affirmed the examiner's decision. The Court of Customs and Patent Appeals reversed that decision, and the Acting Commissioner of Patents and Trademarks (P) filed a petition for certiorari and the writ was granted.

🏛 RULE OF LAW
A mirco-organism that is not naturally occurring and is the product of manufacture is patentable subject matter.

FACTS: Chakrabarty (D) discovered a method of developing a bacterium that could break down multiple components of crude oil. Chakrabarty (D) filed a patent claim for the process of developing the bacterium, for an inoculum comprised of a carrier material and the bacterium, and for the bacterium itself. The patent examiner allowed the first two claims but rejected the patent claim for the bacterium itself. The basis for the rejection of the claim for the bacterium was that it was a living organism and, therefore, not patentable subject matter. Chakrabarty (D) appealed the examiner's decision to the Patent Office Board of Appeals. The decision was upheld but reversed by the Court of Customs and Patent Appeals. The Acting Commissioner of Patents and Trademarks (P) petitioned for certiorari review to resolve the issue. The writ was granted.

ISSUE: Does a micro-organism constitute a "manufacture" or "composition of matter" such that it can be the subject matter of a patent?

HOLDING AND DECISION: (Burger, C.J.) Yes. Congress intends a broad interpretation of the term "manufacture" in the context of the statute governing patentable subject matter (35 U.S.C. Section 101). The term is interpreted as having the same meaning it is given in the dictionary: "The production of articles for use from raw or prepared materials by giving to these materials new forms, qualities, properties, or combinations, whether by hand-labor or machinery." This allows for a very broad reading of the statute. Notwithstanding this broad construction, laws of nature and physical phenomena are not considered patentable subject matter. The petitioner (P)

argues that the micro-organism in question is not patentable subject matter because it is a living organism precluded from patenting by the 1930 Plant Patent Act. The Court rejected this argument because the relevant distinction made by Congress, in passing the Plant Patent Acts, was not between living and inanimate things but between products of nature and products of human ingenuity. In this case, Chakrabarty (D) applied for a patent for a product of his own ingenuity. The micro-organism in question does not occur naturally. Petitioner's (P) final argument is that micro-organisms are not patentable until Congress expressly authorizes patent protection for such organisms. Petitioner (P) contends that Congress could not have foreseen this type of technology when it enacted the statute at issue. The Court disagreed, believing that a finding that unforeseen inventions are not protected frustrates the purpose of patent law, which is to promote progress and ingenuity. The Court therefore rejected petitioner's (P) arguments and found that the micro-organism in question is patentable subject matter. Affirmed.

DISSENT: (Brennan, J.) The dissenting opinion held that the majority misread the applicable legislation, finding that the case did not deal simply with the problem of "unanticipated inventions" but with the question of whether a bacteria, a living organism, is patentable subject matter. The Plant Patent Acts clearly indicate that Congress did not intend living organisms to be patentable. Congress's purpose in passing the Plant Patent Acts was to address the problem of scientists attempting to patent living organisms. In addition, the 1970 Act specifically excludes bacteria from patent protection.

▌ ANALYSIS

Naturally occurring organisms and plants are not patentable subject matter. As this case illustrates, however, when an organism is created through human ingenuity, it becomes patentable subject matter. The public policy behind intellectual property law is to promote human productivity and progress. This case underscores the fact that patent laws are designed to protect human ingenuity and scientific advances.

■=■

Quicknotes

CERTIORARI A discretionary writ issued by a superior court to an inferior court in order to review the lower

Continued on next page.

court's decisions; the United States Supreme Court's writ ordering such review.

INTELLECTUAL PROPERTY A body of law pertaining to the ownership of rights in intangible products of the human intellect.

PATENT A limited monopoly conferred on the invention or discovery of any new or useful machine or process that is novel and non-obvious.

■━■

White v. Samsung Electronics America, Inc.

Celebrity (P) v. Corporation (D)

971 F.2d 1395 (9th Cir. 1992).

NATURE OF CASE: Appeal from summary judgment in favor of defendants in an action brought for the violation of the common law right of publicity and of state and federal statutes.

FACT SUMMARY: When Vanna White's (P) "identity" was used in an advertisement without her consent, she sued Samsung Electronics (D) for allegedly attempting to capitalize on her fame to enhance their fortune.

> 🏛 **RULE OF LAW**
> The right of publicity protects a celebrity's property interest in his or her identity from commercial exploitation, regardless of the method by which it is appropriated.

FACTS: Samsung Electronics (D) ran advertisements in several publications featuring a robot dressed to resemble Vanna White (P), the hostess of the popular game show "Wheel of Fortune." Since White (P) had neither consented to the ads nor was paid for them, she sued, alleging infringement of various intellectual property rights. The district court granted Samsung's (D) motion for summary judgment on White's (P) claims under California Civil Code § 3344, the California common law right of publicity, and the Lanham Act. White (P) appealed, claiming that her California common law right of publicity had been violated because Samsung (D) had appropriated part of her identity for its own profit in selling its product.

ISSUE: Does the right of publicity protect a celebrity's property interest in his or her identity from commercial exploitation, regardless of the method by which it is appropriated?

HOLDING AND DECISION: (Goodwin, J.) Yes. The right of publicity protects a celebrity's property interest in his or her identity from commercial exploitation, regardless of the method by which it is appropriated. Prior case law has established that the California common law right of publicity cause of action may be pleaded by alleging the defendant's use of the plaintiff's identity; the appropriation of plaintiff's name or likeness to defendant's advantage, commercially or otherwise; lack of consent; and resulting injury. The district court erred in reasoning that Samsung (D) had not appropriated White's (P) "name or likeness" with their robot ad and in finding that White's (P) claim failed to satisfy the second prong. The right of publicity does not require that appropriations of identity be accomplished through particular means to be actionable. A celebrity's identity can be valuable in the promotion of products, and the celebrity has an interest that may be protected from the unauthorized commercial exploitation of that identity. The identities of the most popular celebrities are not only the most attractive for advertisers, but also the easiest to evoke without resorting to obvious means such as name, likeness, or voice. Considering the robot's physical attributes, its dress, and its position on the Wheel of Fortune game show set, there is little doubt about which celebrity the ad is meant to depict. Because White (P) has alleged facts showing that Samsung (D) appropriated her identity, the district court erred by rejecting, on summary judgment, White's (P) common law right of publicity claim. Affirmed in part, reversed in part and remanded.

CONCURRENCE AND DISSENT: (Alarcon, J.) All of the California cases that my research has disclosed hold that a cause of action for appropriation of the right to publicity requires proof of the appropriation of a name or likeness. In each of the federal cases relied upon by the majority, the advertisement affirmatively represented that the person depicted therein was the plaintiff. In this case, it is clear that a metal robot and not the plaintiff, Vanna White (P), is depicted in the commercial advertisement. The record does not show an appropriation of Vanna White's (P) identity. In reaching its conclusion, the majority confuses Vanna White (P), the person, with the role she has assumed as the current hostess on the "Wheel of Fortune" television game show. Those things White (P) claims identify her are not unique to her. They are, instead, attributes of the role she plays. The representation of those attributes, therefore, does not constitute a representation of Vanna White (P). I would affirm the district court's judgment in all respects.

▎ *ANALYSIS*

This case was decided by a three-judge panel. Samsung (P) petitioned for a rehearing of the case before all of the judges of the Ninth Circuit. The petition was denied.

■==■

Quicknotes

APPROPRIATION The act of making something one's own or making use of something to serve one's own interest.

COMMON LAW A body of law developed through the judicial decisions of the courts as opposed to the legislative process.

Continued on next page.

SUMMARY JUDGMENT Judgment rendered by a court in response to a motion made by one of the parties, claiming that the lack of a question of material fact in respect to an issue warrants disposition of the issue without consideration by the jury.

■≡■

Moore v. Regents of the University of California

Leukemia patient (P) v. Medical center owners (D)

Cal. Sup. Ct., 793 P.2d 479 (1990), *cert. denied*, 499 U.S. 936 (1991).

NATURE OF CASE: Review of order reversing dismissal of action seeking damages for conversion, fraud, and breach of fiduciary duty.

FACT SUMMARY: Researchers at the University of California, Los Angeles (UCLA), unbeknownst to Moore (P), used specimens of his tissue to produce a potentially lucrative cell line.

RULE OF LAW
A person whose tissue is used for profitable research and development without his knowledge may not maintain a conversion action therefor.

FACTS: In 1976 Moore (P) began treatment at UCLA for a life-threatening form of leukemia. Doctors there realized that his tissue had certain unique properties that showed promise of profitable development. While undergoing treatment, Moore (P) often had tissue removed, such as blood samples, as well as his spleen. While he consented to all these procedures, he was unaware of the nontreatment research being performed on his tissues. Eventually a cell line was developed, which showed promise of benefit in immunology. A patent on the cell line was issued. When he became aware of the use to which his tissue had been put, Moore (P) filed an action seeking damages for conversion, fraud, and breach of fiduciary duty. The trial court dismissed for failure to state a cause of action. The court of appeal reversed, holding that Moore (P) had stated a cause of action for conversion and breach of fiduciary duty. The California Supreme Court granted review.

ISSUE: May a person whose tissue is used for profitable research and development without his knowledge maintain a conversion action therefor?

HOLDING AND DECISION: (Panelli, J.) No. A person whose tissue is used for profitable research and development without his knowledge may not maintain a conversion action therefor. [The court first held that Moore (P) could maintain a breach of fiduciary duty cause of action based on nondisclosure, and then discussed the conversion cause of action.] This court is of the opinion that existing law would not permit such an action. To maintain such an action, a plaintiff must prove interference with ownership or right of possession. A plaintiff in a position such as Moore (P) clearly had no right of possession, so a conversion action would necessitate interference with a proprietary interest. It cannot be said, however, that a person's tissue is "property." Such a notion is at odds with common views on ethics. Beyond that, Health and Safety Code § 7054.4 severs the interest of a person and his removed body parts. Since existing law does not create a conversion action under the circumstances here, an extension of existing law would be required to allow Moore (P) to proceed. This court declines to do so. First, if so held would stifle beneficial research. Conversion is a strict liability tort, and the specter of a conversion suit might dissuade researchers from undertaking important investigations. Secondly, fiduciary duty principles protect a patient, so a conversion cause of action is not necessary. Finally, the present area is one better left to the legislature. For these reasons, this court concludes that Moore (P) has not stated a conversion cause of action. Affirmed in part; reversed in part.

CONCURRENCE: (Arabian, J.) Human tissue should never be viewed as property, even by the person whose tissue is at issue.

DISSENT: (Mosk, J.) Current conversion law should be applied to a person's tissue, as a person should have at the least the right to do with his own tissue what any other person can do with it. Assuming that current conversion law doesn't extend to body tissue, it should be extended. To allow a person to economically benefit from the non-consensual use of another's tissue can be considered a modern version of slavery or indentured servitude.

ANALYSIS

Probably more than any other area of law, property law carries the weight of tradition in its classifications. Modern technology often creates situations that are difficult to apply to traditional legal categories. The present case represents a prime example. The tort of conversion was created in a time when what was and was not capable of being called "property" was pretty clear; things are not so simple today.

Quicknotes

CONVERSION The act of depriving an owner of his property without permission or justification.

FIDUCIARY DUTY A legal obligation to act for the benefit of another, including subordinating one's personal interests to that of the other person.

FRAUD A false representation of facts with the intent that another will rely on the misrepresentation to his detriment.

Qualitex Co. v. Jacobson Products Co., Inc.

Dry cleaning product manufacturer (P) v. Competitor (D)

514 U.S. 159 (1995).

NATURE OF CASE: Review of order reversing finding of a trademark violation.

FACT SUMMARY: Qualitex Co. (P) sought to register a trademark on a color.

 RULE OF LAW
Color alone may be registered as a trademark.

FACTS: Qualitex Co. (P) manufactured and sold pads used by dry cleaners on their presses. The pads made by Qualitex Co. (P) were of a distinctive green-gold color. When Qualitex (P) discovered that Jacobson Products Co. (Jacobson) (D) was also selling pads of the same color, it brought an unfair competition action and also sought to register the color as a trademark. The district court held Jacobson (D) to be in violation of Qualitex's (P) trademark. The Ninth Circuit reversed, holding that color alone could not be registered as a trademark. The United States Supreme Court accepted review.

ISSUE: May color alone be registered as a trademark?

HOLDING AND DECISION: (Breyer, J.) Yes. Color alone may be registered as a trademark. The Lanham Act, which establishes federal trademark law, is quite liberal with respect to the universe of things that can be trademarked. Any symbol that carries a secondary meaning linking it with a particular product may be trademarked. There seems to be no reason why a color cannot fall within this definition. Jacobson's (D) arguments to the contrary are mostly based on pre-Lanham Act common law. Jacobson (D) also argues that since the number of colors is finite, color should not be trademarked. It is not necessary to establish a blanket prohibition for a rare problem. Reversed.

► ANALYSIS

Numerous things of tenuous tangibility have become trademarks: a bottle shape (Coca-Cola) and sound (NBC Broadcasting Co.). Given this, allowing color to be the subject of a trademark is not unusual.

Quicknotes

LANHAM ACT Name of the Trademark Act of 1946 that governs federal law regarding trademarks.

Pocono Springs Civic Association, Inc. v. MacKenzie

Development association (P) v. Vacant-lot owners (D)

Pa. Super. Ct., 667 A.2d 233 (1995).

NATURE OF CASE: Appeal from judgment awarding back homeowner's fees against a property owner.

FACT SUMMARY: The MacKenzies (D) contended that their nonuse of their property, refusal to pay taxes, and offers to sell created abandonment.

 RULE OF LAW
A landowner cannot abandon property to which he holds perfect title.

FACTS: The MacKenzies (D) purchased a vacant lot in a development known as Pocono Springs, which was under the control of the Pocono Springs Civic Association, Inc. (Association) (P). The MacKenzies (D) planned to build on the property. However, it turned out that the property was unable to support a sewage system. Believing their investment to be worthless, they tried to deed the property to the Association (P), which refused to accept it. They then stopped paying taxes on it, and the local government tried to sell it at a foreclosure sale, but there were no takers. The MacKenzies (D) then mailed a "notice of abandonment" to all interested parties, notifying them that they were renouncing all claim to the land. The Association (P) later filed an action seeking to collect delinquent association dues. The trial court entered summary judgment awarding the dues. The MacKenzies (D) appealed.

ISSUE: Can a landowner abandon property to which he has perfect title?

HOLDING AND DECISION: (Rowley, J.) No. A landowner cannot abandon property to which he holds perfect title. Abandoned property is defined as property to which the owner has abandoned all right, title, claim, and possession. When the owner still has title, the property has not been abandoned. Here, the MacKenzies (D) remain owners of real property in fee simple, with a recorded deed and perfect title, so they have not effected abandonment. Consequently, they are still liable for association dues. Affirmed.

▌ ANALYSIS

The law at issue here seems to leave the MacKenzies (D) with little in the way of options. It seems that even not paying taxes will not get them out of the property. This would appear to be a good illustration of the concept of *caveat emptor.*

Quicknotes

ABANDONMENT The voluntary relinquishment of a right without the intent of reclaiming it.

CAVEAT EMPTOR Let the buyer beware; doctrine that a buyer purchases something at his own risk.

PERFECT TITLE Total right of possession and disposition over particular property.

Hawkins v. Mahoney

Prison inmate (P) v. State prison (D)

Mont. Sup. Ct., 990 P.2d 776 (1999).

NATURE OF CASE: Appeal from lower court decision finding that a prison inmate abandoned his personal property after escaping from the prison.

FACT SUMMARY: After Hawkins (P) escaped from prison, prison officials placed his personal property in storage. Hawkins (P) was captured and returned to the prison two days after his escape. Prison officials refused to return his property.

RULE OF LAW
Abandoned personal property may be appropriated by anyone with the intent to acquire title to the property, unless such property has been reclaimed by the former owner.

FACTS: After Hawkins (P) escaped from prison, prison officials placed his personal property in storage. The items included a television, stereo, word processor, and books. Hawkins (P) was captured and returned to the prison two days after his escape. Officials brought Hawkins (P) to the storage room and allowed him to remove any legal documentation. The officials refused to return the rest of his personal property. This was done pursuant to prison policy that considered all personal property of an escapee to be abandoned. The property was eventually destroyed or sold. Hawkins (P) brought this suit alleging that his property was destroyed without affording him due process of law. A lower court agreed with the prison officials that Hawkins (P) had abandoned his property at the time of his escape. Hawkins (P) appealed to the Supreme Court of Montana.

ISSUE: May abandoned personal property be appropriated by anyone with the intent to acquire title to the property, unless such property has been reclaimed by the former owner?

HOLDING AND DECISION: (Trieweiler, J.) Yes. Abandoned personal property may be appropriated by anyone with the intent to acquire title to the property, unless such property has been reclaimed by the former owner. Here, the analysis focuses on both the intent of the person allegedly abandoning the property as well as the one who allegedly took possession of the property. The intent to abandon property is a required element of abandonment. Here, Hawkins's (P) intent to abandon his property can only be inferred or presumed. The question is: can that presumption, based on one's escape from prison, be rebutted? This court finds that the presumption can be rebutted prior to the time when someone else takes possession of the abandoned property. Here, the State (D) did not evidence its own intent to take possession of the

property. It merely labeled Hawkins's (P) property and placed it in storage. Prior to Hawkins's (P) request that his items be returned, the prison took no steps to destroy or sell the property. Based on these facts, Hawkins (P) effectively rebutted the presumption that he abandoned his property by requesting the return of that property. Reversed.

▶ ANALYSIS

Other states have found that the presumption of abandonment cannot be rebutted. On these facts, the state prison had not taken any steps to dispose of Hawkins's (P) property. If the state had done so prior to Hawkins (P) requesting the return of the property, the case would have been resolved in the state's favor.

■=■

Quicknotes

ABANDONMENT The voluntary relinquishment of a right without the intent of reclaiming it.

PRESUMPTION A rule of law requiring the court to presume certain facts to be true based on the existence of other facts, thereby shifting the burden of proof to the party against whom the presumption is asserted to rebut.

■=■

Eyerman v. Mercantile Trust Co.

Adjoining property owners (P) v. Executor of will (D)

Mo. Ct. App., 524 S.W.2d 210 (1975).

NATURE OF CASE: Appeal from lower court decision denying property owners' petition to prevent demolition of testator's home as directed by the testator in her will.

FACT SUMMARY: The will of Louise Johnson directed that after her death, the executor of her will should raze her home in St. Louis and sell the land. Adjoining property owners (P) filed suit to prevent the destruction of the home on the grounds the vacant lot would decrease the value of their properties.

> ## RULE OF LAW
> Because the taking of property by inheritance is not a natural right but one created by the state, the state may modify, add conditions, or prohibit testamentary orders or bequests if they are found to be against public policy.

FACTS: The will of Louise Johnson directed that after her death, the executor of her will should raze her home in St. Louis and sell the land. At the time of her death in 1973, the uncontradicted testimony at trial revealed the house and land together were valued at $40,000. If the house was razed, the land would only be worth $5,000. The adjoining property owners (P) alleged the value of their property would decrease due to the presence of the vacant lot. They also alleged the lot could become a public nuisance by attracting unwanted elements into the neighborhood. The home was also part of a subdivision, called Kingsbury Place, that required homeowners to maintain their homes at a certain level. The adjoining property owners (P) filed suit to prevent the destruction of the home. The lower court found that Johnson had the right to order the destruction of the home via her will and denied their motion for an injunction. The property owners (P) appealed.

ISSUE: Because the taking of property by inheritance is not a natural right but one created by the state, may the state modify, add conditions, or prohibit testamentary orders or bequests if they are found to be against public policy?

HOLDING AND DECISION: (Rendlen, J.) Yes. Because the taking of property by inheritance is not a natural right but one created by the state, the state may modify, add conditions, or prohibit testamentary orders or bequests if they are found to be against public policy. Although a person may deal capriciously with his own property during his or her lifetime, that person's own self-interest will usually restrain them from doing so. However, there are no such restraints after death. Where a testator creates an order or bequest that is capricious and serves no valid purpose to the detriment of the public, the state has the authority to prohibit such testamentary provisions. The phrase "against public policy" typically means actions that conflict with the morals of the time and goes against societal interests. Public policy is identified by examining the federal and state constitutions, state statutes, and judicial decisions. This court's review of judicial decisions from other jurisdictions supports the conclusion that this type of senseless destruction of property is generally disfavored. No individual or group of individuals benefits from the destruction of Ms. Johnston's home. Instead, the beneficiaries of the will and the adjoining property owners will be financially harmed due to the capriciousness of the deceased testator. The executor has presented no reason, valid or otherwise, to raze the property. Accordingly, because the provision is against public policy, the provision is held invalid and the property owners' petition to prohibit the razing of the house is granted. Reversed.

DISSENT: (Clemens, J.) The majority improperly grants a benefit to the beneficiaries of the will who were not even a party to this case. In addition, while the majority's opinion rests on the nebulous public policy doctrine, the plaintiffs submitted no evidence that the vacant lot would create a nuisance. There was no requisite showing of probable harm to the plaintiffs. The plaintiffs' entire case was based on conjecture rather than actual evidence. Turning to public policy, courts are on very fragile ground when they only rely upon other judicial decisions as support for the existence of the alleged public policy. The proper role of the judiciary is not to create public policy. Rather, courts may only determine what the public policy is by reviewing the legislative acts of the state or national legislatures. Because the plaintiffs offered no evidence of actual harm, the will of the testator should have been given effect.

ANALYSIS

The crux of the dissent's position is that the court's decision was not based on evidence. While this portion of the decision did not delve into the elements of a preliminary injunction, typically the moving must show: (1) a likelihood of irreparable harm; (2) the balance of harms favors the moving party; (3) a likelihood of success on the merits of the case; and (4) the public interest favors the injunction. Here, the portion of the majority's decision in the casebook focused on the public interest element, while the dissent focused on the irreparable harm element.

Continued on next page.

Quicknotes

PRELIMINARY INJUNCTION A judicial mandate issued to require or restrain a party from certain conduct; used to preserve a trial's subject matter or to prevent threatened injury.

TESTAMENTARY DISPOSITION A disposition of property that is effective upon the death of the grantor.

■━━■

Subsequent in Time: Acquisition of Property by Find, Adverse Possession, and Gift

Quick Reference Rules of Law

PAGE

1. *Armory v. Delamirie.* A finder of chattel has title superior to all but the rightful owner upon which he may maintain an action at law or in equity.   28

2. *Hannah v. Peel.* The finder of a lost article is entitled to it as against all persons except the real owner.   29

3. *Fulkerson v. Van Buren.* To establish title by adverse possession, one must prove that he or she had been in possession of the property continuously for over seven years and that the possession was visible, notorious, exclusive, hostile and with an intent to hold the property against the owner.   30

4. *Hollander v. World Mission Church of Washington, D.C.* To establish title by adverse possession, one must prove that he or she had been in possession of the property continuously for over 15 years and that the possession was visible, notorious, exclusive, hostile and with an intent to hold the property against the owner.   32

5. *McAvoy v. Medina.* Misplaced goods (items intentionally placed by the owner where they were found and then forgotten or left there) are deemed to be in the bailment of the owner of the property on which they are found for the true owner.   33

6. *Van Valkenburgh v. Lutz.* Title to a parcel may vest in an adverse possessor who occupies the parcel under claim of right, protects the parcel by an enclosure, improves or cultivates the parcel, and maintains that state of affairs for the statutory period.   34

7. *Mannillo v. Gorski.* To claim title by adverse possession, the possessor need not have been aware that the land in question was in fact owned by another.   35

8. *Howard v. Kunto.* Where several successive purchasers received record title to tract *A* under the mistaken belief that they were acquiring tract *B*, immediately contiguous thereto, and where possession of tract *B* is transferred and occupied in a continuous manner for more than 10 years by successive occupants, there is sufficient privity of estate to permit tacking and thus establish adverse possession as a matter of law.   36

9. *O'Keeffe v. Snyder.* The discovery rule controls in actions involving the adverse possession of chattels.   37

10. *Newman v. Bost.* A constructive delivery of a gift *causa mortis* will be effective where it plainly appears that it was the intention of the donor to make the gift, and where the things intended to be given are not present, or, where present, are incapable of manual delivery from their size or weight.   38

11. *Gruen v. Gruen.* A valid *inter vivos* gift of chattel may be made where the donor reserves a life estate and the donee never has physical possession until the donor's death.   39

Armory v. Delamirie

Jewel finder (P) v. Goldsmith (D)

King's Bench, 1 Strange 505 (1722).

NATURE OF CASE: Action in trover to recover the value of personal property.

FACT SUMMARY: Armory (P) found a jewel which he took to Delamirie (D), a goldsmith, for appraisal, but Delamirie's (D) apprentice removed the stones which Delamirie (D) refused to return.

🏛 RULE OF LAW
A finder of chattel has title superior to all but the rightful owner upon which he may maintain an action at law or in equity.

FACTS: Armory (P), a chimney sweeper's boy, found a jewel which he took to Delamirie's (D) goldsmith shop to learn what it was. Delamirie's (D) apprentice, under the pretense of weighing the jewel, removed the stones from the setting and told his master the value. Delamirie (D) offered Armory (P) three halfpence for the stones, but he refused. Delamirie (D) returned the setting without the stones.

ISSUE: Could Armory (P), who lacked legal title to the chattel, maintain an action to recover its value?

HOLDING AND DECISION: (Pratt, C.J.) Yes. The finder of lost property, although he does not acquire absolute ownership, does acquire title superior to everyone else except the rightful owner. Such title is a sufficient property interest in the finder upon which he may maintain an action against anyone (except the rightful owner) who violates that interest. Additionally, Delamirie (D) was liable as he was responsible for the actions of his apprentice. As for the measure of damages, if Delamirie (D) did not show the stones were not of the finest value, their value would be so determined.

▶ ANALYSIS

As to ownership, the finder is in a position similar to that of a bailee. The finder does not obtain absolute ownership, but does have the right of ownership against everybody except the true owner. Here, the chattel, the jewel, was subsequently converted against the finder. Yet the finder, if he should subsequently lose the chattel, may reclaim it from a subsequent finder. The finder has a choice of remedies. He may recover the chattel in specie if it is still in the converter's possession, or he may recover full value from the wrongdoer. Notice that an action in trover, which is an action at law, is to recover the value of the chattel. If it is desired to have the item returned, an action in replevin must be brought in equity.

■▬■

Quicknotes

BAILEE Person holding property in trust for another party.

■▬■

Hannah v. Peel

Brooch finder (P) v. Homeowner (D)

King's Bench, K.B. 509 (1945).

NATURE OF CASE: Action to recover personal property.

FACT SUMMARY: Hannah (P) found a brooch at Peel's (D) home during World War II, and sought to recover it after police handed it over to Peel (D).

🏛 RULE OF LAW
The finder of a lost article is entitled to it as against all persons except the real owner.

FACTS: During the Second World War, Peel's (D) home was requisitioned for use by the military. In August 1940, lance corporal Hannah (P) found a brooch in a crevice in a bedroom of the house. Hannah (P) gave the brooch to his commanding officer a month later, and in August 1942, the police handed the brooch to Peel (D), who subsequently sold it. There was no evidence that Peel (D) had any knowledge of the existence of the brooch before it was found by Hannah (P). Hannah (P) refused a reward offer from Peel (D), and maintained his right to possession of the brooch as against all persons other than the owner, who was unknown. On October 21, 1943, Hannah (P) filed suit to recover the brooch or its value and damages for its detention.

ISSUE: Is the finder of a lost article entitled to it as against all persons except the real owner?

HOLDING AND DECISION: (Birkett, J.) Yes. The general rule is that the finder of a lost article is entitled to it as against all persons except the real owner. This is because an occupier of land does not in all cases possess an unattached thing on his land even though the true owner has lost possession. Although a man possesses everything which is attached to or under his land, a man does not necessarily possess a thing which is lying unattached on the surface of his land even though the thing is not possessed by someone else. Here, the brooch was lost in the ordinary meaning of that term, and it had been lost for a very considerable time. Peel (D) was never physically in possession of the premises at any time. It is clear that the brooch was never his, in the ordinary meaning of the term, in that he did not have the prior possession. Peel (D) had no knowledge of it, until it was brought to his attention by Hannah (P). Accordingly, judgment is rendered for Hannah (P).

▶ ANALYSIS

The issue of finder's rights presented many problems for the English commentators. "The reason why these writers did not have better success in their efforts at definition was that they tried to state the essentials of all the possession cases in too simple a form; they tried, characteristically emphasizing human will, to reduce the essentials of possession to the form of a unilateral act. For them the type case was the act of taking-occupation." Shartel, "Meanings of Possession," 16 *Minn. L. Rev.* 611, 615, 619 (1932).

Quicknotes

POSSESSION The holding of property with the right of disposition.

Fulkerson v. Van Buren

Property owner (P) v. Adverse possessor (D)

Ark. Ct. App., 961 S.W.2d 780 (1998).

NATURE OF CASE: Appeal from lower court decision granting adverse possessor ownership of disputed parcel of land.

FACT SUMMARY: Fulkerson (P) owned a 4.5-acre piece of property that included a vacant building. In 1985, a religious group moved on to the property and used the building as a church for over seven years without any express permission from Fulkerson (P).

🏛 RULE OF LAW
To establish title by adverse possession, one must prove that he or she had been in possession of the property continuously for over seven years and that the possession was visible, notorious, exclusive, hostile and with an intent to hold the property against the owner.

FACTS: Fulkerson (P) owned a 4.5-acre piece of property that included a vacant building. There is no dispute Fulkerson (P) held proper title to the property. In 1985, a religious group, the Progressive Church, Inc. (the Church) (D), moved on to the property and used the building as a church for over seven years without any express permission from Fulkerson (P). The Church (D) made improvements to the building and the surrounding land. It also constructed a new building adjacent to the Church (D) to house its administrative offices. Van Buren (D), the Church Pastor, testified at trial that he became aware in 1990 or 1991 that Fulkerson (P) owned the property. He also testified that the Church (D) was not sure of its status on the land prior to that time. Van Buren (D) requested that Fulkerson (P) sell the property to the Church (D) but Fulkerson (P) refused. Eventually, Fulkerson (P) sent an eviction notice to the Church (D) in 1994. This action commenced in 1996. After a trial, the lower court found that the Church (D) has adversely possessed the property for the requisite seven years and granted ownership to the Church (D). Fulkerson (P) appealed.

ISSUE: To establish title by adverse possession, must one must prove that he or she had been in possession of the property continuously for over seven years and that the possession was visible, notorious, exclusive, hostile and with an intent to hold the property against the owner?

HOLDING AND DECISION: (Jennings, J.) Yes. To establish title by adverse possession, one must prove that he or she had been in possession of the property continuously for over seven years and that the possession was visible, notorious, exclusive, hostile and with an intent to hold the property against the owner. The key issue in this case is whether or not the Church's (D) possession was hostile with the intent to hold possession against the true owner. The intent required for adverse possession is the intention to claim the land outright as opposed to possessing it in conformity with or recognition of the superior right of the true owner of the land. Here, the evidence reveals the Church (D) was unaware of its status as occupiers from 1985 to 1991. Then, in 1991, Van Buren (D) became aware that Fulkerson (P) owned the property. Accordingly, by at least 1991, Van Buren (D) and the Church (D) had recognized the ownership right of the titleholder to the land. Their intent to hold the land adversely therefore did not reach the required seven years. By 1991, the Church's (D) possession of the land was in recognition of Fulkerson's (P) superior right to the land. Reversed and remanded.

DISSENT: (Meads, J.) From 1985 through the commencement of this action, the Progressive Church (D) possessed the land at issue and defied any attempts at eviction by Fulkerson (P). The majority incorrectly concludes that the Church (D) "recognized" Fulkerson's (P) ownership in 1991. Separate testimony from Van Buren (D) at the trial reveals he may not have discovered Fulkerson's (P) ownership until 1992. Even after discovering that, the Church (D) continued to remain on the premises without interruption through 1996. The Church (D) clearly demonstrated the hostile intent to possess the property. To be hostile, the possessor need only claim the land as its own, as distinguished from possessing the land in conformity with the alleged superior rights of another. Here, the evidence reveals the Church's (D) actions on the land have never been taken in recognition of Fulkerson's (P) superior title. The lower court decision should have been affirmed.

▶ ANALYSIS

States differ regarding their interpretation of adverse possession. Many states require up to 20 continuous years of possession before one may be granted title. In addition, states differ regarding the requisite intent shown by an adverse possessor. Some states view only the objective acts of the possessor, including notorious and open possession and improvements made upon the land. Other states include a subjective viewpoint of the possessor, including whether the possessor knew that someone else had superior title to the land.

Continued on next page.

Quicknotes

ADVERSE POSSESSION A means of acquiring title to real property by remaining in actual, open, continuous, exclusive possession of the property for the statutory period.

■═■

Hollander v. World Mission Church of Washington, D.C.

Adjoining property owner (D) v. Church (P)

Va. Sup. Ct., 498 S.E.2d 419 (1998).

NATURE OF CASE: Appeal from lower court decision finding that adjoining property owner did not fulfill the requirements for adverse possession of a disputed piece of land.

FACT SUMMARY: For more than 15 years, Hollander (D) mistakenly believed that her property ran all the way to a line of trees on property owned by World Mission Church of Washington, D.C. (P). Hollander (D) had mowed and otherwise maintained the disputed strip of land between the properties as if she owned it.

> 🏛 **RULE OF LAW**
> To establish title by adverse possession, one must prove that he or she had been in possession of the property continuously for over 15 years and that the possession was visible, notorious, exclusive, hostile and with an intent to hold the property against the owner.

FACTS: For more than 15 years, Hollander (D) mistakenly believed that her property ran all the way to a line of trees on property owned by World Mission Church of Washington, D.C. (the Church) (P). Hollander's (D) property actually stopped some distance before the line of trees. Hollander (D) and her predecessors in interest had mowed and otherwise maintained the disputed strip of land between the properties as if Hollander (D) owned it. This continued for more than 15 years. The Church (P) filed this action to recover the strip of land. Hollander (D) opposed the action on the grounds of adverse possession. The trial court found that Hollander (D) failed to prove the required element of intent to adversely possess the disputed strip of land. The court reached this conclusion because her possession was only based on a mistaken belief that her property ran to the tree line. This mistake negated the requisite intent. Hollander (D) appealed.

ISSUE: To establish title by adverse possession, must one must prove that he or she had been in possession of the property continuously for over 15 years and that the possession was visible, notorious, exclusive, hostile and with an intent to hold the property against the owner?

HOLDING AND DECISION: (Whiting, S.J.) Yes. To establish title by adverse possession, one must prove that he or she had been in possession of the property continuously for over 15 years and that the possession was visible, notorious, exclusive, hostile and with an intent to hold the property against the owner. Typically, if one possesses land via a mistake without the intention to claim such land, the possessor will not have the required intent to hold the land via adverse possession. However, if one holds land by mistake but also believes and intends that he or she owns such property regardless of the actual deed descriptions or actual boundary line, then that person has the required intent to adversely possess the land. Here, Hollander (D) and her predecessors in interest maintained the disputed strip of land as if it were their own for more than 15 years. The required intend was present. Reversed.

▶ ANALYSIS

Most jurisdictions now follow the objective approach to adverse possession. The adverse nature of possession is judged by the conduct and actions of the parties as opposed to their subjective beliefs.

■═■

Quicknotes

ADVERSE POSSESSION A means of acquiring title to real property by remaining in actual, open, continuous, exclusive possession of the property for the statutory period.

■═■

McAvoy v. Medina

Wallet finder (P) v. Barber shop owner (D)

Mass. Sup. Jud. Ct., 93 Mass. (11 Allen) 548 (1866).

NATURE OF CASE: Action to recover money.

FACT SUMMARY: A wallet was inadvertently left at a barber shop, a customer (P) found it, and the barber (D) asserted ownership.

🏛 RULE OF LAW
Misplaced goods (items intentionally placed by the owner where they were found and then forgotten or left there) are deemed to be in the bailment of the owner of the property on which they are found for the true owner.

FACTS: McAvoy (P) was a customer in Medina's (D) barber shop. McAvoy (P) found a wallet which was lying on a table. McAvoy (P) showed Medina (D) where he found the wallet and told Medina (D) to keep the wallet and the money in it and to give it to the real owner. Medina (D) promised to attempt to find the owner. McAvoy (P) later made three demands for return of the money, but Medina (D) refused. The wallet had been placed on the table by a transient customer of the barber shop, and had been accidentally left there. The true owner was never found.

ISSUE: Does the finder of misplaced goods on another's property obtain title to the goods?

HOLDING AND DECISION: (Dewey, J.) No. The owner of the premises on which misplaced goods are found is deemed to be the bailee of the goods for the true owner. This wallet was not lost. It had been voluntarily placed upon a table and then accidentally left there. This is different from lost property which had not been voluntarily placed by the owner where it was later found. When goods are misplaced, the finder acquires no original right to the property. Holding the owner of the premises as bailee of the goods is better adapted to secure the rights of the true owner. Exceptions overruled.

▌ ANALYSIS

The focus of lost or misplaced property cases is to determine whether it is likely that the true owner can ever be found. Therefore, because the finder was the first in possession, he will have paramount rights. On the other hand, where goods have been voluntarily placed and then forgotten, the true owner is much more likely to be found. As the true owner would be more likely to return to where he remembered placing the article, the owner of the premises will be deemed a bailee for the true owner.

■■■

Quicknotes

BAILEE Person holding property in trust for another party.

BAILMENT The delivery of property to be held in trust and which is designated for a particular purpose, following the satisfaction of which the property is either to be returned or disposed of as specified.

■■■

Van Valkenburgh v. Lutz

Tract owner (P) v. Adverse possessor (D)

N.Y. Ct. App., 106 N.E.2d 28 (1952).

NATURE OF CASE: Appeal from judgment establishing title by adverse possession.

FACT SUMMARY: Beginning around 1920, Lutz (D) traveled across a triangular tract to reach his home on a nearby parcel, and also built a shed and kept a garden on the tract, but in 1947 Van Valkenburgh (P) purchased the tract at a tax sale, and when Van Valkenburgh (P) demanded that Lutz (D) vacate the land, Lutz (D) obtained a judgment that granted him a right of way by prescription over the tract and then in a judicial proceeding established title to the tract by adverse possession.

RULE OF LAW
Title to a parcel may vest in an adverse possessor who occupies the parcel under claim of right, protects the parcel by an enclosure, improves or cultivates the parcel, and maintains that state of affairs for the statutory period.

FACTS: Lutz (D) and his family owned and occupied a parcel of land near a triangular tract in the City of Yonkers. Beginning around 1920, Lutz (D) used the tract to cross to his land. He then cleared part of the tract and built a shed thereon and maintained a garden, knowing that he had no title to the tract. In 1937, Van Valkenburgh (P) moved onto a parcel contiguous to the triangular tract and a small feud developed for unrelated reasons between the parties. In 1947, Van Valkenburgh (P) purchased the triangular tract at a tax sale and gave Lutz (D) notice to vacate the tract. At a meeting between the parties and counsel, Lutz (D) agreed to remove the shed and garden, but claimed a right of way by right of prescription across the tract. Though Van Valkenburgh (P) agreed, he erected a fence across the right of way path, whereupon Lutz (D) obtained a judgment awarding him a right of way, which was affirmed. Van Valkenburgh (P) then brought this suit to compel removal of encroachments and delivery of possession of the triangular tract. The trial court held for Lutz (D) granting title by adverse possession, and Van Valkenburgh (P) appealed.

ISSUE: May title to a parcel vest in an adverse possessor who occupies the parcel under claim of right, protects the parcel with an enclosure, improves or cultivates the parcel, and maintains that state of affairs for the statutory period?

HOLDING AND DECISION: (Dye, J.) Yes. In this case there was no proof offered of any protection of the parcel by enclosure by Lutz (D), and the proof shows that he did not cultivate the entire premises claimed. Fur-

thermore there was no improvement of the land because the shed thereon, the only structure of any kind involved here, was built by Lutz (D) with the conceded knowledge that he did not own the land under it. Title to a parcel may vest in an adverse possessor who occupies the parcel under claim of right, protects the parcel with an enclosure, improves or cultivates the parcel, and maintains that state of affairs for the statutory period. In this case, the elements permitting taking title by adverse possession were not present. Reversed, judgment directed for Van Valkenburgh (P).

DISSENT: (Fuld, J.) The weight of the evidence establishes Lutz's (D) right to the property in question by adverse possession. There was a "traveled way" across the property. Lutz (D) operated a truck farm there of substantial size. The fact that Lutz (D) knew he had no title to the tract is irrelevant so long as he intended to acquire title in himself, as he did. Lutz (D) actually occupied the property and title vested in him.

ANALYSIS

The traditional requirements for adverse possession are that the possession be actual, open, notorious, exclusive, adverse or hostile, continuous, under a claim of right, and for the statutory period. These requirements are variously expressed in the statutes and in the cases.

Quicknotes

ADVERSE POSSESSION A means of acquiring title to real property by remaining in actual, open, continuous, exclusive possession of property for the statutory period.

CLAIM OF RIGHT Person claiming a right in property is in possession and intends to claim ownership of that property without regard to the record title owner.

EASEMENT The right to utilize a portion of another's real property for a specific use.

Mannillo v. Gorski

Lot owner (P) v. Encroacher (D)

N.J. Sup. Ct., 255 A.2d 258 (1969).

NATURE OF CASE: Review of judgment denying claimed title by adverse possession.

FACT SUMMARY: Since Gorski (D) had created a structure encroaching upon Mannillo's (P) property, not knowing that the structure so encroached, Mannillo (P) argued that Gorski (D) lacked the requisite hostile intent to obtain title by adverse possession.

RULE OF LAW
To claim title by adverse possession, the possessor need not have been aware that the land in question was in fact owned by another.

FACTS: Mannillo (P) and Gorski (D) owned adjoining lots. At one point Gorski (D) erected a set of steps and a concrete walk to her dwelling that, unbeknownst to her, encroached upon Mannillo's (P) property. Years later, upon discovering that the steps encroached, Mannillo (P) filed a complaint seeking an injunction against the trespass. Gorski (D) counterclaimed for a declaratory judgment of title by adverse possession. The trial judge entered judgment for Mannillo (P), believing that an adverse possessor had to have been aware that her possession was hostile to be entitled to possession. The state supreme court granted review.

ISSUE: To claim title by adverse possession, must the possessor have been aware that the land in question was in fact owned by another?

HOLDING AND DECISION: (Haneman, J.) No. To claim title by adverse possession, the possessor needs not have been aware that the land in question was in fact owned by another. To hold to the contrary, i.e., to require that the adverse possession claim must be accompanied by a knowing intentional hostility, is called the "Maine Rule" and has been the law of this state for many years, but is of questionable historical pedigree and leads to undesirable results. Specifically, it places a knowing wrongdoer in a better position than an innocent party, a result the law ought not to condone. *Stare decisis* is an important principle, but in cases where people do not frame their conduct in reliance thereon, it is of lesser vitality as a doctrine. With respect to adverse possession, it is unlikely that the state of the law in this regard will impact people's behavior in any manner, as adverse possession is more of an after-the-fact situation than one done through preplanning. Since the law here is bad law, and *stare decisis* does not mandate adherence thereto, this court concludes that knowledge of the adversity of one's possession is not an element of adverse possession. However, no presumption of knowledge on the part of the true owner arises from a minor encroachment along a common boundary. In such a case, only where the true owner has actual knowledge thereof may the possession be said to be open and notorious. Remanded for trial.

▶ ANALYSIS

The competing rules here are the "Maine Rule," discussed but rejected in the above case, and the "Connecticut Rule," which the court adopted. The Maine Rule at one time enjoyed widespread adherence, but it has increasingly been abandoned for the reasons explained in the opinion here. The problem with the "Connecticut Rule," however, is that the true owner may not be put on notice that someone is in possession of a very small strip of land. Hence, the court rejected the traditional presumption of knowledge as fallacious and unjustified.

■=■

Quicknotes

ADVERSE POSSESSION A means of acquiring title to real property by remaining in actual, open, continuous, exclusive possession of property for the statutory period.

ENCROACHMENT The unlawful intrusion onto another's property.

INJUNCTION A court order requiring a person to do or prohibiting that person from doing a specific act.

STARE DECISIS Doctrine whereby courts follow legal precedent unless there is good cause for departure.

TRESPASS Unlawful interference with, or damage to, the real or personal property of another.

■=■

Howard v. Kunto

Record title owner (P) v. Adverse-possessor (D)

Wash. Ct. App., 477 P.2d 210 (1970).

NATURE OF CASE: Action to quiet title.

FACT SUMMARY: The land occupied by Kunto (D) was not that to which he had record title, but he appealed a judgment quieting title in Howard (P) who did have record title.

> ## 🏛 RULE OF LAW
> Where several successive purchasers received record title to tract *A* under the mistaken belief that they were acquiring tract *B*, immediately contiguous thereto, and where possession of tract *B* is transferred and occupied in a continuous manner for more than 10 years by successive occupants, there is sufficient privity of estate to permit tacking and thus establish adverse possession as a matter of law.

FACTS: The Kuntos (D) took possession of a summer home under a deed that unbeknownst to them described the adjoining property. After discovering the mistake, Howard (P) obtained a conveyance of the deed that described the property occupied by the Kuntos (D), then sought and obtained a judgment quieting title in himself. Several successive purchasers, over a period of over ten years, had taken possession of the disputed tract under the same mistaken deed. The Kuntos (D) appealed.

ISSUE: Where several successive purchasers received record title to tract *A* under the mistaken belief that they were acquiring tract *B*, immediately contiguous thereto, and where possession of tract *B* is transferred and occupied in a continuous manner for more than 10 years by successive occupants, is there sufficient privity of estate to permit tacking and thus establish adverse possession as a matter of law?

HOLDING AND DECISION: (Pearson, J.) Yes. Where several successive purchasers received record title to tract *A* under the mistaken belief that they were acquiring tract *B*, immediately contiguous thereto, and where possession of tract *B* is transferred and occupied in a continuous manner for more than ten years by successive occupants, there is sufficient privity of estate to permit tacking and thus establish adverse possession as a matter of law. The deed running between parties purporting to transfer land traditionally furnishes the privity of estate that connects the possession of successive occupants. The technical requirement of "privity" should not be used to upset the long periods of occupancy of those who in good faith received an erroneous deed description. The use of a summer cottage only in summer is uninterrupted possession sufficient to establish adverse possession. There is a public interest favoring early certainty as to the location of land ownership. Reversed with directions.

▶ ANALYSIS

The *Howard* case provides a good example of how the sometimes seemingly unjust doctrine of adverse possession can produce a just result.

Quicknotes

PRIVITY OF ESTATE Common or successive relation to the same right in property.

QUIET TITLE Equitable action to resolve conflicting claims to an interest in real property.

RECORD TITLE Title to real property that is recorded in the public land records.

TAKING A governmental action that substantially deprives an owner of the use and enjoyment of his or her property, requiring compensation.

O'Keeffe v. Snyder

Artist (P) v. Adverse-possessor (D)

N.J. Sup. Ct., 416 A.2d 862 (1980).

NATURE OF CASE: Appeal from reversal of award of replevin.

FACT SUMMARY: Snyder (D) contended that he had acquired three of O'Keeffe's (P) paintings by adverse possession.

 RULE OF LAW
The discovery rule controls in actions involving the adverse possession of chattels.

FACTS: The painter Georgia O'Keeffe (P) brought an action against Snyder (D) for replevin, or return of three small pictures painted by O'Keeffe (P). In her complaint, filed in March, 1976, O'Keeffe (P) alleged that she was the owner of the paintings, and that they had been stolen from a New York art gallery in 1946. Snyder (D) asserted that he was a purchaser for value of the paintings, that he had acquired title by adverse possession, and that O'Keeffe's (P) action was barred by the expiration of the six-year period of limitations pertaining to an action in replevin. The appellate court, in reversing the trial court, concluded that the paintings were stolen, the defenses of expiration of the statute of limitations and title by adverse possession were identical, and that Snyder (D) had not proved the elements of adverse possession.

ISSUE: Does the discovery rule control in actions involving the adverse possession of chattels?

HOLDING AND DECISION: (Pollock, J.) Yes. The discovery rule provides that, in an appropriate case, a cause of action will not accrue until the injured party discovers, or by exercise of reasonable diligence and intelligence should have discovered, facts that form the basis of a cause of action. Here, O'Keeffe's (P) cause of action accrued when she first knew, or reasonably should have known through the exercise of due diligence, of the cause of action, including the identity of the possessor of the paintings. The focus of the inquiry will no longer be whether the possessor has met the tests of adverse possession, but whether the owner has acted with due diligence in pursuing his or her personal property. Under the discovery rule, if an artist diligently seeks the recovery of a lost or stolen painting, but cannot find it or discover the identity of the possessor, the statute of limitations will not begin to run. Under the discovery rule, the burden is on the owner as the one seeking the benefit of the rule to establish facts that would justify deferring the beginning of the period of limitations. However, if the period of limitations does begin to run, the expiration of the six-year statutory limitation period should vest title as effectively under the discovery rule as under the doctrine of adverse possession. Reversed and remanded for further proceedings.

▶ ANALYSIS

Prior to the ruling in this case, the discovery rule had been applied primarily in tort actions where the injuries allegedly suffered by the plaintiff were difficult to discover. The court in this case, after reviewing the difficulty of applying principles of adverse possession to cases involving artwork, ruled that the application of the discovery rule would mitigate the unjust results that would flow from strict adherence to the rules of adverse possession.

■=■

Quicknotes

ADVERSE POSSESSION A means of acquiring title to real property by remaining in actual, open, continuous, exclusive possession of property for the statutory period.

CHATTEL An article of personal property, as distinguished from real property; a thing personal and moveable.

DUE DILIGENCE The standard of care as would be taken by a reasonable person in accordance with the attendant facts and circumstances.

REPLEVIN An action to recover personal property wrongfully taken.

■=■

Newman v. Bost

Donee (P) v. Estate administrator (D)

N.C. Sup. Ct., 29 S.E. 848 (1898).

NATURE OF CASE: Appeal from a finding of a valid gift *causa mortis*.

FACT SUMMARY: Newman (P) sought to recover the value of certain gifts *causa mortis* sold by the decedent's administrator (D) who did not believe any valid gifts were made to Newman (P).

🏛 RULE OF LAW

A constructive delivery of a gift *causa mortis* will be effective where it plainly appears that it was the intention of the donor to make the gift, and where the things intended to be given are not present, or, where present, are incapable of manual delivery from their size or weight.

FACTS: The decedent was stricken with paralysis and died within a month. While so stricken, he directed his nurse, Houston, to call Newman (P), his housekeeper, into his bedroom. The decedent handed to Newman (P) his private keys and told her to take them and keep them, that he desired her to have them and everything in the house. He then pointed out certain articles of furniture, including a bureau, and repeated that everything was hers. One of the keys unlocked a bureau drawer in which was decedent's life insurance policy, payable to his estate, and a few notes. Newman (P) brought suit against Bost (D), the decedent's administrator, to recover $3,000, the proceeds of the life insurance policy; $300, the value of a piano which decedent allegedly gave Newman (P) and which was destroyed by fire; $200.94, the value of household property sold by Bost (D); and $45, the value of the bedroom furniture sold by Bost (D). The court found that decedent made a valid gift *causa mortis*, and Bost (D) appealed.

ISSUE: Will a constructive delivery of a gift *causa mortis* be effective where it plainly appears that it was the intention of the donor to make the gift, and where the things intended to be given are not present, or where present, are incapable of manual delivery from their size and weight?

HOLDING AND DECISION: (Furches, J.) Yes. A constructive delivery of a gift *causa mortis* will be effective where it plainly appears that it was the intention of the donor to make the gift, and where the things intended to be given are not present, or, where present, are incapable of manual delivery from their size or weight; but where the articles are present, and are capable of manual delivery, manual delivery must be made. Here, as for the life insurance policy, it could have been removed from the drawer and easily handed to Newman (P). The failure to do so

prevented the policy from passing to her. However, the bureau and any other furniture that the keys would fit did pass to her because actual delivery would have been unreasonable because of their size and weight. The keys were thus an effective constructive delivery of those items. All other furniture, except that in Newman's own bedroom in the house, remained in the estate. The furniture in Newman's (P) bedroom passed to her, rather, as a gift *inter vivos* for she had use and control of it before decedent contemplated his death. As for the piano, it was not ever within her dominion and control and there was never any delivery, and so it did not pass to her. Remanded for a new trial.

▶ ANALYSIS

The court above took a fairly restrictive view of the concept of delivery and believed that the concept of gifts *causa mortis* should be strictly construed. The court expressed the fear that to allow symbolic delivery would be to open the door to all sorts of fraud. Where one is holding the donor's property as a bailee, and the donor wishes to give to the bailee that property already in the possession of the bailee, it is not necessarily for the intended donee-bailee to return the property to the donor so that delivery of the gift can be made. To so require, it has been held, would be a senseless formality. *Matter of Mill's Estate*, 158 N.Y.S. 1100 (App. Div. 1916).

■=■

Quicknotes

CONSTRUCTIVE DELIVERY The transfer of title or possession of property by means other than actual delivery indicative of the parties' intent to effect a transfer.

GIFT *CAUSA MORTIS* A gift made contingent on the donor's anticipated death.

GIFT *INTER VIVOS* A gift that is made, and is to take effect, while the parties are living.

STATUTE OF WILLS An English law stating the requirements for a valid testamentary disposition.

SYMBOLIC DELIVERY A method of constructive delivery whereby the transfer of title or possession of property is effectuated by delivering an article symbolic of the property.

■=■

Gruen v. Gruen

Son/donee (P) v. Stepmother (D)

N.Y. Ct. App., 496 N.E.2d 869 (1986).

NATURE OF CASE: Appeal from an enforcement of an *inter vivos* gift.

FACT SUMMARY: Mrs. Gruen (D) contended her husband could not make a valid *inter vivos* gift to his son (P) and still retain present exclusive possession of the property for his life.

🏛 **RULE OF LAW**
A valid *inter vivos* gift of chattel may be made where the donor reserves a life estate and the donee never has physical possession until the donor's death.

FACTS: Michael Gruen (P) received a letter from his father indicating the latter wished to make a gift of a painting, but that he wished to use it for his life. Gruen (P) never took possession of the painting. After his father's death, he requested the painting from his stepmother, Mrs. Gruen (D), who refused. Gruen (P) sued, contending a valid *inter vivos* gift had been made. His stepmother defended, contending no valid gift could be made if the donor retained a life estate and no physical delivery was made during life. The trial court held against Gruen (P), while the appellate court reversed. Mrs. Gruen (D) appealed.

ISSUE: May a valid *inter vivos* gift of chattel be made where the donor reserves a life estate and the donee does not take physical possession?

HOLDING AND DECISION: (Simons, J.) Yes. A valid *inter vivos* gift of chattel may be made where the donor reserves a life estate and the donee never takes physical possession until after the donor's death. In this case, donative intent was established constructively through the document of transfer, the letter. Acceptance is implied because the painting had value. Thus, a valid gift was made. Affirmed.

▶ **ANALYSIS**

Various estates in chattel can be created just as various estates in land are. The property in this case happened to be personal rather than real, yet the creation of a remainder interest was valid. It is clear the elder Mr. Gruen intended to make a current transfer of such interest, while retaining a possessory interest.

■■■

Quicknotes

CHATTEL An article of personal property, as distinguished from real property; a thing personal and moveable.

DONATIVE INTENT Donor's intent to make a gift.

GIFT *INTER VIVOS* A gift that is made, and is to take effect, while the parties are living.

REMAINDER INTEREST An interest in land that remains after the termination of the immediately preceding estate.

■■■

Possessory Estates

Quick Reference Rules of Law

PAGE

1. *White v. Brown.* Unless the words and context of a will clearly evidence an intention to convey only a life estate it will be interpreted as conveying a fee estate. 42

2. *Baker v. Weedon.* A court may order the sale of property that is held subject to a future interest, but only if a sale is necessary for the best interests of both the life tenant and the remainderman. 43

3. *Mahrenholz v. County Board of School Trustees.* Only where the grantor creates a possibility of reverter will he or his successors become possessory owners of the property immediately upon the breaking of the condition. 44

4. *Mountain Brow Lodge No. 82, Independent Order of Odd Fellows v. Toscano.* A limitation on the use of property, although it might serve to impede its transfer, will not be void as a restraint against alienation. 45

5. *Ink v. City of Canton.* Where land, restricted by a deed, is taken by eminent domain, a court shall divide the eminent domain damages award between the owner of the fee and the holder of the right of reverter. 46

White v. Brown

Beneficiary (P) v. Heir at law (D)

Tenn. Sup. Ct., 559 S.W.2d 938 (1977).

NATURE OF CASE: Appeal from a will interpretation.

FACT SUMMARY: The trial court held that Lide's will created a life estate in White (P) based on the fact the will specified the property was not to be sold.

🏛 RULE OF LAW
Unless the words and context of a will clearly evidence an intention to convey only a life estate it will be interpreted as conveying a fee estate.

FACTS: Lide died leaving a will that provided, "I wish Evelyn White to have my home to live in and not be sold." Lide's niece, Brown (D), claimed the will created a life estate and she obtained a remainder interest. White (P) sued to quiet title, contending the will created a fee estate. The trial court found for Brown (D), and White (P) appealed.

ISSUE: Will a will be interpreted as conveying a fee estate unless the words and context clearly evidence an intention to convey a lesser estate?

HOLDING AND DECISION: (Brock, J.) Yes. Unless the words and context of a will clearly evidence an intention to convey only a life estate, it will be interpreted as conveying a fee estate. Interpreting the will language presented here as creating only a life estate would create a partial intestacy. There is a general policy against creating intestacy where a reasonable alternative interpretation exists. Taking these two policies together, the trial court should have construed the will as creating a fee estate in White (P). Reversed and remanded.

DISSENT: (Harbison, J.) The express language of the will indicated an insurmountable constraint on alienation, indicating a clear intent to create less than a fee estate.

▌ANALYSIS

This case illustrates two common rules of construction to which courts resort in interpreting conveyances. The intent of the testator is derived from the entire document, and extrinsic evidence is admissible only under limited circumstances. Because of this restraint on extrinsic evidence of intent, courts must resort to the rules of construction previously noted. Where the instrument is drafted by a layperson, such rules of construction are essential to provide uniformity in construction.

∎≡∎

Quicknotes

ALIENATION Conveyance or transfer of property.

EXTRINSIC EVIDENCE Evidence that is not contained within the text of a document or contract but which is derived from the parties' statements or the circumstances under which the agreement was made.

HOLOGRAPHIC WILL A will that is handwritten by the testator or testatrix.

INTESTACY To die without leaving a valid testamentary instrument.

LIFE ESTATE An interest in land measured by the life of the tenant or a third party.

QUITCLAIM A deed whereby the grantor conveys whatever interest he or she may have in the property without any warranties or covenants as to title.

TESTATRIX A woman who dies having drafted and executed a will or testament.

∎≡∎

Baker v. Weedon

Life tenant (P) v. Remaindermen (D)

Miss. Sup. Ct., 262 So. 2d 641 (1972).

NATURE OF CASE: Sale of property bequeathed by will.

FACT SUMMARY: Weedon's will gave his property to his wife (P) for life, remainder to his grandchildren (D). The court was asked to permit sale of certain real property.

🏛 RULE OF LAW
A court may order the sale of property that is held subject to a future interest, but only if a sale is necessary for the best interests of both the life tenant and the remainderman.

FACTS: Weedon's will bequeathed all his property, both real and personal, to his third wife, Anna (P), for life. The remainder interest was willed to Anna's (P) children, if any, with Weedon's grandchildren (D) designated as beneficiaries in the event that Anna (P) died without issue. Weedon expressly failed to provide for his own children by a previous marriage, none of whom had enjoyed a happy relationship with him. Weedon died in 1932, and Anna (P) continued to live on a farm which he had bequeathed to her. Anna (P) remarried, but this second union, although it lasted for 20 years, resulted in no children. In 1964, the Mississippi State Highway Department (the Department) sought a right-of-way through the farm occupied by Anna (P). The Department contacted Weedon's surviving grandchildren (D), who thus became aware, for the first time, of their interests as remaindermen. Anna (P) was by now aged and destitute, and the grandchildren (D) willingly agreed to let Anna (P) receive a substantial proportion of the amount paid by the Department for the right-of-way. Anna (P) then sought an order permitting her to sell all of part of the farm property, contending that such a sale was necessary for her support. Since the property, although of negligible value for agricultural purposes, was of substantial and rapidly increasing worth as a commercial site, Weedon's grandchildren (D) opposed its sale. The chancellor, noting Anna's (P) age and that the property was of little value as agricultural property, approved its sale. The grandchildren (D) then appealed, challenging the right of the court to order the sale of property in which they held a future interest.

ISSUE: May a court order the sale of property that is encumbered by a future interest?

HOLDING AND DECISION: (Patterson, J.) Yes. A court may order the sale of property that is held subject to a future interest, but only if a sale is necessary for the best interests of both the life tenant and the remainderman.

In this case, the farm property is increasing in value and a significant financial loss to the remaindermen would result from the premature sale of the entire tract of land. This action should, therefore, be remanded so that the chancery court may entertain a motion by Anna Weedon (P) to sell only enough of the property to provide adequate support for her, unless a satisfactory compromise can be reached by all the interested parties. Reversed and remanded.

▶ ANALYSIS

When property that is subject to a future interest is constantly diminishing in worth, most courts will consider permitting its sale according to the doctrine of ameliorative (or ameliorating) waste. The concept of ameliorative waste presumes that a decline in the value of a property will eventually prove detrimental to the best interests of the remaindermen as well as the life tenants. However, before the doctrine will be applied, most courts require that the property be demonstrated to be worthless, or at least of only negligible value, for any purpose.

■══■

Quicknotes

AMELIORATIVE WASTE An unauthorized change in a physical structure which, though technically "waste," in fact increases the value of the land.

CONTINGENT REMAINDERMAN One who has an interest in property to commence upon the termination of a present possessory interest and subject to condition precedent.

DECREE PRO CONFESSO A decree founded upon a bill in equity to which the defendant fails to answer.

ECONOMIC WASTE An act done by someone in lawful possession of an interest in land, causing injury to other estate holders in the same property, that diminishes the value of the mineral resources that may be produced from the property.

FUTURE INTEREST An interest in property the right to possession or enjoyment of which is to take place at sometime in the future.

■══■

Mahrenholz v. County Board of School Trustees

Possibility-of-reverter holder (P) v. Grantee (D)

Ill. App. Ct., 417 N.E.2d 138 (1981).

NATURE OF CASE: Appeal from dismissal of action to quiet title.

FACT SUMMARY: Mahrenholz (P) contended he obtained a possessory interest in land when the School District (D) ceased using the property for classes, allegedly breaching a deed restriction.

🏛 **RULE OF LAW**
Only where the grantor creates a possibility of reverter will he or his successors become possessory owners of the property immediately upon the breaking of the condition.

FACTS: Mahrenholz (P) sued to quiet title to land deeded to the School District (D) "for school purposes." The land grant specifically stated that "this land to be used for school purpose only; otherwise to revert to Grantors herein." The heir of the grantors subsequently conveyed his interest in the land to Mahrenholz's (P) predecessor in interest. Mahrenholz (P) contended that the original conveyance created a fee simple determinable which gave rise to a possibility of reverter. This allowed him to become the possessory owner of the property by operation of law when the site ceased being used to hold classes. The trial court held that the conveyance created a fee simple subject to a condition subsequent and because the heir had not affirmatively enforced his right of re-entry, he had no possessory interest to convey. Mahrenholz (P) appealed.

ISSUE: Will a grantor automatically obtain possessory ownership of the estate only where the grant created a possibility of reverter?

HOLDING AND DECISION: (Jones, J.) Yes. Only where the grantor creates a possibility of reverter will he or his successors become possessory owners immediately upon the breach of the deed restriction. A grant of use for an exclusive purpose followed by an express provision for reverter creates a fee simple determinable and a possibility of reverter. The deed in this case created such use and therefore the heir held a possibility of reverter. His conveyance to Mahrenholz's (P) predecessor conveyed this interest which became possessory, if at all, when the land was no longer used for classes. Therefore, the trial court erred in dismissing the action. Reversed and remanded.

▶ *ANALYSIS*

This case illustrates the difference in theory between the possibility of reverter created by a fee simple determinable and the right of re-entry created by a fee simple subject to a condition subsequent. In the former, the breach of con-

dition precedent automatically terminates the possessory estate. In the latter, termination is merely a right which must be exercised by the holder. This is purely an academic distinction as any possessory interest will have to be formally terminated before the estate holder will abandon the estate.

◼◼◼

Quicknotes

DETERMINABLE FEE An interest in property that may last forever or until the happening of a specified event.

FEE SIMPLE DEFEASIBLE ESTATE A fee simple interest in land that is subject to being terminated upon the happening of a future event.

FEE SIMPLE SUBJECT TO A CONDITION SUBSEQUENT An estate in land that represents total ownership, except that it is capable of being defeated upon the occurrence or nonoccurrence of a specified condition.

QUIET TITLE Equitable action to resolve conflicting claims to an interest in real property.

REVERSIONARY INTEREST An interest retained by a grantor of property in the land transferred, which is created when the owner conveys less of an interest than he or she owns and which returns to the grantor upon the termination of the conveyed estate.

RIGHT OF REENTRY An interest in property reserved in the conveyance of a fee that gives the holder the right to resume possession of property upon the happening of a condition subsequent.

◼◼◼

Mountain Brow Lodge No. 82, Independent Order of Odd Fellows v. Toscano

Grantee (P) v. Possibility-of-reverter holders (D)

Cal. Ct. App., 64 Cal. Rptr. 816 (1967).

NATURE OF CASE: Appeal from denial of order to quiet title.

FACT SUMMARY: Mountain Brow Lodge (P) sought to have a clause in a gift deed declared void as a restraint on alienation, thereby quieting its title in the property.

🏛 RULE OF LAW
A limitation on the use of property, although it might serve to impede its transfer, will not be void as a restraint against alienation.

FACTS: Mountain Brow Lodge (Lodge) (P) acquired real property by a gift deed from Toscano. Included in the deed was a clause that purportedly restricted the use and ownership of the property to the Lodge (P). Upon violation of the restriction, the property was to revert to Toscano's estate (D). The Lodge (P) sought a court ruling that the restrictive condition was void as a restraint against alienation and that the Lodge (P) therefore owned the property outright. The trial court held that the conditions were not void and refused to quiet title. The Lodge (P) appealed.

ISSUE: Is a limitation on the use of property that also has the effect of restricting its transfer void as a restraint against alienation?

HOLDING AND DECISION: (Gargano, J.) No. Courts in this jurisdiction and many others have long recognized that limitations on the use of property, although they might also serve to impede its transfer, will not be void as a restraint against alienation. Thus, the part of the clause that limits the use of the property to Lodge (P) purposes is valid. However, the language that expressly restricts the sale or transfer of the property at issue will be stricken as an impermissible restraint against alienation. Affirmed as modified.

DISSENT: (Stone, J.) The restriction on use that appears in the deed is for all practical purposes a restraint against alienation and should be voided. Therefore the Lodge's (P) title should be quieted.

▌ ANALYSIS

Other jurisdictions have found that a use restriction that effectively serves to limit the alienation of the property to a small group of people is void as an impermissible indirect restriction on alienation. See, e.g., *Falls City v. Missouri Pacific Railway So.*, 453 F.2d. 771 (8th Cir. 1971). In *Falls*

City, the court framed the test as whether the imposed condition materially and adversely affected the marketability of the property. If it did, then it was an invalid limitation and the fee simple determinable was transmuted into a fee simple absolute.

■■■

Quicknotes

ALIENATION Conveyance or transfer of property.

HABENDUM CLAUSE A clause contained in a deed that specifies the parties to the transaction and defines the interest in land to be conveyed.

QUIET TITLE Equitable action to resolve conflicting claims to an interest in real property.

RESTRAINT AGAINST ALIENATION A provision restricting the transferee's ability to convey interests in the conveyed property.

RESTRICTIVE CONDITION A promise contained in a deed to limit the uses to which the property will be made.

USE RESTRICTION A restriction on the right to utilize one's personal or real property.

■■■

Ink v. City of Canton
Individuals (P) v. City (D)

Ohio Sup. Ct., 212 N.E.2d 574 (1965).

NATURE OF CASE: Plaintiff's appeal of lower court decisions in favor of defendant.

FACT SUMMARY: Harry Ink granted the City of Canton (the City) (D) 33 acres of land to be used only as a public park, with his heirs holding a right of reverter. The state of Ohio took a large portion of the land by eminent domain and a lower court granted all of the damages to Canton (D).

🏛 RULE OF LAW
Where land, restricted by a deed, is taken by eminent domain, a court shall divide the eminent domain damages award between the owner of the fee and the holder of the right of reverter.

FACTS: Harry Ink granted the City (D) 33 acres of land. The deed stated that the City (D) could only use the land for a public park. If the city used the land otherwise, the land would revert to Mr. Ink's heirs (P). The state of Ohio then took all but six acres of the land for a highway project. The courts below awarded all of the eminent domain damages, $130,822, to the City (D). The heirs (P) appeal.

ISSUE: When land, restricted by a deed, is taken by eminent domain, must a court divide the eminent domain damages award between the owner of the fee and the holder of the right of reverter?

HOLDING AND DECISION: (Taft, C.J.) Yes. When land, restricted by a deed, is taken by eminent domain, a court shall divide the eminent domain damages award between the owner of the fee and the holder of the right of reverter. The common law rule was that all eminent domain damages would go to the grantee of the deed, here, the City (D). The holder of the reverter would receive nothing. Many jurisdictions have refused to apply this harsh rule. Instead, Ohio has previously recognized that such a scenario would result in a significant windfall to the grantee of the restricted deed, who paid nothing for the land. In this matter, we hold that the eminent domain action does not force a reversion of the remaining property back to Mr. Ink's heirs (P). However, the City (D) must use the damages award solely for maintenance of the remaining six acres of the park. In the event that the $130,822 exceeds the city's maintenance costs, the city should turn that excess over to the holders of the right of reverter. Reversed and remanded.

ANALYSIS

Most jurisdictions respond to this scenario in similar fashions, eschewing the common law rule in favor of a more equitable result. One other factor the court relied upon was the fiduciary duty the City (D) owed the plaintiffs to maintain the park. Accordingly, the City (D) had to use the damages award for the park's benefit.

Quicknotes

EMINENT DOMAIN The governmental power to take private property for public use so long as just compensation is paid therefor.

REVERTER A reversionary interest referring to an interest in land that remains in the grantor until the happening of a condition precedent.

Future Interests

Quick Reference Rules of Law

PAGE

1. *Broadway National Bank v. Adams.* A founder of a trust may lawfully restrict the grantee's power of anticipatory alienation of the trust benefits and bar creditors from reaching the trust funds.   48

2. *The Symphony Space, Inc. v. Pergola Properties, Inc.* Commercial option agreements are not exempted from the Rule Against Perpetuities.   49

Broadway National Bank v. Adams

Creditor (P) v. Debtor (D)

Mass. Sup. Jud. Ct., 133 Mass. 170 (1882).

NATURE OF CASE: Appellate court's consideration of plaintiff's bill in equity.

FACT SUMMARY: Adams (D) owed Broadway National Bank (Broadway) (P) money. Broadway (P) sought to reach and apply a portion of a trust that Adams's (D) brother created for Adams's (D) benefit.

🏛 RULE OF LAW
A founder of a trust may lawfully restrict the grantee's power of anticipatory alienation of the trust benefits and bar creditors from reaching the trust funds.

FACTS: Adams (D) owed Broadway (P) money. Adams's (D) brother created a lifetime trust for Adams, with the provision that such funds may not be alienated to satisfy a debt. Adams would receive semi-annual payments from the trust only. Broadway (P) filed this bill in equity to reach the trust funds to satisfy the debt.

ISSUE: May a founder of a trust lawfully restrict the grantee's power of anticipatory alienation of the trust benefits and bar creditors from reaching the trust funds?

HOLDING AND DECISION: (Morton, C.J.) Yes. A founder of a trust may lawfully restrict the grantee's power of anticipatory alienation of the trust benefits and bar creditors from reaching the trust funds. The common law rule was that one could not attach to a grant or transfer of property a restriction that the property not be alienated. Some courts in England and in our own country have applied this rule to similar circumstances. However, we hold the rule does not apply for a lifetime trust created by one for the benefit of another where the grantor restricts the grantee's ability to alienate the trust funds. In this matter, Adams's (D) brother, as the owner of the property in question, has the right to dispose of the property in any manner he sees fit. His clear intention was not to give Adams (D) complete control of the trust funds, but only semi-annual payments. The court should give effect to his intention unless those intentions run afoul of public policy. Broadway (P) argues the provision may defraud creditors and induce them to give credit to Adams (D) based on his apparent wealth. However, the creditors, by their due diligence, may ascertain the precise nature of his estate prior to giving credit. Whether a man may transfer funds into a trust for his own benefit, simply to place funds beyond the reach of creditors, is a different question that we do not answer today. Broadway's (P) bill in equity is dismissed.

▶ ANALYSIS

This case is still good law and is a seminal case regarding the creation of spendthrift trusts. A spendthrift trust is created with limitations on the grantee's access to the trust funds. The grantee's creditors may not reach the trust funds until the funds are distributed from the trust to the grantee. The trust document requires a specific provision denoting such limitations.

■=■

Quicknotes

BILL IN EQUITY First pleading in a lawsuit in which a plaintiff seeks equitable remedies.

SPENDTHRIFT PROVISION A provision in a trust providing for the beneficiary's support, but with restrictions imposed so as to safeguard against the beneficiary's alienation of his interest therein.

SPENDTHRIFT TRUST A trust formed for the beneficiary's support, but with restrictions imposed so as to safeguard against the beneficiary's alienation of his interest therein.

■=■

The Symphony Space, Inc. v. Pergola Properties, Inc.

Buyer (P) v. Seller (D)

N.Y. Ct. App., 669 N.E.2d 799 (1996).

NATURE OF CASE: Suit for declaratory judgment.

FACT SUMMARY: Symphony Space, Inc. (Symphony) (P) sought a declaratory judgment that an option clause in its agreement to purchase property from Broadwest Realty Corp. (Broadway) was unenforceable in violation of the Rule Against Perpetuities.

RULE OF LAW
Commercial option agreements are not exempted from the Rule Against Perpetuities.

FACTS: Symphony (P), a nonprofit organization dedicated to the arts, leased a theatre from Broadwest. Broadwest sold the building to Symphony (P) and leased back the income producing property, minus the theatre, for one year. The purpose of the agreement was to provide Symphony (P) with a tax exemption. The agreement also contained an option clause allowing Broadwest to purchase the property during specified periods. Pergola Properties, Inc. (Pergola) (D), a nominee of Broadwest, notified Symphony (P) of its intent to exercise the option, and Symphony (P) brought suit seeking a declaratory judgment that the option violated New York's Rule Against Perpetuities. The Appellate Division held the clause unenforceable.

ISSUE: Are commercial option agreements exempted from the Rule Against Perpetuities?

HOLDING AND DECISION: (Kaye, C.J.) No. Commercial option agreements are not exempted from the Rule Against Perpetuities. Options to purchase are to be treated differently than preemptive rights, which impede transferability only minimally in contrast to purchase options, which vest substantial control over the alienability of the property upon the option holder. Only where the preemptive right arises in a governmental or commercial agreement is the minor restraint offset by the holder's incentive to improve the property. The option agreement here creates the type of control over the transferability over property that the rule against remote vesting has sought to prevent. An option "appurtenant" to purchase land that originates in a lease provision that is not exercisable after the expiration of the lease, and is incapable of separation from the lease agreement, is still generally valid even though the holder's interest may vest beyond the perpetuities period. Here the option does not qualify as an option appurtenant, since it significantly deters the development of the property. Affirmed.

ANALYSIS

The exception to the Rule Against Perpetuities for preemptive rights was developed in order to provide an incentive for the development of property. At common law, options to purchase land were subject to the rule, since they worked as a disincentive to such development. Although such options are typically found in commercial contracts, they are still subject to the rule against remote vesting.

Quicknotes

FREE ALIENABILITY Unrestricted transferability.

OPTION A contract pursuant to which a seller agrees that property will be available for the buyer to purchase at a specified price and within a certain time period.

RULE AGAINST PERPETUITIES The doctrine that a future interest that is incapable of vesting within twenty-one years of lives in being at the time it is created is immediately void.

VESTING The attaining of the right to pension or other employer-contribution benefits when the employee satisfies the minimum requirements necessary in order to be entitled to the receipt of such benefits in the future.

Co-ownership and Marital Interests

Quick Reference Rules of Law

PAGE

1. *Riddle v. Harmon.* A joint tenancy may be terminated by the conveyance by one joint tenant of his interest in the joint tenancy property to himself. — 52

2. *Harms v. Sprague.* A mortgage on a joint tenant's interest does not survive the mortgagor. — 53

3. *Delfino v. Vealencis.* Partition sales are employed only where partition in kind is unworkable. — 54

4. *Spiller v. Mackereth.* Absent an owner physically barring a cotenant from entry upon the owned premises, that owner is not liable to the cotenant for rent. — 55

5. *Swartzbaugh v. Sampson.* The act of one joint tenant without express or implied authority from, or consent of, his cotenant cannot bind or prejudicially affect the rights of that cotenant; but, a lease to all of the joint property by one joint tenant is not a nullity but rather is valid to the extent of his interest in the joint property. — 56

6. *Sawada v. Endo.* Tenancy-by-the-entirety property may not be reached by the separate creditors of either spouse. — 58

7. *In re Marriage of Graham.* An educational degree cannot be marital property subject to division upon divorce. — 59

8. *Elkus v. Elkus.* Celebrity status with the accompanying economic opportunities may be a marital asset subject to equitable dissolution. — 60

9. *Varnum v. Brien.* Iowa's marriage statute, defining marriage as between one man and one woman, violates the equal protection clause of the Iowa constitution. — 61

Riddle v. Harmon

Joint tenant (P) v. Estate executrix (D)

Cal. Ct. App., 162 Cal. Rptr. 530 (1980).

NATURE OF CASE: Appeal from summary judgment upholding joint tenancy and quieting title.

FACT SUMMARY: Riddle (P) sought to enforce a joint tenancy right of survivorship against Harmon (D), the executrix of his wife's estate, after the wife had deeded her one-half joint tenancy interest in the Riddle property to herself in order to sever and terminate Riddle's (P) right to succeed to the whole.

🏛 RULE OF LAW
A joint tenancy may be terminated by the conveyance by one joint tenant of his interest in the joint tenancy property to himself.

FACTS: Riddle's (P) wife, the decedent, owned certain real property in joint tenancy with Riddle (P). When she was planning her estate, she did not want her interest in the parcel to pass to Riddle (P). Her attorney advised her to terminate the joint tenancy by granting herself an undivided one-half interest in the property, making her a tenant in common. A grant deed was drawn up to that effect, and a will devising her tenancy in common to a third party was executed. Riddle (P), upon his wife's death, challenged her estate plan, and the trial court quieted title in him. Harmon (D), the wife's executrix, appealed.

ISSUE: May a joint tenancy be terminated by the conveyance by one joint tenant of his interest in the joint tenancy property to himself?

HOLDING AND DECISION: (Poche, J.) Yes. A joint tenancy may be terminated by the conveyance by one joint tenant of his interest in the joint tenancy property to himself. At common law, the creation of joint tenancy required the "four unities": interest, time, title, and possession. This required that both tenants acquire their interest at the same moment, which in turn required that one party holding the whole had to convey his interest to a third person ("straw man") who would convey to the joint tenants in order for such party to create a joint tenancy between himself and another. Modern law has abandoned this obsolete requirement as to creation. There is little virtue in adhering to cumbersome feudal law requirements. One joint tenant may unilaterally sever the joint tenancy without the use of an intermediary device. A "straw man" is not necessary. Reversed.

▶ ANALYSIS

The purchaser of an interest in property from a joint tenant becomes a tenant in common with the other joint tenants, who remain joint tenants as to each other only. A minority

of jurisdictions not requiring reconveyance to a straw man for severance permit termination of a joint tenancy by the filing of a declaration of an intention to do so, eliminating even the fiction of having to convey to sever.

■■■

Quicknotes

FOUR UNITIES The four unities that must be present in order for a joint tenancy to be formed include unity of interest, possession, time, and title.

GRANT DEED A deed conveying an interest in real or personal property.

JOINT TENANCY An interest in property whereby a single interest is owned by two or more persons and created by a single instrument; joint tenants possess equal interests in the use of the entire property, and the last survivor is entitled to absolute ownership.

LIVERY OF SEISIN A ceremony in which an interest in land is formally delivered usually by delivering a piece of earth.

QUIET TITLE Equitable action to resolve conflicting claims to an interest in real property.

SEVERANCE Dividing or separating.

STRAW MAN A third party to whom a transfer of property is made in order to effectuate a transaction that may not otherwise be allowed.

TENANCY IN COMMON An interest in property held by two or more people, each with equal right to its use and possession; interests may be partitioned, sold, conveyed, or devised.

■■■

Harms v. Sprague

Joint tenant (P) v. Mortgage assignee (D)

Ill. Sup. Ct., 473 N.E.2d 930 (1984).

NATURE OF CASE: Appeal of reversal of court order quieting title.

FACT SUMMARY: John Harms, deceased former joint tenant in property with William Harms (P) had executed a mortgage in favor of the predecessor in interest of Sprague (D) who claimed the mortgage survived John.

> ## 🏛 RULE OF LAW
> A mortgage on a joint tenant's interest does not survive the mortgagor.

FACTS: William (P) and John Harms owned property in joint tenancy. John executed a mortgage favoring Simmons, who later assigned his interest to Sprague (D). After John died, William (P) contended that the mortgage had died with John and brought an action to quiet title. The trial court held that Sprague's (D) mortgage survived John's death and entered judgment in favor of Sprague (D). The appellate court reversed. Sprague (D) appealed.

ISSUE: Does a mortgage on a joint tenant's interest survive the mortgagor?

HOLDING AND DECISION: (Moran, J.) No. A mortgage on a joint tenant's interest does not survive the mortgagor. One requirement for joint tenancy is a unity of title. If a mortgage constituted a change in title, it would destroy this unity. However, this state recognizes that a mortgage will not constitute a change of title until foreclosure plus the running of any redemption period. Since a mortgage does not sever a joint tenancy, the entire estate of the decedent joint tenant passes to the survivor. This effects a nullification of any liens thereon. For this reason, Sprague's (D) interest was extinguished upon John's death. Affirmed.

▶ ANALYSIS

An issue regarding both real property law and secured transaction law is the "lien" vs. "title" theories. As discussed in the case, mortgages have been seen as both transfers of title and mere encumbrances. It seems that most jurisdictions adhere to the lien theory.

■══■

Quicknotes

JOINT TENANCY An interest in property whereby a single interest is owned by two or more persons and created by a single instrument; joint tenants possess equal interests in the use of the entire property, and the last survivor is entitled to absolute ownership.

LIEN A claim against the property of another in order to secure the payment of a debt.

MORTGAGE An interest in land created by a written instrument providing security for the payment of a debt or the performance of a duty.

QUIET TITLE Equitable action to resolve conflicting claims to an interest in real property.

REDEMPTION PERIOD The period during which a mortgagor has the right to reclaim forfeited property, following a default on mortgage payments, by the payment of the mortgage debt and any other interest, fees, and costs.

UNITY OF TITLE Requirement that cotenants in a joint tenancy or tenancy by the entirety obtain their interests in the property under the same legal title.

■══■

Delfino v. Vealencis

Tenant in common (P) v. Cotenant (D)

Conn. Sup. Ct., 436 A.2d 27 (1980).

NATURE OF CASE: Appeal from judicially ordered partition sale.

FACT SUMMARY: The trial court held the rights of the parties would be best protected by a partition sale rather than a partition in kind.

🏛 RULE OF LAW
Partition sales are employed only where partition in kind is unworkable.

FACTS: The Delfinos (P) owned an undivided 99/144 interest in land, in which Vealencis (D) owned an undivided 45/144 interest. The property was held as a tenancy in common. Delfino (P) wanted to develop residential housing on the tract and sought a partition sale. Vealencis (D) defended, contending partition in kind. She used her portion of the property for the operation of a rubbish removal business. The court held the partition in kind was unavailable and a partition sale was necessary. Vealencis (D) appealed, contending the property, rectangular in shape and having only three cotenants, could easily be subjected to partition in kind.

ISSUE: Are partition sales employed only where partition in kind is unworkable?

HOLDING AND DECISION: (Healey, J.) Yes. Partition sales are employed only where partition in kind is unavailable. Partition sales should be employed only in extraordinary circumstances, as the forced sale of a party's interest should be avoided. In this case, the limited number of competing interests, and the relative ease of division makes partition in kind very workable. Reversed and remanded.

▶ ANALYSIS

The court rejected the proposition that the property could not be used jointly. The trial court had found that the use for residential property was mutually exclusive with use as rubbish removal business. The shape of the property allowed for easy partition.

■■■■

Quicknotes

PARTITION IN KIND A separation of undivided interests in land so that the parties may possess their interests separately.

PARTITION SALE A court-ordered sale of property held in joint tenancy, as a cotenant or in tenancy by the entirety, if the property is incapable of being divided; the income is distributed in proportion to the parties' interests in the sold property.

■■■■

Spiller v. Mackereth

Cotenant in possession (D) v. Tenant in common (P)

Ala. Sup. Ct., 334 So. 2d 859 (1976).

NATURE OF CASE: Appeal from judgment awarding damages for back rent.

FACT SUMMARY: Spiller (D), cotenant of a warehouse with Mackereth (P), ignored her demand that he cease using the whole premises or pay her rent.

> 🏛 **RULE OF LAW**
> Absent an owner physically barring a cotenant from entry upon the owned premises, that owner is not liable to the cotenant for rent.

FACTS: Spiller (D) and Mackereth (P) were tenants in common of a warehouse. When their tenant vacated, Spiller (D) began using the entire warehouse as a storage facility. Mackereth (P) demanded that he either vacate half the premises or pay rent. He ignored the demand. Mackereth (P) sued for rent. A trial court awarded $2,100 back rent. Spiller (D) appealed.

ISSUE: Absent an owner physically barring a cotenant from entry upon the owned premises, is that owner liable to the cotenant for rent?

HOLDING AND DECISION: (Jones, J.) No. Absent an owner physically barring a cotenant from entry upon the owned premises, the owner is not liable to the cotenant for rent. As a general rule, a cotenant has the full right to use the premises and cannot be liable to cotenants for rent. The only exception to this occurs when there is an "ouster." For there to be an ouster, a cotenant must physically bar the other cotenant from entry. Merely ignoring an order to partially vacate does not constitute ouster. Here, there is no evidence that Spiller (D) physically barred Mackereth (P) from entry, so there was no ouster. Reversed.

▶ ANALYSIS

Ouster can exist in different degrees. When it is not done under a claim of absolute ownership, it can support an action for back rent. When done under a claim of such ownership, it can give rise to adverse possession, if the other elements required therefor are present.

■ ▬ ■

Quicknotes

ABSOLUTE OWNERSHIP Ownership of property that exists exclusively to one party.

ADVERSE POSSESSION A means of acquiring title to real property by remaining in actual, open, continuous, exclusive possession of property for the statutory period.

OUSTER The unlawful dispossession of a party lawfully entitled to possession of real property.

PER MY ET PER TOUT By half and by whole; refers to the holding of interests in a joint tenancy whereby a joint tenant is entitled to the whole property for purposes of survivorship and to his or her share for purposes of alienation.

■ ▬ ■

Swartzbaugh v. Sampson

Joint tenant (P) v. Cotenant/lessor (D) and lessee (D)

Cal. Ct. App., 54 P.2d 73 (1936).

NATURE OF CASE: Action to cancel a lease made by a co-joint tenant with a third party.

FACT SUMMARY: Mrs. Swartzbaugh (P) refused to agree to a lease between Sampson (D) and Mr. Swartzbaugh (D), her husband, for land held by the Swartzbaughs in joint tenancy.

🏛 **RULE OF LAW**
The act of one joint tenant without express or implied authority from, or consent of, his cotenant cannot bind or prejudicially affect the rights of that cotenant; but, a lease to all of the joint property by one joint tenant is not a nullity but rather is valid to the extent of his interest in the joint property.

FACTS: Mrs. Swartzbaugh (P) and Mr. Swartzbaugh (D) had acquired title to certain real property as joint tenants. (They are husband and wife.) Subsequently, Mr. Swartzbaugh (D) and Sampson (D) executed two leases for parcels of this property. At all times however, Mrs. Swartzbaugh (P) objected to the lease, refused to participate in it, and made these facts well known to both Mr. Swartzbaugh (D) and Sampson (D). At no time has she received any rent from this lease. She sued to cancel the lease, claiming it was a total nullity without her participation as a joint tenant. From a nonsuit decision, she appealed.

ISSUE: Can one joint tenant who has not joined in leases executed by her cotenant and a third party maintain an action to cancel the leases where the third party is in exclusive possession of the leased property?

HOLDING AND DECISION: (Marks, J.) No. The act of one joint tenant without express or implied authority from, or consent of, his cotenant cannot bind or prejudicially affect the rights of that cotenant; but, a lease of all of the joint property by one joint tenant is not a nullity but rather is valid to the extent of his interest in the joint property. Each joint tenant has an equal right to possession of the fee involved. As such, a joint tenant is free to convey his interest in the property by lease or other transfer free of any challenge by his cotenant. While it is true that he may owe an accounting to his cotenant for any rents received from third parties from such a lease, and that such cotenant may bring an action in ejectment to be allowed to re-enter and jointly occupy the fee, the lease or transfer itself is not challengeable. Here, there is no evidence that either Sampson (D) or Mr. Swartzbaugh (D) ever attempted to interfere with Mrs. Swartzbaugh's (P) enjoyment of her interest. While she may be entitled to an accounting for rents received, she has no right to challenge the lease itself. The nonsuit was properly granted. Affirmed.

▶ **ANALYSIS**

This case points up the general rule that a joint tenancy cannot be severed by the unilateral transfer of one joint tenant's interest to a third party. An estate in joint tenancy may be destroyed by voluntary or involuntary acts of all joint tenants which destroy one of the necessary unities of joint tenancy (interest, time, title, and possession) but only in extraordinary cases (adverse possession) may it be done unilaterally. Note further that even when a unilateral act results in a transfer of a joint tenant's interest (as here), it will not result in any partition of property which the other cotenant must recognize. Here, therefore, the leasing of certain parts of property does not in any way divide or affect the cotenants' undivided cotenant interest in the property.

■=■

Quicknotes

ACCOUNTING The evaluation of assets for the purpose of assigning relative interests.

CO-JOINT TENANT Two or more persons who own a single interest in property which is created by a single instrument; joint tenants possess equal interests in the use of the entire property and the last survivor is entitled to absolute ownership.

EJECTMENT An action to oust someone in unlawful possession of real property and to restore possession to the party lawfully entitled to it.

EXPRESS AUTHORITY Authority that is delegated pursuant to expressly stated words.

FOUR UNITIES The four unities that must be present in order for a joint tenancy to be formed include unity of interest, possession, time, and title.

IMPLIED AUTHORITY Inferred power granted to an agent to act on behalf of the principal in order to effectuate the principal's objective.

JOINT TENANCY An interest in property whereby a single interest is owned by two or more persons and created by a single instrument; joint tenants possess equal interests in the use of the entire property, and the last survivor is entitled to absolute ownership.

MOIETY A one-half interest.

Continued on next page.

NONSUIT Judgment against a party who fails to make out a case.

NULLITY An act having no legal effect.

PRESCRIPTION The acquisition of an easement in or on another's property as a result of continuous use for the statutory period.

■━■

Sawada v. Endo

Judgment creditors (P) v. Judgment debtor (D)

Haw. Sup. Ct., 561 P.2d 1291 (1977).

NATURE OF CASE: Action to set aside conveyance of real property.

FACT SUMMARY: Endo (D) and his wife conveyed tenancy-by-the-entirety property to their son after Endo (D) had been sued.

🏛 RULE OF LAW
Tenancy-by-the-entirety property may not be reached by the separate creditors of either spouse.

FACTS: Endo (D), who had no liability insurance, severely injured Helen (P) and Masako Sawada (P). Suits for personal injuries were filed against Endo (D). Endo's (D) only real asset was real property held as a tenant by the entirety with his wife. This was conveyed to their son, for no consideration, shortly after the Sawadas (P) had filed suit. Endo (D) and his wife continued to live on the land even though they had not reserved an estate in it. The Sawadas (P) each recovered a judgment against Endo (D) but they were unable to satisfy it. The Sawadas (P) subsequently brought an action to set aside the conveyance of Endo's (D) property to the son, alleging that it was fraudulent. Endo's (D) wife had died prior to the action. Endo (D) alleged that the conveyance could not be deemed fraudulent because the separate creditor of either spouse may not reach property held as tenants by the entirety.

ISSUE: May the separate creditor of either spouse reach property held in tenancy by the entirety?

HOLDING AND DECISION: (Menor, J.) No. While this is a question of first impression, and there are four separate views, we hold that the separate creditors of either spouse cannot reach property held as a tenancy by the entirety. The other views are that: (1) the creditor may reach the entire property subject to the wife's contingent right of survivorship if the husband is the debtor; (2) the creditor may reach the property subject only to the other spouse's right of survivorship; and (3) the right of survivorship may be levied upon. Tenancy-by-the-entirety property is generally the family residence and public policy considerations of promoting family solidarity, as well as *stare decisis*, favor the result reached herein. Since the Sawadas (P) could not have reached the property, the conveyance to the son was not fraudulent. Affirmed.

DISSENT: (Kidwell, J.) Under the Married Women's Act there is equality between the spouses. On this basis, the court should choose to allow creditors of either spouse to reach their right of survivorship.

▶ ANALYSIS

In *Hurd v. Hughes*, 12 Del. Ch. at 193, the court stated in support of its decision not to allow creditors of one spouse to reach tenancy-by-the-entirety property, "But creditors are not entitled to special consideration. If the debt arose prior to the creation of the estate, the property was not a basis of credit, and if the debt arose subsequently, the creditor presumably had notice of the characteristics of the estate which limited his right to reach the property."

━■━

Quicknotes

FRAUDULENT CONVEYANCE Conveyances made within one year of filing the bankruptcy petition with intent to defraud creditors and which may be voidable.

MARRIED WOMEN'S PROPERTY ACT Legislation which secured to women the separate and independent control of their property.

STARE DECISIS Doctrine whereby courts follow legal precedent unless there is good cause for departure.

TENANCY BY THE ENTIRETY The ownership of property by a husband and wife whereby they hold undivided interests in the property with right of survivorship.

━■━

In re Marriage of Graham

Wife (P) v. Husband with an educational degree (D)

Colo. Sup. Ct., 574 P.2d 75 (1978).

NATURE OF CASE: Appeal of ruling dividing property in marital dissolution.

FACT SUMMARY: Anne Graham (P) provided substantial support for Dennis Graham (D), her husband, while he attained an education leading to B.S. and M.B.A. degrees.

🏛 **RULE OF LAW**
An educational degree cannot be marital property subject to division upon divorce.

FACTS: During most of the marriage of Anne and Dennis Graham, Anne (P) provided financial support while Dennis (D) pursued an education that led to B.S. and M.B.A. degrees with lucrative earning potential. Not long after Dennis (D) had completed his education, the spouses separated and the marriage ended. In dividing marital assets, the trial court ruled that Anne (P) was entitled to an interest in Dennis' (D) degrees, and awarded her installment payments based on the estimated increased earning capacity of Dennis (D), who appealed. The court of appeals reversed, and Anne appealed.

ISSUE: Can an educational degree be marital property subject to division upon divorce?

HOLDING AND DECISION: (Lee, J.) No. An educational degree cannot be marital property subject to division upon divorce. There are limits on what can be considered "property." Property may be defined as "everything that has an exchangeable value or which goes to make up wealth or estate." A degree is not exchangeable and has no value on an open market and cannot be willed. It is simply an intellectual achievement that can assist in property acquisition, but is not property itself. While it can be taken into account in awarding support, it cannot be considered property. Affirmed.

DISSENT: (Carrigan, J.) It is not the degree itself, but the increased earning capacity upon which focus should be given. Since damages for lost earning capacity can be awarded, there is no reason that increased earning capacity cannot be divided.

▶ **ANALYSIS**

Several other jurisdictions have considered this issue. The great majority have agreed with the court here. Some have seen fit to award the supporting spouse reimbursement under a variety of theories, such as return on investment.

Quicknotes

EQUITABLE Just; fair.

GOODWILL An intangible asset reflecting a corporation's favorability with the public and expectation of continued patronage.

MAINTENANCE The upkeep or preservation of property.

MARITAL DISSOLUTION Legal termination of the marital relationship.

MARITAL PROPERTY Property accumulated by a married couple during the term of their marriage.

Elkus v. Elkus

Opera star/wife (P) v. Manager/husband (D)

N.Y. App. Div., 572 N.Y.S.2d 901 (1991).

NATURE OF CASE: Appeal from order dividing marital property.

FACT SUMMARY: Elkus (P), an opera diva, contended that her artistic career was not a marital asset.

🏛 RULE OF LAW
Celebrity status with the accompanying economic opportunities may be a marital asset subject to equitable dissolution.

FACTS: Frederica Elkus (P) was a major opera star with the New York Metropolitan Opera Company. She had married in 1973, when her career was just beginning. Her husband, a voice coach, gave up his career to concentrate on coaching her, as well as taking the primary role in childrearing. In 1989, Mrs. Elkus (P) sued for divorce. The trial court rejected Mr. Elkus's (D) contention that Mrs. Elkus's (P) celebrity status and career were marital assets and incorporated that holding into its property division award. Mr. Elkus (D) appealed.

ISSUE: May celebrity status with the accompanying economic opportunities, be a marital asset subject to equitable distribution?

HOLDING AND DECISION: (Rosenberger, J.) Yes. Celebrity status with the accompanying economic opportunities may be a marital asset subject to equitable dissolution. Section 236 of the New York Domestic Relations law broadly defines marital property acquired during a marriage, regardless of the form it takes. The law was intended to give effect to the notion that marriage is a joint economic enterprise and that both partners thereto are entitled to enjoy, upon dissolution, the fruits of their endeavor. Marital property may be any thing of value, even if it falls outside of traditional concepts of property. The New York Court of Appeals has already held that a medical license and practice acquired during a marriage may be a marital asset; the same analysis applies to a show business career. Here, Mrs. Elkus (P) rose to fame in some part due to the sacrifices made by Mr. Elkus (D), and her career may properly be considered a marital asset. Reversed and remanded.

▶ ANALYSIS
Here, Mr. Elkus (D) took an active role in helping his wife's career, and his having a stake in that career comports with common notions of fairness. The decision does not seem to limit itself to such a situation, however. Its language would seem to make it applicable even when the claiming spouse did not actively contribute to the other spouse's career.

Quicknotes

CELEBRITY STATUS Any person who is generally known in the community.

EQUITABLE DISTRIBUTION The means by which a court distributes all assets acquired during a marriage by the spouses equitably upon dissolution.

MARITAL PROPERTY Property accumulated by a married couple during the term of their marriage.

Varnum v. Brien

Same-sex couples (P) v. State county (D)

Iowa Sup. Ct., 763 N.W.2d 862 (2009).

NATURE OF CASE: Appeal of lower court decision in favor of plaintiffs.

FACT SUMMARY: Polk County (D) in the state of Iowa denied marriage licenses to six same-sex couples.

🏛 RULE OF LAW

Iowa's marriage statute, defining marriage as between one man and one woman, violates the equal protection clause of the Iowa constitution.

FACTS: Six same-sex couples (P) applied for marriage licenses in Polk County, Iowa (the County) (D). The County (D) denied their requests. Varnum (P), the lead plaintiff representing the couples, brought suit, alleging the state's marriage statute violated their right to equal protection and denied them the fundamental right to marry. The federal district court granted summary judgment to the plaintiffs. The County (D) appealed.

ISSUE: Does Iowa's marriage statute, defining marriage as between one man and one woman, violate the equal protection clause of the Iowa constitution?

HOLDING AND DECISION: (Cady, J.) Yes. Iowa's marriage statute, defining marriage as between one man and one woman, violates the equal protection clause of the Iowa constitution. The equal protection clause of the Iowa constitution requires that similarly situated people be treated equally under the law. First, as a threshold matter, we hold that same-sex couples are similarly situated to heterosexual couples. The plaintiffs here are in long term relationships and are raising families just like heterosexual couples. Second, we hold that intermediate scrutiny shall apply. There is no question the gay and lesbian community has been the subject of past discrimination. Moreover, it is clear the legislature's refusal to grant same-sex couples the right to marry is because of their sexual orientation. Therefore, to uphold the statute, the County (D) must prove that the marriage statute is substantially related to an important governmental interest. Third, the County (D) has failed to advance any important governmental interests to survive intermediate scrutiny. Maintaining the traditional definition of marriage, without anything more, is not an important governmental interest. Also, the plaintiffs have adequately shown by scientific studies that the interests of children are "served equally by same-sex parents and opposite-sex parents." The marriage statute itself does not prevent same-sex couples from having, adopting and/or raising children. Using the "over and under" inclusive type of analysis, denying marriage to same-sex couples simply because they cannot procreate is under-inclusive.

There are many reasons heterosexual couples may not procreate, such as age, disability, or choice. The legislature has not moved to deny those couples marriage rights. Also, there is no evidence granting marriage licenses to same-sex couples would put a strain on state resources. Lastly, while many may oppose same-sex marriages on religious grounds, civil marriage is judged under our state constitution, and not on any religious belief. Accordingly, we hold that Iowa's marriage statute violates our constitution's equal protection clause. Affirmed.

▶ ANALYSIS

Iowa became the third state to grant marriage rights to same-sex couples. Currently, 35 states have statutes or constitutional amendments that define marriage as between one man and one woman. There have been attempts in Iowa since this decision to pass a constitutional amendment limiting marriage to one man and one woman. Recently, California has been the epicenter of the national debate on same-sex marriages. After the state's highest court granted same-sex couples the right to marry, California's residents passed Proposition 8, which added a constitutional amendment defining marriage as between one man and one woman. As of February 2010, a court challenge to Proposition 8 was under way in federal court in San Francisco. An appeal of the trial court's decision, either way, may rise to the United States Supreme Court.

■═■

Quicknotes

EQUAL PROTECTION CLAUSE A constitutional provision that each person be guaranteed the same protection of the laws enjoyed by other persons in like circumstances.

INTERMEDIATE SCRUTINY A standard of reviewing the propriety of classifications pertaining to gender or legitimacy under the Equal Protection Clause of the United States Constitution which requires a court to ascertain whether the classification furthers an important state interest and is substantially related to the attainment of that interest.

■═■

Tradition, Tension, and Change in Landlord–Tenant Law

Quick Reference Rules of Law

PAGE

1. *Kajo Church Square, Inc. v. Walker.* A lease that terminates at death is a tenancy at will rather than a tenancy for life. — 64

2. *Garner v. Gerrish.* A lease may provide for termination at the will of the tenant only. — 65

3. *Hannan v. Dusch.* A landlord is obligated only to place a tenant in legal possession of rented real property. — 66

4. *Ernst v. Conditt.* An assignment arises when a lessee transfers his entire interest under a lease. — 67

5. *Kendall v. Ernest Pestana, Inc.* Absent contractual language to the contrary, a lessor may not arbitrarily withhold consent to an assignment. — 68

6. *Berg v. Wiley.* A landlord may not remove a breaching or defaulting tenant's possessions or bar such tenant's access to the leasehold without resorting to judicial remedies. — 69

7. *Sommer v. Kridel.* A landlord has a duty to mitigate damages when he seeks to recover rents due from a defaulting tenant. — 70

8. *Village Commons, LLC v. Marion County Prosecutor's Office.* If an act or omission by the landlord materially deprives the lessee from the beneficial use or enjoyment of the leased property, the lessee may abandon the property and avoid any further obligations under the lease. — 71

9. *Hilder v. St. Peter.* An implied warranty of habitability exists in residential leases. — 72

10. *Chicago Board of Realtors, Inc. v. City of Chicago.* [Not included in casebook excerpt.] — 73

Kajo Church Square, Inc. v. Walker

Property owner (D) v. Leaseholders (P)

Tex. Ct. App., 2003 WL 1848555 (2003).

NATURE OF CASE: Appeal from lower court decision finding that neighbors retained life estates and leaseholds for life in property that they conveyed to a church.

FACT SUMMARY: The Walkers (P) and another property owner (the Eakins) (P) conveyed two parcels of land to Grace Covenant Fellowship Church (the church) whose property abutted theirs. The church then leased a portion of the property back to the Walkers (P) for life. When Kajo Church (D) purchased the church property, it terminated the leases with the Walkers (P) and the other property owner.

🏛 RULE OF LAW
A lease that terminates at death is a tenancy at will rather than a tenancy for life.

FACTS: Don and Patsy Walker (P) and another property owner, Joe and Meriam Eakin (P), conveyed two parcels of land to Grace Covenant Fellowship Church (the church) whose property abutted theirs. The deed did not reference any life estates allegedly retained by the Walkers (P) and the Eakins (P) in the conveyed property. The church then leased one of the parcels back to the Walkers (P) and the Eakins (P). The lease document stated it would not terminate until the death of the last of the lessees. When Kajo Church Square, Inc. (Kajo Church) (D) purchased the church property, the former owner assigned the lease to Kajo Church (D). Kajo Church (D) then terminated the lease. The Walkers (P) and the Eakins (P) brought suit alleging that they retained life estates in the property. They also argued the lease was for their lifetimes and could not be terminated by Kajo Church (D), the new property owner. Both parties filed motions for summary judgment. The lower court granted summary judgment to the Walkers (P) and the Eakins (P). Kajo Church (D) appealed.

ISSUE: Is a lease that terminates at death a tenancy at will rather than a tenancy for life?

HOLDING AND DECISION: (Griffith, J.) Yes. A lease that terminates at death is a tenancy at will rather than a tenancy for life. While it is certain that death will occur at some point, an event that is uncertain as to its occurrence may not be used as the termination point of a lease. Landlord-tenant law does not recognize leaseholds for life. They are not a recognized property right. Such leases have been deemed tenancies at will by other jurisdictions as well. Accordingly, Kajo Church (D) was within its right to terminate the tenancy at will. Separately, the Walk-

ers (P) and the Eakins (P) argue they retained a life estate in the disputed piece of property. However, the deed from them to the former owner of the church property does not reference any such retention of rights. Like any contract, when the language of the deed is clear and unequivocal, a court must look only to the document itself to ascertain the intention of the parties. The Walkers (P) and the Eakins (P) put into evidence a condition statement executed by Kajo Church (D) and the former owner, which stated that the Walkers (P) and the Eakins (P) retained life estates in the property. However, the deed is unambiguous. Accordingly, extrinsic evidence such as this condition statement cannot be used to determine the intent of the parties. Lastly, Kajo Church (D) did not breach its lease with the Walkers (P) because, as noted, it was within Kajo Church's (D) right to terminate a tenancy at will. Reversed.

▶ ANALYSIS

The case supports the basic rule that leases for life are usually construed as tenancies at will. Regarding the life estates, the court properly excluded the extrinsic evidence of the condition statement. Whenever a contract or other type of agreement is clear, extrinsic evidence typically may not be reviewed. Some jurisdictions do allow extrinsic evidence to supplement a legal document. No jurisdiction allows extrinsic evidence that contradicts a provision in an unambiguous legal document.

Quicknotes

EXTRINSIC EVIDENCE Evidence that is not contained within the text of a document or contract, but which is derived from the parties' statements or the circumstances under which the agreement was made.

TENANCY AT WILL Someone who is in possession of property with the consent of the owner or landlord for an unfixed period of time.

Garner v. Gerrish

Estate administrator (P) v. Lessee (D)

N.Y. Ct. App., 473 N.E.2d 223 (1984).

NATURE OF CASE: Appeal of eviction proceeding.

FACT SUMMARY: A dispute arose as to whether Gerrish's (D) tenancy was terminable at the will of the lessor.

🏛 RULE OF LAW
A lease may provide for termination at the will of the tenant only.

FACTS: Donovan granted a lease of a house to Gerrish (D). The lease contained a clause granting Gerrish (D) the ability to terminate the lease at the date of his choice. No such right was reserved for the lessor. Upon Donovan's death, the administrator (P) attempted to evict Gerrish (D), claiming that the will was indefinite as to time, and, therefore, a tenancy at will had been created. The trial court held for the administrator (P), and Gerrish (D) appealed.

ISSUE: May a lease provide for its termination at the will of the tenant only?

HOLDING AND DECISION: (Wachtler, J.) Yes. A lease may provide for termination at the will of the tenant only. Ancient authority held to the contrary. However, this rule grew out of medieval rituals involving livery of seisin, a symbolic act no longer followed. Since livery of seisin has long been abandoned, it is appropriate to interpret leases based on the will of the parties as expressed by the terms of the lease. Here, the language unequivocally reserves the right of termination to Gerrish (D), so he may not be evicted. Reversed.

▶ ANALYSIS

Livery of seisin was a ritual necessary in ancient times for conveying land. The grantor had to present a clod of earth or other symbol to the grantee. A tenancy which could last a tenant's lifetime was considered legally equivalent to a life estate, so the old rule maintained that such a tenancy could not be created without livery of seisin.

■■■■

Quicknotes

EVICTION The removal of a person from possession of property.

LEASE An agreement or contract which creates a relationship between a landlord and tenant (real property) or lessor and lessee (real or personal property).

LIVERY OF SEISIN A ceremony in which an interest in land is formally delivered usually by delivering a piece of earth.

TENANCY AT WILL Someone who is in possession of property with the consent of the owner or landlord for an unfixed period of time.

■■■■

Hannan v. Dusch

Tenant (P) v. Lessor (D)

Va. Sup. Ct. App., 153 S.E. 824 (1930).

NATURE OF CASE: Appeal from decision denying action for damages for breach of contract and deed.

FACT SUMMARY: Hannan (P), the lessee, alleged that Dusch (D), the lessor, failed to deliver possession of rented property by allowing a former tenant to remain in possession.

🏛 RULE OF LAW
A landlord is obligated only to place a tenant in legal possession of rented real property.

FACTS: On August 31, 1927, Dusch (D) leased certain real estate to Hannan (P), for a period of 15 years, the term to begin on January 1, 1928. Hannan (P) alleged that Dusch (D) had allowed the prior tenants to remain in possession of the premises after January 1, 1928, and had refused to take any legal or other actions to remove them. There was no express covenant in the rental agreement regarding either delivery of the premises or quiet enjoyment of the premises. Dusch (D) demurred to the complaint on the grounds that he was under no duty to deliver actual possession to Hannan (P).

ISSUE: Is a landlord obligated only to place a tenant in legal possession of rented real property?

HOLDING AND DECISION: (Prentis, C.J.) Yes. Under the American rule, a landlord does not impliedly covenant against the wrongful acts of others, and is not responsible for the tortious acts of third parties unless he expressly contracts so. Where a new tenant fails to obtain possession of rented premises solely because a former tenant wrongfully holds over, his remedy is against the former tenant and not against the landlord. Under the English rule, in the absence of express provisions to the contrary, there is in every lease an implied covenant by the landlord that the premises will be open to entry by the tenant at the time fixed by the lease for the beginning of the term. Here, Hannan (P) should have brought an action for unlawful entry or unlawful detainer against the former tenant, rather than seeking relief from Dusch (D). Affirmed.

▌ ANALYSIS

There still exists a split of authority over application of the American or English rule for delivery of possession. The American rule provides that a tenant may sue to recover possession and damages from the person wrongfully in possession. The English remedy allows the tenant to terminate the lease, and sue the landlord for damages, or, if the third party is in possession of only part of the premises, to take possession of the remainder with a proportionate abatement in rent and damages.

■=■

Quicknotes

DEMURRER The assertion that the opposing party's pleadings are insufficient and that the demurring party should not be made to answer.

EXPRESS COVENANT A promise created by the express words of a document.

HOLDOVER TENANT A tenancy that arises upon the expiration of a lawful tenancy and the tenant remains in possession of the property.

IMPLIED COVENANT A promise inferred by law from a document as a whole and the circumstances surrounding its implementation.

LEGAL POSSESSION Party having possession of property that it is legally entitled to.

TORTIOUS ACTS Acts that constitute legal wrongs, resulting in breach of a duty.

UNLAWFUL DETAINER The unlawful withholding of real or personal property from an individual who is lawfully entitled to it.

■=■

Ernst v. Conditt

Lessor (P) v. Sublessees (D)

Tenn. Ct. App., 390 S.W.2d 703 (1964).

NATURE OF CASE: Appeal from award of damages for past due rent and removal of improvements constructed on leased real property.

FACT SUMMARY: After Ernst (P) leased property to Rogers, who assigned his lease to Conditt (D), Ernst (P) sought damages from Conditt (D) for past due rent and removal of improvements.

🏛 RULE OF LAW
An assignment arises when a lessee transfers his entire interest under a lease.

FACTS: On June 18, 1960, Ernst (P) leased a tract of land to Frank D. Rogers for a term of one year and seven days, beginning on June 23, 1960. On August 4, 1960, Rogers, having sold his business to Conditt (D), executed a document which extended the term of the lease to two years, and "sublet" the premises to Conditt (D). The document, which stated that Rogers remained personally liable under the terms of the amended lease, was signed by Rogers, Ernst (P) and Conditt (D). At the end of the lease term, Ernst (P) filed suit against Conditt (D), seeking past due rent and removal of improvements constructed on the property. The trial court, holding that the document constituted an assignment, rather than a sublease, held that Conditt (D), and not Rogers, was directly liable for the monies owed.

ISSUE: Does an assignment arise when a lessee transfers his entire interest under a lease?

HOLDING AND DECISION: (Chattin, J.) Yes. Under the common-law rule, if an instrument purports to transfer the lessee's interest for the entire remainder of the lease term, an assignment has occurred. However, if the instrument purports to transfer the lessee's interest for any length of time less than the remainder of the lease term, a sublease has been established. Under the modern rule, the intention of the parties governs in construing deeds, leases, and other written transfers of property interests. Here, under both the common law and modern rule, the agreement between Rogers and Conditt (D) is an assignment, rather than a sublease. Rogers did not retain any interest in the lease, and he also did not reserve a right of re-entry in the event of a breach of any of the conditions or covenants of the lease by Conditt (D). The use of the word "sublet" is not conclusive, because it appears from all of the facts and circumstances and the instrument itself that all of the parties intended an assignment rather than a sublease. Affirmed.

▶ ANALYSIS
This case illustrates the two methods used to distinguish an assignment from a sublease. Under the common law test, an assignment arises when a lessee transfers his right to possession for the entire term of the lease. Under the less commonly used modern rule, the intention of the parties governs, although the actual words used are often persuasive in the final determination.

Quicknotes

ASSIGNMENT A transaction in which a party conveys his or her entire interest in property to another.

RIGHT OF REENTRY An interest in property reserved in the conveyance of a fee that gives the holder the right to resume possession of property upon the happening of a condition subsequent.

SUBLEASE A transaction in which a tenant or lessee conveys an interest in the leased premises that is less than his own or retains a reversionary interest.

Kendall v. Ernest Pestana, Inc.

Tenant (P) v. Lessor (D)

Cal. Sup. Ct., 709 P.2d 837 (1985).

NATURE OF CASE: Appeal of denial of injunctive relief and damages.

FACT SUMMARY: Ernest Pestana, Inc. (D) arbitrarily withheld permission from Kendall (P), its tenant, to sublet its leasehold.

🏛 RULE OF LAW
Absent contractual language to the contrary, a lessor may not arbitrarily withhold consent to an assignment.

FACTS: Through a series of leases and assignments, Ernest Pestana, Inc. (D) became lessor of certain hangar space at a municipal airport, with Kendall (P) and other lessees. The lease contained a consent clause regarding subleases. At one point, Kendall (P) and other lessees approached management of Ernest Pestana, Inc. (D), requesting permission to sublet. Permission was denied for no apparent commercially reasonable reason. Kendall (P) and the others sued Ernest Pestana, Inc. (D) for injunctive and declaratory relief, as well as damages. The trial court sustained Ernest Pestana, Inc.'s (D) demurrer, and the appellate court affirmed. The state supreme court granted review.

ISSUE: Absent contractual language to the contrary, may a lessor arbitrarily withhold consent to an assignment?

HOLDING AND DECISION: (Broussard, J.) No. Absent contractual language to the contrary, a lessor may not arbitrarily withhold consent to an assignment. The basic social policy in this area is that interests in property, including those of a leasehold nature, should be freely alienable. Restrictions on alienability are to be strictly construed against the lessor. The lessor does have a reversionary interest in the property, and therefore is entitled to assurance that a lessee will not sublet to an irresponsible individual who may commit waste. This is a commercially reasonable rationale for denying permission to sublet. There are no doubt others. Absent some sort of reasonable basis for denial of permission, however, it seems that public policy favoring free alienability should override whatever minor interest a lessor might have in arbitrarily denying permission to sublet. The major arguments in favor of retaining the right are unpersuasive. The lessor's common law right to look to no one but the lessee for rent has been curtailed. The argument that the lessee could have bargained for free subletting rights does not stand up to scrutiny. What the parties contemplated is not always clear, and doubts should be resolved in favor of alienability. Finally, the argument based on *stare decisis* is also to be found wanting. When changed conditions warrant overruling precedent, a court may do so. Here, since the complaint alleged that Ernest Pestana, Inc. (D) had unreasonably withheld approval, a cause of action was stated. Reversed.

▶ ANALYSIS

The rule of the present case could well prove to have a more limited application than one might gather at first glance. The opinion does give a lessor the option of contracting in the power to arbitrarily veto a sublease. Also, it only applies to commercial leases. How the court would rule in residential leases is a matter of speculation.

■=■

Quicknotes

ASSIGNMENT A transaction in which a party conveys his or her entire interest in property to another.

DEMURRER The assertion that the opposing party's pleadings are insufficient and that the demurring party should not be made to answer.

FREE ALIENABILITY Unrestricted transferability.

INJUNCTIVE RELIEF A court order issued as a remedy, requiring a person to do, or prohibiting that person from doing, a specific act.

STARE DECISIS Doctrine whereby courts follow legal precedent unless there is good cause for departure.

■=■

Berg v. Wiley

Locked-out tenant (P) v. Landlord (D)

Minn. Sup. Ct., 264 N.W.2d 145 (1978).

NATURE OF CASE: Appeal from award of damages for wrongful eviction.

FACT SUMMARY: Wiley (D), lessor of commercial property to Berg (P) for the purpose of operating a restaurant thereon, locked Berg (P) out of the premises when Berg (P) delayed making certain remodeling changes to meet health code requirements.

> ## 🏛 RULE OF LAW
> A landlord may not remove a breaching or defaulting tenant's possessions or bar such tenant's access to the leasehold without resorting to judicial remedies.

FACTS: Wiley (D) leased commercial property to Berg (P) for the purpose of operating an establishment called "A Family Affair Restaurant." Wiley (D) made demand that Berg (P) make certain remodeling changes to alleviate alleged health code violations and notified Berg (P) of his intention to retake possession if the changes were not made within a two-week period. At the end of the period, Berg (P) closed the restaurant and put up a sign that said "Closed for Remodeling." Wiley (D) then entered the premises in Berg's (P) absence and changed the locks. Berg (P) brought this action to recover lost profits, damage to chattels and emotional distress due to the wrongful eviction. The trial court awarded Berg (P) $31,000 for lost profits and $3,540 for loss of chattels, and the jury specially found that Berg (P) neither abandoned nor surrendered the premises. Wiley (D) appealed.

ISSUE: May a landlord remove a breaching or defaulting tenant's possessions or bar such tenant's access to the leasehold without resorting to judicial remedies?

HOLDING AND DECISION: (Rogosheske, J.) No. The evidence amply supports the jury's finding that Berg (P) did not abandon or surrender the premises, and the lockout was thus not justified on the ground of abandonment and surrender. As to self-help procedures employed by landlords to remove defaulting tenants, the common-law rule was to permit such removal if accomplished peaceably. Wiley (D) contended that only actual or threatened violence constitutes a nonpeaceable entry. This is not correct. In response to a long-applied policy to discourage landlords from taking the law into their own hands, the modern trend in this area of the law has been to bar self-help to dispossess a breaching tenant, and this represents the rule that should be applied here. A landlord may not remove a breaching or defaulting tenant's possessions or bar the tenant's access to the leasehold without resorting to judicial remedies. Wiley's (D) failure to resort to judicial remedies rendered the lockout wrongful as a matter of law. Affirmed.

▶ ANALYSIS

In this respect, the trend of the law on leaseholds is moving toward the property law concept that the covenant to pay rent and the right to quiet possession are not interdependent. The notion of the sanctity of one's home and the emphasis in recent legal history on the right of privacy have doubtless swayed legislators, commentators, and courts in this area.

Quicknotes

SELF-HELP Acting without recourse to the legal system.

TENANT IN POSSESSION A party in possession of property by title or right.

WRONGFUL EVICTION The unlawful dispossession of a person from property.

Sommer v. Kridel

Landlord (P) v. Repudiating-lessee (D)

N.J. Sup. Ct., 378 A.2d 767 (1977).

NATURE OF CASE: Appeal from award of damages for past due rent.

FACT SUMMARY: Kridel (D), the lessee, vacated the apartment, which he leased from Sommer (P), before the end of the lease term.

🏛 RULE OF LAW
A landlord has a duty to mitigate damages when he seeks to recover rents due from a defaulting tenant.

FACTS: On March 10, 1972, Kridel (D), the lessee, entered into a lease with Sommer (P), for the rental of an apartment. The term of the lease was from May 1, 1972 to April 30, 1974. One week after signing the agreement, Kridel (D) paid Sommer (P) a sum of money to satisfy the first month's rent and security deposit. On May 19, 1972, Kridel (D) repudiated the lease and acknowledged the forfeiture of the sum already paid to Sommer (P). Although a third party was subsequently interested in renting the same apartment, Sommer (P) did not re-let the apartment until September 1, 1973. Sommer (P) brought suit against Kridel (D) to recover the total amount due for the full two-year term of the lease. The trial court's ruling in favor of Kridel (D) was reversed at the appellate level, and Kridel (D) appealed.

ISSUE: Does a landlord have a duty to mitigate damages when he seeks to recover rents due from a defaulting tenant?

HOLDING AND DECISION: (Pashman, J.) Yes. A landlord does have an obligation to make a reasonable effort to mitigate damages when a tenant defaults on a lease. The landlord's duty to mitigate consists of making reasonable efforts to re-let the apartment. The burden of proof shall be upon the landlord to establish that he used reasonable diligence in attempting to re-let the premises. Among the factors to be considered in determining whether the landlord has exercised reasonable diligence are whether the landlord offered or showed the apartment to any prospective tenants, or whether the availability of the apartment was advertised in local newspapers. Here, despite the availability of a prospective tenant who was ready, willing, and able to rent the apartment, Sommer (P) allowed the apartment to lie empty in order to increase the amount of damages. Sommer (P) could have reasonably avoided the damages which accrued by virtue of the apartment lacking a tenant. Reversed.

▶ ANALYSIS

This case illustrates the modern trend of analyzing landlord-tenant issues under contract, rather than real property law. Increasingly, the courts agree that the contract rule requiring mitigation of damages for residential leases best effectuates notions of basic fairness and equity. The contract rule also promotes efficiency considerations by giving landlords an incentive to make use of any available property.

Quicknotes
DEFAULT Failure to carry out a legal obligation.
MITIGATION Reduction in penalty.

Village Commons, LLC v. Marion County Prosecutor's Office

Landlord (P) v. Tenant (D)

Ind. Ct. App., 882 N.E.2d 210 (2008).

NATURE OF CASE: Appeal from lower court decision finding that landlord actually and constructively evicted tenant from premises after a series of unremedied water leaks over the course of several years.

FACT SUMMARY: The Marion County Prosecutor's Office (D) (MCPO) rented a basement space from Village Commons, LLC (P). Over the course of two years, there were multiple water leaks from ceilings and pipes that were not repaired by Village Commons (P). MCPO (D) eventually left the space and ceased paying rent.

🏛 RULE OF LAW
If an act or omission by the landlord materially deprives the lessee from the beneficial use or enjoyment of the leased property, the lessee may abandon the property and avoid any further obligations under the lease.

FACTS: The Marion County Prosecutor's Office (D) (MCPO) rented a basement space from Village Commons, LLC (P) in Indiana. Over the course of two years, there were multiple water leaks from ceilings and pipes that were not repaired by Village Commons (P). The leaks occurred in office spaces, evidence rooms, and bathrooms. While Village Commons (P) attempted some repairs in October 2002, it eventually informed MCPO (D) that it should cease using the most damaged areas. MCPO (D) eventually left the space in January of 2003 and ceased paying rent. Three years remained on the lease at the time, including $380,477 in unpaid rental payments. Village Commons (P) brought suit alleging that MCPO (D) breached the lease by terminating it. According to the lease, MCPO (D) was not able to terminate the lease or set off rental payments due to any damage to the premises. After a bench trial, the trial court found that Village Commons (P) constructively and actually evicted MCPO (D). Village Commons (P) appealed.

ISSUE: If an act or omission by the landlord materially deprives the lessee from the beneficial use or enjoyment of the leased property, may the lessee abandon the property and avoid any further obligations under the lease?

HOLDING AND DECISION: (Riley, J.) Yes. If an act or omission by the landlord materially deprives the lessee from the beneficial use or enjoyment of the leased property, the lessee may abandon the property and avoid any further obligations under the lease. There was substantial evidence in the record that there were repeated and unremedied water leaks in the space over the course of two

years. The trial court's findings in this regard were not clearly erroneous. The constructive eviction occurred in January of 2003, when MCPO (D) was forced to leave the premises due to the leaks that Village Commons (P) continuously failed to repair. It is clear that the leaks were not transitory or fleeting as Village Commons (P) argues. In addition, Village Commons (P) informed MCPO (D) to cease using portions of the leased premises where the leaks were occurring. This is a form of actual eviction. Village Commons (P) is correct that MCPO (D) did not have the power under the lease to terminate it unilaterally. However, that is not what occurred here. Rather, it was the acts and omissions of Village Commons (P) that ended MCPO's (D) obligation to pay rent under the lease. Accordingly, the trial court's findings and rulings were correct. Affirmed.

▶ ANALYSIS

Under constructive eviction, the tenant must leave within a reasonable time period after the tenant's beneficial use of the property has been disrupted. As always, the tenant must give proper notice to the landlord of any maintenance or repair issues. Most states allow the landlord time to repair the damages. In this case, the repeated water leaks and Village Commons' (P) failure to repair them over several years, all with notice, provided substantial evidence of a constructive eviction.

■═■

Quicknotes

CONSTRUCTIVE EVICTION An action whereby the landlord renders the property unsuitable for occupancy, either in whole or in part, so that the tenant is forced to leave the premises.

EVICTION The removal of a person from possession of property.

■═■

Hilder v. St. Peter

Lessee (P) v. Lessor (D)

Vt. Sup. Ct., 478 A.2d 202 (1984).

NATURE OF CASE: Action by tenant to recover rent.

FACT SUMMARY: Hilder (P) leased from St. Peter (D) a residential premise that had serious deficiencies.

🏛 RULE OF LAW
An implied warranty of habitability exists in residential leases.

FACTS: Hilder (P) leased an apartment from St. Peter (D). During the course of the tenancy various problems with the apartment manifested themselves, including sewage leaks, nonfunctioning toilets, water leaks, falling plaster, and broken locks. These were brought to St. Peter's (D) attention, but nothing was done. Hilder (P) paid the agreed rent, but after 14 months of renting the premises, she brought an action seeking recovery of the rental monies. The trial court awarded damages to Hilder (P), and St. Peter (D) appealed.

ISSUE: Does an implied warranty of habitability exist in residential leases?

HOLDING AND DECISION: (Billings, C.J.) Yes. An implied warranty of habitability exists in residential leases. The old view of leases was that the lessee took the property as he found it. This view was proper in an agrarian society, but in a modern urban setting is improper. The modern tenant bargains for viable habitation, and if he receives less, he is not getting that for which he contracts in a lease. For this reason a rented dwelling which is not habitable amounts to a breach of contract by the lessor, and standard contract damages are available, as well as tort damages arising therefrom. Affirmed in part, reversed in part, and remanded.

▶ *ANALYSIS*

The seminal case in this area was *Green v. Superior Ct.,* 10 Cal. 3d 616 (1974). The analysis of the court there was the same as the analysis here. Residential tenancies, the court determined, were no longer land conveyances but rather contracts with certain inherent expectations embodied in them.

■=■

Quicknotes

IMPLIED WARRANTY OF HABITABILITY A warranty implied by a landlord that the premises are suitable, and will remain suitable, for habitation.

■=■

Chicago Board of Realtors, Inc. v. City of Chicago

Property owner (P) v. Municipality (D)

819 F.2d 732 (7th Cir. 1987).

NATURE OF CASE: Appeal from denial of injunction against enforcement of a landlord-tenant ordinance.

FACT SUMMARY: Chicago Board of Realtors (Realtors) (P), a group of property owners, challenged the constitutionality of Chicago's Residential Landlord and Tenant Ordinance (D), contending that it violated various clauses of the Constitution.

 RULE OF LAW
[Rule of law not included in casebook excerpt.]

FACTS: Realtors (P), a group of property owners, challenged the constitutionality of Chicago's Residential Landlord and Tenant Ordinance (D), arguing that it violated the Contracts Clause, procedural and substantive due process, void-for-vagueness doctrine, equal protection, the Takings Clause, and the Commerce Clause. The district court denied a motion for a preliminary injunction, concluding that Realtors (P) did not have a reasonable likelihood of prevailing on the merits. Realtors (P) appealed, contesting the district court's ruling with respect to all but the Takings and Commerce Clause issues. The court of appeals affirmed. Realtors (P) appealed.

ISSUE: [Issue not included in casebook excerpt.]

HOLDING AND DECISION: (Cudahy, J.) [The majority opinion, in which the lower court decisions were upheld on the basis that the ordinance was sufficiently reasonable in light of its stated purpose (to promote public safety, health, and welfare), was not included in the casebook excerpt. The policy analysis of J. Posner in his separate opinion was included and follows below.]

SEPARATE OPINION: (Posner, J.) The majority's opinion, although reaching the correct result, does not go far enough. It makes the rejection of the appeal seem easier than it is, by refusing to acknowledge the strong case that can be made for the unreasonableness of the ordinance. While the stated purpose of the ordinance is the promotion of public health, safety, and welfare and the quality of housing in Chicago, it is unlikely that this is the real purpose, and it is not the likely effect. Forbidding landlords to charge interest at market rates on late payment of rent could hardly be thought to be calculated to improve the health, safety, and welfare of Chicagoans, and it may have the opposite effect. The initial consequence of the rule will be to reduce the resources that landlords devote to improve the quality of housing by making the provision of rental housing more costly. Landlords will try to offset the higher cost by raising rents. The ordinance is not in the interest of

poor people. The principal beneficiaries will be the middle class. Affirmed.

ANALYSIS

In the separate opinion by Judge Posner, which was joined by Judge Easterbrook (like Judge Posner, a former professor at the University of Chicago), the judge seemed more concerned with analyzing the economic impact of the ordinance than its constitutional impact. In addition, both judges seemed more concerned with making Judge Cudahy aware of the economic impact that the ordinance will have on the city than discussing his legal analysis. Judge Posner cited different literature to show that the Chicago (D) ordinance may not be unsound, but if economic theory holds true, the poorer and newer tenants will be hurt by the ordinance.

Quicknotes

COMMERCE CLAUSE Article 1, Section 8, clause 3 of the United States Constitution, granting Congress the power to regulate commerce with foreign countries and between the states.

PRELIMINARY INJUNCTION A judicial mandate issued to require or restrain a party from certain conduct; used to preserve a trial's subject matter or to prevent threatened injury.

TAKINGS CLAUSE Provision of the Fifth Amendment to the United States Constitution prohibiting the government from taking private property for public use without providing just compensation therefor.

The Land Transaction

Quick Reference Rules of Law

PAGE

1. *Licari v. Blackwelder.* Real estate brokers must fully, fairly, and promptly inform their clients of all known facts that might be material to the transaction for which the brokers were employed. — 77

2. *Hickey v. Green.* An oral contract for the transfer of interest in land may be specifically enforced despite the Statute of Frauds if the party seeking performance changed his position in reasonable reliance on the contract and injustice can be avoided only through specific performance. — 79

3. *Lohmeyer v. Bower.* A party cannot convey good merchantable title if violations of covenants or zoning ordinances exist on the subject property at the time it is to be sold. — 80

4. *Stambovsky v. Ackley.* Where a condition that has been created by the seller materially impairs the value of the contract and is peculiarly within the knowledge of the seller or unlikely to be discovered by a prudent purchaser exercising due care with respect to the subject transaction, nondisclosure constitutes a basis for rescission as a matter of equity. — 81

5. *Johnson v. Davis.* Where the seller of a home knows of the facts affecting the value of a home that are not readily observable, the seller is under a duty to disclose. — 82

6. *Lempke v. Dagenais.* A subsequent purchaser of property may recover from one performing defective contractor services for the prior owner if the work contained latent defects not apparent at the time of purchase. — 83

7. *Jones v. Lee.* The non-defaulting party under a real estate contract is entitled to an award of damages following a breach of the contract. — 84

8. *Kutzin v. Pirnie.* A buyer who materially breaches a real estate purchase contract can recover in restitution for benefits he conferred on the seller through either part performance on the contract or reliance beyond the loss that his own breach caused. — 86

9. *Brown v. Lober.* The mere existence of a superior title does not constitute a breach of the covenant of quiet enjoyment. — 88

10. *Frimberger v. Anzellotti.* Latent violations of state or municipal land use regulations (1) that do not appear on the land records, (2) that are unknown to the seller of the property, (3) as to which the agency charged with enforcement has taken no official action to compel compliance at the time the deed was executed, and (4) that have not ripened into an interest that can be recorded on the land records do not constitute an encumbrance for the purpose of the deed warranty. — 89

11. *Rockafellor v. Gray.* The breach of the covenant of seisin creates a chose in action which passes by assignment to subsequent grantees of the deed. — 91

12. *Sweeney v. Sweeney.* Where a deed has been formally executed and delivered, the presumption that the grantee assented to delivery can be overcome only by evidence that no delivery was in fact intended. — 92

13. *Rosengrant v. Rosengrant.* Grantors do not legally deliver a deed if they reserve the right to retrieve the deed, require that the delivery may become operative only when the grantors have died, and keep using the property as if it were still their own. — 93

CHAPTER 7

14. *Murphy v. Fin. Dev. Corp.* Mere compliance with statutory requirements may not discharge a mortgagee's duty to exercise good faith and due diligence in selling the property at foreclosure.   *94*

15. *Commonwealth v. Fremont Investment & Loan.* Mortgage loans with the following four characteristics would likely be "unfair" under Massachusetts' Consumer Protection Act: (1) the loans were adjustable with a preliminary rate for three years; (2) the initial rate was typically three points lower than the usual mortgage rate on 30-year loans; (3) the debt to income ratio would exceed 50 percent after the introductory period expired; and (4) the loan-to-value ratio was 100 percent.   *95*

16. *U.S. Bank Natl. Assn. v. Ibanez.* Any foreclosure proceeding initiated by a party that lacks the jurisdiction and authority to conduct the foreclosure shall be null and void.   *97*

17. *Bean v. Walker.* The vendee under a land sale contract acquires an interest in the property of such a nature that it must be extinguished before the vendor may resume possession.   *99*

Licari v. Blackwelder

Real estate sellers (P) v. Real estate brokers (D)

Conn. App. Ct., 539 A.2d 609 (1988).

NATURE OF CASE: Suit to recover damages for the defendants' breaches of their fiduciary duties as real estate brokers.

FACT SUMMARY: Six siblings enlisted a real estate broker to help them sell a home they had inherited, and the broker in turn enlisted another broker for further assistance. The second broker himself bought the home for less than market value and sold it six days later for $45,000 more than his purchase price.

🏛 **RULE OF LAW**
Real estate brokers must fully, fairly, and promptly inform their clients of all known facts that might be material to the transaction for which the brokers were employed.

FACTS: Six brothers and sisters, who were unsophisticated laypersons with little experience in real estate, inherited a home and related property from their parents. Wanting to sell the property, though they knew nothing of its potential value, they contacted a real estate broker, Schwartz, for help in finding a buyer. Schwartz in turn contacted another real estate broker, Blackwelder (D), who was knowledgeable about real estate values near the plaintiffs' property. Blackwelder (D) and Schwartz entered a "co-broke" agreement under which they would evenly divide the commissions from a sale to one of Blackwelder's (D) prospective buyers. During an exclusive 24-hour window to sell the property for $125,000, an agent of Schwartz showed the property to a prospective buyer generated by Blackwelder (D). Within that 24-hour period, Blackwelder (D) himself offered $115,000 for the property. The plaintiffs accepted the offer. At no time did Blackwelder (D) either negotiate on the plaintiffs' behalf with the prospective buyer Blackwelder (D) had arranged or disclose the true value that Blackwelder (D) himself had assigned the property. The plaintiffs accepted a cash payment of $11,500 and a purchase money mortgage for the $103,500 balance of Blackwelder's (D) $115,000 purchase price; at the time of the transaction, the plaintiffs thought that their property had sold at market value and that Blackwelder (D) himself would use the property. Blackwelder (D), however, immediately contracted to sell the property for $160,000 to a buyer the plaintiffs had forbidden Schwartz from considering as a potential buyer for the property. The plaintiffs sued Blackwelder (D) and an associate of his, alleging that the defendants had breached their duties by withholding information from them and by intentionally misrepresenting who would purchase the property. The trial court found for the plaintiffs, holding that Blackwelder (D) had breached obligations to the plaintiffs that arose in their initial relationship with Schwartz. Judgment was entered for the plaintiffs in the amount of $45,000, which the trial judge found to be Blackwelder's (D) unconscionable profit from the transaction. Blackwelder (D) appealed.

ISSUE: Must real estate brokers fully, fairly, and promptly inform their clients of all known facts that might be material to the transaction for which the brokers were employed?

HOLDING AND DECISION: (Bieluch, J.) Yes. Real estate brokers must fully, fairly, and promptly inform their clients of all known facts that might be material to the transaction for which the brokers were employed. Real estate brokers are fiduciaries, and accordingly they must act with the highest fidelity and good faith in promoting their clients', and not their own, interests. Those duties flow to a broker who acts as a subagent of another broker if the subagent has the primary broker's express permission to act on the clients' behalf. The broker—the subagent—therefore has an obligation to disclose to the client all known facts about a potentially more advantageous transaction before concluding a sale that is less advantageous for the client. This record contains evidence supporting the trial court's findings that Blackwelder (D) breached those duties here. There is no error.

▶ **ANALYSIS**

Licari illustrates a fiduciary's constant obligation to know—and remember—where his loyalties lie. They won't lie with his self-interest. Giving Blackwelder (D) some benefit of the doubt in this case, it is at least conceivable that he saw some duty of loyalty to the prospective ultimate buyers. The duties of the primary broker (Schwartz), however, which ran to the plaintiffs, would have negated even that hypothetical defense for Blackwelder (D) here.

■■■

Quicknotes

BREACH OF FIDUCIARY DUTY The failure of a fiduciary to observe the standard of care exercised by professionals of similar education and experience.

BROKERAGE A business in which brokers or agents are paid for entering transactions on behalf of others.

FIDUCIARY DUTY A legal obligation to act for the benefit of another, including subordinating one's personal interests to that of the other person.

Continued on next page.

INTENIONAL MISREPRESENTATION   A statement or conduct
by one party to another that constitutes a false representation of fact.

■≡■

Hickey v. Green

Would-be buyer (P) v. Breaching seller (D)

Mass. App. Ct., 442 N.E.2d 37 (1982), *rev. denied*, 445 N.E.2d 156 (1983).

NATURE OF CASE: Appeal from grant of specific performance of a real estate contract.

FACT SUMMARY: Green (D) contended that the real estate sales contract she orally entered into with Hickey (P) was unenforceable based on the Statute of Frauds.

🏛 **RULE OF LAW**
An oral contract for the transfer of interest in land may be specifically enforced despite the Statute of Frauds if the party seeking performance changed his position in reasonable reliance on the contract and injustice can be avoided only through specific performance.

FACTS: Green (D) orally agreed to sell a parcel to Hickey (P), and accepted a check as a deposit. In reliance on the contract, Hickey (P) accepted a deposit on his home from a purchaser, intending to build a new home on the land he purchased from Green (D). Subsequently, Green (D), knowing Hickey (P) sold his house in reliance on the contract, refused to sell the land to Hickey (P). Hickey (P) sued for specific performance. Green (D) defended, contending the contract was unenforceable under the Statute of Frauds. The trial court granted specific performance, and Green (D) appealed.

ISSUE: Can an oral contract for the sale of real estate be specifically enforced if the party seeking enforcement changed his position in reasonable reliance upon the contract?

HOLDING AND DECISION: (Cutter, J.) Yes. An oral contract for the transfer of an interest in land may be specifically enforced, despite the Statute of Frauds requirement of writing, if the party seeking enforcement changed his position in reasonable reliance on the contract and injustice can be avoided only through specific performance. In this case, Hickey (P) clearly changed his position in reliance on the contract by selling his house in anticipation of occupying another on Green's (D) land. The reliance was reasonable, and Green (D) was fully aware of this change in position when she refused to honor the contract. As a result, it would be manifestly unjust to refuse specific performance in this case. Therefore, it must be ordered. Remanded.

▶ **ANALYSIS**

This case could have been decided on different grounds. Some commentators, spurred by dicta in the opinion, contend that the check which Hickey (P) gave Green (D) as a deposit on the land constituted an adequate memorandum to satisfy the requirements of the Statute of Frauds.

Quicknotes

RELIANCE Dependence on a fact that causes a party to act or refrain from acting.

SPECIFIC PERFORMANCE An equitable remedy whereby the court requires the parties to perform their obligations pursuant to a contract.

STATUTE OF FRAUDS A statute that requires specified types of contracts to be in writing in order to be binding.

Lohmeyer v. Bower

Property buyer (P) v. Seller (D)

Kan. Sup. Ct., 227 P.2d 102 (1951).

NATURE OF CASE: Specific performance of real estate contract.

FACT SUMMARY: Lohmeyer (P), claiming unmerchantable title, sued for rescission of real estate sales contract, which Bower (D) cross-complained for specific performance.

🏛 RULE OF LAW
A party cannot convey good merchantable title if violations of covenants or zoning ordinances exist on the subject property at the time it is to be sold.

FACTS: Lohmeyer (P) contracted to buy a specific parcel of property from Bower (D). The contract provided that Bower (D) would convey, by warranty deed good merchantable title, free and clear of encumbrances, but subject to all recorded restrictions and easements applying to the property. The contract further stated that Bower (D) would be allowed sufficient time to correct any defects in the title. Upon examination of the title, Lohmeyer (P) learned that the subject property was in violation of both a city zoning ordinance and a restrictive covenant previously imposed on the lot. He then sued for rescission of the contract and return of his money. Bower (D) contested Lohmeyer's (P) right to rescind and cross-complained for specific performance. The trial court held for Bower (D) and ordered specific performance of the contract. Lohmeyer (P) appealed.

ISSUE: May property which is in violation of restrictive covenants or city zoning ordinances be conveyed under good merchantable title?

HOLDING AND DECISION: (Parker, J.) No. In order for a title to be merchantable, it must be free from reasonable doubt and must not expose the prospective purchaser to the hazard of potential litigation. A title to property which is in violation of city zoning ordinances or restrictive covenants clearly does not meet the requirement of merchantability. It is obvious that Lohmeyer (P) would be exposed to potential litigation upon purchase of the property in question. It must be stressed that it is the existence of the violation of the ordinance and covenant which makes the title unmerchantable, not the presence of the ordinance or covenant, themselves. Furthermore, the contract provision allowing Bower (D) to correct any defect in title is immaterial in the present case, since any action Bower (D) might take to correct the title defects would materially alter the subject property and effect a breach of contract. Accordingly, the trial court is reversed and Lohmeyer's (P) plea for rescission is granted.

▶ ANALYSIS

As stated in the principal case, the existence of zoning laws generally does not make a title unmarketable. There are several exceptions to this general principle. First, if violations of the laws exist, as in *Lohmeyer*, title may be deemed unmarketable. This is due, however, to the risk of litigation, rather than the presence of the ordinances in and of themselves. Also, where zoning regulations are imposed after the contract is entered into and where they would materially frustrate the buyer's intended use of the property, many courts will not enforce the contract. This again is done for reasons other than unmarketable title. Finally, where the seller knows of relevant zoning laws which would interfere with the buyer's intended use of the property but informs the buyer such use would be permitted, the courts will refuse to enforce the contract.

■=■

Quicknotes

EARNEST MONEY A payment made by a buyer to a seller to evidence the intent to fulfill the obligations of a contract to purchase property.

EASEMENT The right to utilize a portion of another's real property for a specific use.

MERCHANTABLE TITLE Title, that although not perfect, would be acceptable to a reasonably well-informed buyer exercising ordinary business prudence.

RESCISSION The canceling of an agreement and the return of the parties to their positions prior to the formation of the contract.

RESTRICTIVE COVENANT A promise contained in a deed to limit the uses to which the property will be made.

SPECIFIC PERFORMANCE An equitable remedy whereby the court requires the parties to perform their obligations pursuant to a contract.

■=■

Stambovsky v. Ackley

Repudiating homebuyer (P) v. Haunted house owner (D)

N.Y. App. Div., 572 N.Y.S.2d 672 (1991).

NATURE OF CASE: Appeal from the dismissal action for rescission of contract of sale.

FACT SUMMARY: Stambovsky (P), purchaser, contended that he should be entitled to rescind the contract of sale and recover his down payment because Ackley (D), the owner of the house, did not disclose that the house was haunted.

🏛 **RULE OF LAW**
Where a condition that has been created by the seller materially impairs the value of the contract and is peculiarly within the knowledge of the seller or unlikely to be discovered by a prudent purchaser exercising due care with respect to the subject transaction, nondisclosure constitutes a basis for rescission as a matter of equity.

FACTS: Stambovsky (P) discovered that the house he had recently contracted to purchase was widely reputed to be possessed by poltergeists, reportedly seen by Ackley (D), the seller, and members of her family on numerous occasions over the previous nine years. Stambovsky (P) promptly sought rescission of the contract of sale. The New York Supreme Court dismissed the complaint, holding that Stambovsky (P) had no remedy at law within the jurisdiction. Stambovsky (P) appealed.

ISSUE: Does nondisclosure of a condition that has been created by the seller and is peculiarly within the knowledge of the seller or unlikely to be discovered by a prudent purchaser exercising due care with respect to the subject transaction constitute a basis for rescission as a matter of equity?

HOLDING AND DECISION: (Rubin, J.) Yes. Where a condition that has been created by the seller materially impairs the value of the contract and is peculiarly within the knowledge of the seller or unlikely to be discovered by a prudent purchaser exercising due care with respect to the subject transaction, nondisclosure constitutes a basis for rescission as a matter of equity. The unusual facts of this case clearly warrant a grant of equitable relief to Stambovsky (P), who did not have any familiarity with the folklore of the village of Nyack, where the house was located, and could not readily learn that the home he had contracted to buy was haunted. New York law fails to recognize any remedy for damages incurred as a result of the seller's mere silence, applying the doctrine of *caveat emptor*. However, Ackley (D) deliberately fostered the public belief that her home was possessed. Having undertaken to inform the public-at-large, to whom she has no legal relationship, about the supernatural occurrences on her property, she may be said to owe no less a duty to her contract vendee. Where, as here, Ackley (D) not only took unfair advantage of the buyer's (P) ignorance but created and perpetuated a condition about which he was unlikely even to inquire, enforcement of the contract would be offensive to the court's sense of equity. Application of the remedy of rescission, within the bounds of the narrow exception to the doctrine of *caveat emptor*, is entirely appropriate to relieve Stambovsky (P) from the consequences of a most unnatural bargain. Reversed.

DISSENT: (Smith, J.) This court should require something more substantial than a poltergeist before discarding the doctrine of *caveat emptor*.

▌ *ANALYSIS*

The doctrine of *caveat emptor* requires that a buyer act prudently to assess the fitness and value of his purchase and operates to bar the purchaser who fails to exercise due care from seeking the equitable remedy of rescission. It was apparent from this case, however, that the most careful inspection would not reveal the presence of ghosts at the premises. Therefore, there was no sound policy reason to deny the buyer relief for failing to discover a state of affairs which the most prudent purchaser would not be expected even to contemplate.

Quicknotes

CAVEAT EMPTOR Let the buyer beware; doctrine that a buyer purchases something at his or her own risk.

EQUITY Fairness; justice; the determination of a matter consistent with principles of fairness and not in strict compliance with rules of law.

NONDISCLOSURE The failure to communicate certain facts to another person.

POLTERGEIST Noise; ghost responsible for making noises.

RESCISSION The canceling of an agreement and the return of the parties to their positions prior to the formation of the contract.

Johnson v. Davis

Nondisclosing seller (D) v. Repudiating buyer (P)

Fla. Sup. Ct., 480 So. 2d 625 (1985).

NATURE OF CASE: Appeal of order rescinding a land sale contract.

FACT SUMMARY: The Johnsons (D) failed to disclose to the Davises (P) certain roof defects prior to conveyance of the Johnson (D) residence.

🏛 RULE OF LAW
Where the seller of a home knows of facts affecting the value of a home that are not readily observable, the seller is under a duty to disclose.

FACTS: The Davises (P) negotiated with the Johnsons (D) for purchase of the Johnson (D) house. The parties inserted into the sale contract a clause making the Johnsons (D) liable for minor roof repairs. After signing but before conveyance, Ms. Davis (P) noticed certain water spots. Mr. Johnson (D) assured her that they evidenced minor problems already fixed. Not long after conveyance, a storm occurred and water leaked extensively. A roofer concluded that a new roof was necessary. The Davises (P) sued for rescission and return of their deposit, plus costs. The Johnsons (D) counter-claimed, seeking liquidated damages of $5,000. The trial court rescinded, ordered the deposit returned, and awarded liquidated damages. The appellate court reversed the liquidated damages award, and the Johnsons (D) appealed.

ISSUE: Where the seller of a home knows of facts affecting the value of a home that are not readily observable, is the seller under a duty to disclose?

HOLDING AND DECISION: (Adkins, J.) Yes. Where the seller of a home knows of facts affecting the value of a home that are not readily observable, the seller is under a duty to disclose. Common law tort doctrine recognized the difference between nonfeasance and malfeasance, often sanctioning the latter but not the former. However, as more and more courts are realizing, the two circumstances have more similarities than differences, having the same bad motivations and effects. The fact is that in certain situations, a land conveyance being one of them, the seller is in a far better position to be aware of relevant facts than the buyer and should not be permitted to exploit the buyer's poor position. For this reason, the court thinks it fundamentally fair for *caveat emptor* to be abandoned in land sale contracts, and the seller to be placed under a duty to disclose. Affirmed.

▶ ANALYSIS

The court also briefly discussed fraud. The Johnsons (D) apparently fraudulently misrepresented the condition of the roof. They then argued that since the fraud occurred after contract execution it was irrelevant. The court hinted that any fraud prior to conveyance justified rescission, but the broader rule enunciated made a ruling on this issue superfluous.

Quicknotes

CAVEAT EMPTOR Let the buyer beware; doctrine that a buyer purchases something at his or her own risk.

DUTY TO DISCLOSE The duty owed by a fiduciary to reveal those facts that have a material effect on the interests of the party that must be informed.

FRAUDULENT MISREPRESENTATION A statement or conduct by one party to another that constitutes a false representation of fact.

LATENT DEFECTS A defect that cannot be discovered upon ordinary examination.

LIQUIDATED DAMAGES An amount of money specified in a contract representing the damages owed in the event of breach.

MALFEASANCE The commission of an unlawful act.

MISFEASANCE The commission of a lawful act in a wrongful manner.

NONFEASANCE The omission, or failure to perform, an obligation.

RESCISSION The canceling of an agreement and the return of the parties to their positions prior to the formation of the contract.

Lempke v. Dagenais

Subsequent purchaser (P) v. Contractor (D)

N.H. Sup. Ct., 547 A.2d 290 (1988).

NATURE OF CASE: Appeal of dismissal of action against a contractor for unworkmanlike performance.

FACT SUMMARY: Lempke (P) sought to recover from Dagenais (D) the cost of rebuilding a garage Dagenais (D) had built for the prior owner, which Lempke (P) claimed had been built in a substandard manner.

🏛 RULE OF LAW
A subsequent purchaser of property may recover from one performing defective contractor services for the prior owner if the work contained latent defects not apparent at the time of purchase.

FACTS: Lempke's (P) predecessor contracted with Dagenais (D) for the latter to build a garage, which he did. After Lempke (P) purchased the property, structural problems appeared which Lempke (P) claimed were due to substandard work by Dagenais (D). Lempke (P) sued Dagenais (D) for the cost of repair and/or replacement. The trial court dismissed the complaint, ruling that privity was a condition precedent to a cause of action against a builder for unworkmanlike performance. Lempke (P) appealed.

ISSUE: May a subsequent purchaser of property recover from one performing defective contractor services for the prior owner if the work contained latent defects not apparent at the time of purchase?

HOLDING AND DECISION: (Thayer, J.) Yes. A subsequent purchaser of property may recover from one performing defective contractor services for the prior owner if the work contained latent defects not apparent at the time of purchase. New Hampshire, like most states, recognizes in building construction work an implied warranty of workmanlike quality. Much debate has been generated as to whether this warranty is a creature of tort or contract, on the notion that the latter would require privity. However, in a final analysis, the implied warranty, be it tort or contract, arises by operation of law as a matter of public policy. Consequently, whether privity is required is determined by a reference to policy. In this respect, numerous policy reasons for not imposing a privity requirement exist. First, our society is increasingly mobile, and a builder/vendor should not be surprised by a change in ownership. Second, experience teaches us that latent defects often will not show up for years, so a sale to an unsuspecting purchaser is not unlikely. Third, a builder is in a better position to control the quality of the work than a subsequent buyer. Fourth, a contractor is already under an obligation to perform in a workmanlike manner, so the nature of his obligation is not changed by dispensing with privity. Finally, to impose a privity requirement would encourage sham first sales. These policy concerns lead this court to conclude that privity should not be required for a homeowner to sue a vendor/builder for latent defects resulting from substandard work. [The court went on to hold that the measure of damages would be the cost of repair or replacement, and also noted that a vendor/builder's duty did not go on indefinitely, but only for a reasonable time.] Reversed and remanded.

DISSENT: (Souter, J.) This issue was addressed by this court only two years ago, in *Ellis v. Robert C. Morris, Inc.*, 513 A.2d 951 (1986), and the result was the opposite. Adequate justification for departure therefrom has not been shown.

▶ *ANALYSIS*

All jurisdictions recognize some form of implied warranty such as that discussed here. Whether privity is required to assert it varies among the jurisdictions. The trend is generally toward disposing of the requirement. Some jurisdictions take the warranty out of contract and put it into tort. Others simply dispense with the requirement, as this court did.

■━■

Quicknotes

CONDITION PRECEDENT The happening of an uncertain occurrence, which is necessary before a particular right or interest may be obtained or an action performed.

IMPLIED WARRANTY An implied promise made by one party to a contract that the other party may rely on a fact, relieving that party from the obligation of determining whether the fact is true and indemnifying the other party from liability if that fact is shown to be false.

LATENT DEFECTS A defect that cannot be discovered upon ordinary examination.

PRIVITY OF CONTRACT A relationship between the parties to a contract that is required in order to bring an action for breach.

■━■

Jones v. Lee

Real estate sellers (P) v. Real estate buyers (D)

N.M. Ct. App., 971 P.2d 858 (1998).

NATURE OF CASE: Suit to recover damages for breach of a contract to purchase real estate.

FACT SUMMARY: The Lees (D) entered a written contract to buy real estate owned by the Joneses (P) for $610,000. Three months after the Lees (D) backed out of the deal, the Joneses (P) sold the property for $540,000.

🏛 RULE OF LAW
The non-defaulting party under a real estate contract is entitled to an award of damages following a breach of the contract.

FACTS: The parties entered a written agreement under which the Lees (D) would buy a home owned by the Joneses (P) for $610,000, with the Lees (D) paying $6,000 in earnest money to solidify the deal. Two months after entering the written contract, the Lees (D) informed the Joneses (P) that they could not go through with the purchase for financial reasons. The Joneses (P) rejected the Lees' (D) proposed termination agreement and sold the home three months after the breach for $540,000. The Joneses (P) sued the Lees (D) for breach of contract, requesting an award of damages. The trial court returned judgment for the Joneses (P) for the $70,000 difference between the contract price and the actual sale price, for special damages in the amount of $4,109, and for punitive damages, with a total judgment in the amount of $157,118.94. The Lees (D) appealed.

ISSUE: Is the non-defaulting party under a real estate contract entitled to an award of damages following a breach of the contract?

HOLDING AND DECISION: (Donnelly, J.) Yes. The non-defaulting party under a real estate contract is entitled to an award of damages following a breach of the contract. A seller generally can choose from three remedies when a buyer breaches an agreement to purchase real estate: (1) rescission of the contract, (2) specific performance, or (3) damages. In this case, by choosing to pursue damages, the Joneses (P) had the burden of proving the damages they sought. New Mexico analyzes such damages claims under the "loss of the bargain" rule, which requires a showing of the difference between the purchase price and the property's market value when the breach occurred. The parties here agreed that the market value was $610,000 when the breach occurred—which means that the Joneses (P) suffered no compensatory damages, the Lees (D) argued, because the market value and the contract price were identical when the breach occurred. Such an identity of value normally limits a seller's recovery to nominal

damages or retention of the buyer's earnest money; the exception to this rule occurs when, as here, the sellers also have incurred special damages. The trial court in this case failed to enter the required findings of fact on the date of the breach and the property's market value on that date. The case therefore must be remanded on the issue of compensatory damages so that the trial court can enter the appropriate factual determinations. Further, the trial court correctly awarded the Joneses (P) special damages for $1,859 in expenses incurred because of the home's solar system and heating warranty. Such expenses are recoverable if they were reasonably foreseeable, and the purchase agreement rendered them reasonably foreseeable in this case. Special damages here also properly included $2,250 for half of the interest on mortgage payments made by the Joneses (P) after the breach. These damages, too, were reasonably foreseeable. Finally, the record also supports an award of punitive damages against the Lees (D). When they breached the contract, claiming "financial reasons" for terminating the transaction, their checking account held approximately $577,000, and their monthly income totaled more than $16,000. The record shows further that the Lees (D) intimidated the Joneses (P) to induce them to accept the termination agreement. Under the circumstances, the Lees (D) breached the contract in a wanton and utterly reckless manner, thereby justifying an award of punitive damages. Affirmed in part; vacated in part and remanded.

▶ ANALYSIS

On remand, the trial judge in *Jones* must calculate compensatory damages by choosing between the parties' stipulated value for the property at the time of the breach—$610,000—and the eventual actual sale price of $540,000. Though the parties' purpose in stipulating to the property's value at the time of the breach was unclear, a stipulation on a fact-issue should receive special, deferential consideration when a trial court establishes a factual record. The Joneses' (P) compensatory damages on remand thus were very likely limited to retention of the Lees' (D) earnest money because the market value and contract price at the time of the breach would have been identical.

Quicknotes

EARNEST MONEY A payment made by a buyer to a seller to evidence the intent to fulfill the obligations of a contract to purchase property.

Continued on next page.

MEASURE OF DAMAGED Monetary compensation that may be awarded by the court to a party, who has sustained injury or loss to his person, property, or rights due to another party's unlawful act, omission, or negligence.

PUNITIVE DAMAGED Damages exceeding the actual injury suffered for the purposes of punishment of the defendant, deterrence of the wrongful behavior or comfort to the plaintiff.

SPECIAL DAMAGED Damages caused by a specific act that are not the usual consequence of that act and which must be specifically pled and proven.

Kutzin v. Pirnie

Real estate sellers (P) v. Real estate buyers (D)

N.J. Sup. Ct., 591 A.2d 932 (1991).

NATURE OF CASE: Suit by real estate sellers for damages sustained from the breach of a purchase contract.

FACT SUMMARY: The Pirnies (D) paid a $36,000 deposit toward the purchase of the Kutzins' (P) house. After the Pirnies (D) defaulted on the purchase, the trial court ordered the Kutzins (P) to return $18,675 of the Pirnies' (D) deposit.

RULE OF LAW
A buyer who materially breaches a real estate purchase contract can recover in restitution for benefits he conferred on the seller through either part performance on the contract or reliance beyond the loss that his own breach caused.

FACTS: The Pirnies (D) entered a written agreement to purchase the Kutzins' (P) house for $365,000. Under the contract, the Pirnies (D) agreed to pay a total deposit of $36,000 within seven days of signing the contract; the contract, however, contained no liquidated-damages clause governing the deposit's return if the sale did not occur. Although the Pirnies (D) performed on their obligation to pay the deposit, they later breached the contract. Six months after the original closing date, the Kutzins (P) sold their house for $352,500 after also incurring extra expenses for utilities, real estate taxes, insurance, and carpeting that they would not have incurred had the Pirnies (D) fulfilled the original purchase agreement. The Kutzins (P) sued, and the trial court awarded them various damages totaling $17,325: $12,500 for the difference between the contract price and the eventual sale price; $3,825 in utilities; and $1,000 for new carpet. The trial court also ordered the Kutzins (P) to return $18,675 to the Pirnies (D) as the difference between the deposit and the Kutzins' (P) actual damages. The Kutzins (P) appealed, claiming that the trial court should have awarded them the entire deposit; the Pirnies (D) cross-appealed, arguing that the contract had been rescinded and that they therefore were entitled to a return of their entire deposit. The appellate court affirmed the trial court's denial of recovery for taxes and insurance, reasoning that such expenses were too speculative, but the appellate court followed well-established law and reversed the trial court's order requiring a return of part of the deposit. The Kutzins (P), the appellate court held, were entitled to keep the entire deposit of $36,000. The Pirnies (D) requested further review in the Supreme Court of New Jersey.

ISSUE: Can a buyer who materially breaches a real estate purchase contract recover in restitution for benefits he conferred on the seller through either part performance

on the contract or reliance beyond the loss that his own breach caused?

HOLDING AND DECISION: (Clifford, J.) Yes. A buyer who materially breaches a real estate purchase contract can recover in restitution for benefits he conferred on the seller through either part performance on the contract or reliance beyond the loss that his own breach caused. The majority rule is that a buyer who breaches his purchase contract may not recover his deposit. A definite recent trend in the law, however, sees an injustice in permitting a seller to retain a deposit in excess of his actual damages. In this respect, Professor Corbin has observed that a defaulting buyer should receive restitution for that portion of his deposit that the evidence shows to be a penalty rather than compensatory damages. Section 374(1) of the Restatement (Second) of Contracts now states this developing position: the party in breach may recover restitution for benefits he conferred through either part performance or reliance beyond the loss that his own breach caused. Any New Jersey cases to the contrary are hereby overruled, and this Court adopts the approach described in Section 374(1) of the Restatement. Accordingly, in this case the Pirnies (D) are entitled to a return of that portion of their deposit that exceeds the Kutzins' (P) actual damages: $18,675. The buyer has the burden of proving entitlement to such a recovery, and the Pirnies (D) have met that burden here. Also worth noting is that the contract in this case contained no liquidated-damages provision; such a provision would have required New Jersey courts to use Section 374(2) of the Restatement. The trial court's damages award should be reinstated. With that modification, the appellate court's judgment is affirmed.

ANALYSIS

Kutzin points up the tension in the law between fairness and administrative or evidentiary expedience. As the *Kutzin* court notes, courts are recognizing an injustice in permitting a non-defaulting seller to withhold a deposit that exceeds his actual damages. As always, though, balanced against the interests of fairness and accuracy are the evidentiary and administrative issues involved with ascertaining actual damages in such cases. According to the casebook, most courts permit retaining the deposit in these cases, partly because of the evidentiary difficulties of proving damages. The New Jersey Supreme Court goes some distance in *Kutzin* to resolve this difficulty by placing

Continued on next page.

86 CASENOTE® LEGAL BRIEFS
Property

the burden of proof on the buyer who demands return of his deposit.

■━■

Quicknotes

FORFEITURE CLAUSE A clause providing for the loss of property or a right without compensation therefor.

LIQUIDATED DAMAGED An amount of money specified in a contract representing the damages owed in the event of breach.

PART PERFORMANCE Partial performance of a contract, promise, or obligation.

RELIANCE Dependence on a fact that causes a party to act or refrain from acting.

RESTITUTION The return or restoration to rightful owner to prevent unjust enrichment.

UNJUST ENRICHMENT Principle that one should not be unjustly enriched at the expense of another.

■━■

Brown v. Lober

Purchaser (P) v. Seller's executor (D)

Ill. Sup. Ct., 389 N.E.2d 1188 (1979).

NATURE OF CASE: Appeal from award of damages for breach of the covenant of quiet enjoyment.

FACT SUMMARY: Brown (P) acquired the subject property under a general warranty deed despite the fact that a two-thirds interest in mineral rights had previously been reserved.

🏛 RULE OF LAW
The mere existence of a superior title does not constitute a breach of the covenant of quiet enjoyment.

FACTS: Brown (P) acquired a parcel of property from Bost under a general warranty deed containing no exceptions. Unknown to Brown (P), the property contained a reservation of a two-thirds interest in mineral rights by Bost's grantor. Seventeen years after purchasing the land, Brown (P) contracted to sell the mineral rights for $6,000, but was forced to lower the price to $2,000 when the parties learned of the prior reservation of rights. Because the 10-year statute of limitations prevented Brown (P) from suing for breach of warranty, he chose to sue Bost's executor, Lober (D), for breach of the covenant of quiet enjoyment of the premises. In effect, Brown (P) claimed that the existence of the rights reservation constituted a constructive eviction. The trial court held for Lober (D) and the appellate court reversed. The case was then appealed to the Illinois Supreme Court.

ISSUE: Does the mere existence of a paramount title in a third-party constitute a breach of the covenant of quiet enjoyment by the vender of property?

HOLDING AND DECISION: (Underwood, J.) No. Brown (P) was in no way hindered from the peaceable possession and enjoyment of his property by someone holding superior title. The mere fact that he had to renegotiate his contract for the assignment of mineral rights does not constitute an interference with quiet enjoyment. Thus the suit was premature. The covenant of quiet enjoyment guarantees only possession and enjoyment of the premises, not a perfect title. Since there was no interference with the use of the property or assertion of an adverse title, there was no breach. The reservation of mineral rights was a matter of public record and Brown (P) could therefore have maintained an action for breach of warranty. However, he let the statute of limitations run and lost his opportunity. He may not now prevail on a premature claim of breach of quiet enjoyment. Reversed.

ANALYSIS

A general warranty deed typically contains the following five covenants: covenant of seisin, covenant of right to convey, covenant against encumbrances, covenant of quiet enjoyment, and covenant of warranty. Sometimes a sixth covenant, of further assurances, is included in the deed. This states that the covenantor will perform any reasonably necessary acts to perfect the purchaser's title. The general warranty deed covenants serve to warrant title against imperfections which occurred before the time which the grantor assumed his title, as well as during his time of title. The first three covenants (seisin, right to convey, and against encumbrances) are deemed present covenants. Thus a breach occurs, if at all, at the time the covenant is made and a cause of action arises at that time. In contrast, the last three covenants are future covenants and are not breached until the time the covenantee's possession is actually interfered with.

Quicknotes

COVENANT OF QUIET ENJOYMENT A promise contained in a lease or a deed that the tenant or grantee will enjoy unimpaired use of the property.

COVENANTEE A party for whom a promise is made pursuant to a written agreement.

FUTURE COVENANTS A written promise to do, or to refrain from doing, a particular activity in the future.

GENERAL WARRANTY DEED A deed that guarantees that the conveyor possesses that title that he purports to convey.

PRESENT COVENANTS Covenant to do an act at the present moment.

RESERVATION OF RIGHTS A clause in a deed or other instrument reserving particular rights to the grantor of the property.

Frimberger v. Anzellotti

Wetlands purchaser (P) v. Seller (D)

Conn. App. Ct., 594 A.2d 1029 (1991).

NATURE OF CASE: Appeal from award of damages for breach of warranty.

FACT SUMMARY: Anzellotti (D) contended that she did not breach the warranty against encumbrances and did not innocently misrepresent the condition of property purchased by Frimberger (P) and subsequently found to be in violation of wetlands statutes.

🏛 RULE OF LAW
Latent violations of state or municipal land use regulations (1) that do not appear on the land records, (2) that are unknown to the seller of the property, (3) as to which the agency charged with enforcement has taken no official action to compel compliance at the time the deed was executed, and (4) that have not ripened into an interest that can be recorded on the land records do not constitute an encumbrance for the purpose of the deed warranty.

FACTS: In 1978, Anzellotti's (D) brother, DiLoreto, subdivided a parcel of land for the purposes of constructing residences. The property abutted a tidal marshland and was, therefore, subject to the provisions of General Statutes §§ 22a-28 controlling the development of wetlands. DiLoreto built a bulkhead and filled that portion of the subject parcel immediately adjacent to the wetlands area and then proceeded with the construction of a dwelling on the property. DiLoreto then transferred the property to Anzellotti (D) by quit claim deed. Anzellotti (D), in turn, transferred the property to Frimberger (P) by warranty deed, free and clear of all encumbrances but subject to all building and zoning restrictions. Deciding to perform repairs on the land, Frimberger (P) requested a survey of the tidal wetlands from the state department of environmental protection (DEP). The survey discovered a violation of §§ 22a-30 of the General Statutes. DEP suggested that to correct the violation, Frimberger (P) submit an application to DEP, demonstrating the necessity of maintaining the bulkhead and fill within the tidal wetlands. Instead of filing the application, Frimberger (P) sued Anzellotti (D), claiming damages for breach of the warranty against encumbrances and innocent misrepresentation. The trial court found for Frimberger (P), holding that Anzellotti (D) breached the warranty against encumbrances and had innocently misrepresented the conditions. The court awarded Frimberger (P) $47,792.60, a figure that included costs to fix the land and diminution of value of the property caused by the violation. Anzellotti (D) appealed.

ISSUE: Do latent violations of state or municipal land use regulations that do not appear on the land records, that are unknown to the seller of the property, as to which the agency charged with enforcement has taken no official action to compel compliance at the time the deed was executed, and that have not ripened into an interest that can be recorded on the land records constitute an encumbrance for the purpose of the deed warranty?

HOLDING AND DECISION: (Lavery, J.) No. Latent violations of state or municipal land use regulations that do not appear on the land records, that are unknown to the seller of the property, as to which the agency charged with enforcement has taken no official action to compel compliance at the time the deed was executed, and that have not ripened into an interest that can be recorded on the land records do not constitute an encumbrance for the purpose of the deed warranty. The New Jersey Supreme Court in *Fahmie v. Wulster*, 81 N.J. 391, 408 A.2d 789 (1979), concluded that it was generally the law throughout the country that a claim for breach of a covenant against encumbrances cannot be predicated on the necessity to repair or alter the property to conform with land use regulations. By so doing, the *Fahmie* court refused to expand the concept of an encumbrance to include structural conditions existing on the property that constitute violations of a statute or governmental regulation. The case at bar raises the same issues as those raised in *Fahmie*. Here, in 1978 the wetlands area was filled without a permit and in violation of state statute. The alleged violation was unknown to Anzellotti (D), was not on the land records, and was discovered only after Frimberger (P) attempted to get permission to perform additional improvements to the wetlands area. The reasoning in *Fahmie* is correct, because to hold otherwise would create uncertainty in the law of conveyances, title searches, and title insurance. The parties to conveyance of real property can adequately protect themselves from such conditions by including protective language in the contract and by insisting on appropriate provisions in the deed. Frimberger (P), an attorney and land developer, who had previously developed waterfront property and was aware of wetlands statutes, could have adequately protected himself from any liability for wetlands violations. As for innocent misrepresentation, at no time was any representation made relating to the wetlands area. Because the warranty of a covenant against encumbrances was not violated, no misrepresentation could have been made. Reversed and remanded.

Continued on next page.

▶ *ANALYSIS*

An encumbrance is defined as "every right to or interest in the land which may subsist in third persons, to the diminution of the value of the land, but consistent with the passing of the fee by the conveyance." All encumbrances may be classed as (1) a pecuniary charge against the premises, such as mortgages, judgment liens, tax liens, or assessments, (2) estates or interests in the property less than the fee, like leases or life estates, or (3) easements or servitudes on the land, such as rights of way, restrictive covenants, and profits. It is important to note that the covenant against encumbrances cannot be breached unless the encumbrance existed at the time of the conveyance.

■━■

Quicknotes

WARRANTY AGAINST ENCUMBRANCES A guarantee in a contract that the interest in property being conveyed is unencumbered.

■━■

Rockafellor v. Gray

Remote grantees (P) v. Remote grantor (D)

Iowa Sup. Ct., 191 N.W. 107 (1922).

NATURE OF CASE: Appeal from award of damages for breach of covenant of seisin.

FACT SUMMARY: Hansen & Gregerson (P), the remote grantees of a deed from Connelly (D), sued for a breach of the covenant of seisin.

🏛 **RULE OF LAW**
The breach of the covenant of seisin creates a chose in action which passes by assignment to subsequent grantees of the deed.

FACTS: Gray held a mortgage on a certain parcel of property which was obtained by Rockafellor. When payments were missed, Gray foreclosed on the mortgage. This resulted in the acquisition of the property by sheriff's deed by Connelly (D). Connelly (D) subsequently conveyed the property by warranty deed to Dixon in 1911 for $4,000. Dixon then sold it to Hansen & Gregerson (hereinafter Hansen) (P) for $7,000. In 1920, Rockafellor filed suit to vacate the foreclosure sale on the ground that the court lacked proper jurisdiction over him. Hansen (P) then filed a cross-petition, praying for a judgment against the remote grantor, Connelly (D), in the event that Rockafellor succeeded in vacating the foreclosure sale. The basis for Hansen's (P) claim was that Connelly (D) breached the covenant of seisin when he sold property to Dixon which in truth he did not own. The trial court vacated the foreclosure sale and rendered judgment on Hansen's (P) cross-complaint against Connelly (D) for $4,000. Connelly (D) appealed from the judgment against him only.

ISSUE: Does the breach of the covenant of seisin pass to remote grantees of the original covenantor as a chose in action?

HOLDING AND DECISION: (Faville, J.) Yes. The state of Iowa follows the English rule—which is the minority rule in America—that the covenant of seisin, runs with the land. Thus when the covenant is broken, it becomes a chose in action and is passed by assignment to subsequent grantees of the deed. Admittedly, there is an exception to this rule, arising from the situation where the original covenantor has neither title nor possession of the premises at the time the deed is executed and delivered. In such a case, the cause of action for the breach of the covenant of seisin arises immediately and is imbued in the immediate grantee. When the grantee subsequently assigns the deed to others, the cause of action for the breach is transferred along with the property. However, because the cause of action accrued immediately, the statute of limitations, which in Iowa is ten years, applies. Thus in the present

case, it is irrelevant whether or not the remote grantor, Connelly (D), had title and possession at the time he delivered the deed to Dixon since the suit was brought nine years after the cause of action accrued, and is therefore valid. Since Hansen (P) acquired the right to sue for the breach of covenant as either a chose in action or a cause of action at the time he acquired the deed, he is entitled to judgment in this case. This is because Connelly (D) warranted that he was properly seized of the property when in fact he was not, as the foreclosure sale by which he acquired the deed was later judged invalid. Finally, the lower court's award of $4,000 was proper despite Connelly's (D) argument to the contrary. He offered evidence that despite the recital of $4,000 as consideration in the deed, the amount actually paid was nominal. Therefore, since Hansen's (P) cause of action accrues through the immediate grantee, he may not recover more damages than the immediate grantee would be entitled to. However, Hansen (P) was entitled to rely on the amount specified in the deed from Connelly (D) to Dixon. Even though Connelly (D) would be entitled to raise the discrepancy between the deed price and the price actually paid in an action against Dixon, it would be unfair to allow him to do so against a remote grantee. Affirmed.

▶ **ANALYSIS**

In the majority of jurisdictions, the breach of the covenant of seisin (a present covenant) occurs at the time of conveyance and therefore cannot be said to run with the land. The cause of action for the breach arises at the time of conveyance and is subject to the restrictions of the statute of limitations. Under the common law, there was no implied assignment of the cause of action when the title was conveyed. However, some jurisdictions follow the English rule, under which such an assignment is implied.

Quicknotes

CHOSE IN ACTION The right to recover, or the item recoverable, in a law suit.

COVENANT OF SEISIN A promise that the conveyor of property has the lawful right to convey the interest he is attempting to transfer.

FORECLOSURE SALE Termination of an interest in property, usually initiated by a lienholder upon failure to tender mortgage payments, resulting in the sale of the property in order to satisfy the debt.

Sweeney v. Sweeney

Grantor's widow (P) v. Grantee (D)

Conn. Sup. Ct. of Errors, 11 A.2d 806 (1940).

NATURE OF CASE: Action to cancel a deed.

FACT SUMMARY: Maurice, Sweeney's (P) intestate, gave property to John Sweeney (D) by deed which was recorded, and John (D) deeded the property back to Maurice, who wished to be protected in the event John (D) predeceased him, but that deed was not recorded.

🏛 RULE OF LAW
Where a deed has been formally executed and delivered, the presumption that the grantee assented to delivery can be overcome only by evidence that no delivery was in fact intended.

FACTS: Sweeney (P) is Maurice Sweeney's widow and administratrix. Maurice deeded property to John Sweeney (D). This deed was recorded. Pursuant to Maurice's request, a second deed was executed which deeded the property back to him. This deed was not recorded. A week or two later, Maurice took John (D) the recorded deed, and a week or two after that he took John (D) the unrecorded deed. John (D) gave the second deed to his attorney. When the latter's office was burned, the deed was destroyed. Maurice's purpose in making the second deed was so that he would be protected if John (D) predeceased him. Maurice continued to live on the deeded property until his death. He made leases in regard to it and exercised full control over it without interference from John (D). The trial court concluded that there was no intention to deliver John's (D) deed to Maurice and there was no delivery or acceptance thereof.

ISSUE: Has a deed been delivered where it was formally executed and manually delivered and where there is no evidence that no delivery was intended?

HOLDING AND DECISION: (Jennings, J.) Yes. It is true that physical possession of a duly executed deed is not conclusive proof that it was legally delivered. Delivery must be made with the intent to pass title if it is to be effective. However, where a deed has been manually delivered, there is a rebuttable presumption that the grantee assented since the deed was beneficial to him. Where deeds are formally executed and delivered, this presumption can be overcome only by evidence that no delivery was in fact intended. In this case the only purpose in making the deed expressed by either party was Maurice's statement that it was to protect him in case John (D) predeceased him. Since this purpose would have been defeated had there been no delivery with intent to pass title, this conclusively establishes the fact that there was legal delivery. John (D) also contended that the delivery was on the condition that John (D) predeceased Maurice. However, a conditional delivery can only be made by placing the deed in the hands of a third person to be kept until the happening of the condition. The court's ruling is reversed and a new trial is ordered.

▶ ANALYSIS

The delivery must be voluntary and must occur with the mutual intention of the parties to pass title. The term "escrow" is sometimes used as importing any deposit of a deed for delivery upon the performance of a condition. There can be no escrow without conditional delivery of the deed to a third person as depositary. "Conditional delivery to a grantee vests absolute title in the latter."

■■■

Quicknotes

DELIVERY The transfer of title or possession of property.

■■■

Rosengrant v. Rosengrant

Conveyance contestants (P) v. Alleged grantee (D)

Okla. Ct. App., 629 P.2d 800 (1981).

NATURE OF CASE: Petition to cancel a deed purporting to transfer real property to only one of the grantors' six nieces and nephews.

FACT SUMMARY: A retired couple tried to convey their farm to one of their nieces and nephews. After the couple died, the other nieces and nephews challenged the conveyance for lack of legal delivery.

🏛 **RULE OF LAW**
Grantors do not legally deliver a deed if they reserve the right to retrieve the deed, require that the delivery may become operative only when the grantors have died, and keep using the property as if it were still their own.

FACTS: A retired couple, Harold and Mildred Rosengrant, who had no children of their own, tried to convey their farm to J.W. ("Jay") Rosengrant (D), one of the couple's six nieces and nephews. Harold and Mildred both signed a deed transferring the property to Jay (D), but they also asked him to leave the deed at their bank, saying that he could record the deed after they died. Harold himself handed the deed to Jay (D) at the bank during their meeting with the banker, apparently in an effort to comply with the legal requirement that a deed be delivered. Jay (D) took the deed from Harold but then handed it to the banker. The banker then held the deed in a safety deposit box in an envelope marked as being for "J.W. Rosengrant or Harold Rosengrant." Six days after Harold died Jay (D) recorded the deed. Nineteen days after recordation, a petition to cancel the deed was filed [by other nieces and nephews of Harold and Mildred Rosengrant]. The petition to cancel alleged that the deed was not legally delivered, and was therefore void, or that the deed was only a testamentary instrument and therefore failed to comply with the Statute of Wills. The trial court agreed with the petitioners' first argument and voided the deed for lack of legal delivery. Jay (D) appealed.

ISSUE: Do grantors legally deliver a deed if they reserve the right to retrieve the deed, require that the delivery may become operative only when the grantors have died, and keep using the property as if it were still their own?

HOLDING AND DECISION: (Boydston, J.) No. Grantors do not legally deliver a deed if they reserve the right to retrieve the deed, require that the delivery may become operative only when the grantors have died, and keep using the property as if it were still their own. The grantor's intent at the time of delivery controls the question of whether legal delivery occurred. Here, as the writing on the envelope clearly signified, Harold could have retrieved the deed at any time. The same conclusion finds support in Harold and Mildred's conditioning the conveyance on two future events: their deaths and the deed's recordation by Jay (D) after they died. Also significant is that Harold and Mildred continued to live on the farm and kept using it as their own even after the alleged conveyance to Jay (D). Under these circumstances, the evidence supports the trial court's judgment finding the deed null and void for lack of delivery. Affirmed.

CONCURRENCE: (Brightmire, J.) Although the facts in cases like this one can be difficult to determine, the applicable law is clear: the grantor must actually or constructively deliver the deed to the grantee, and the grantor must evince an intent to divest himself of his interest. To help the courts determine the pertinent facts in this case, only one of the four people involved in the original conveyance meeting at the bank—Jay (D) himself—is still alive and able to testify. Jay's (D) self-serving statements at the trial in this case therefore suffer inherent problems with credibility. Harold and Mildred's conduct after the meeting only further implies that they did not intend to deliver the deed to Jay (D). Even if they did so intend, they also retained a right to revoke the conveyance. Either way, the deed was not validly delivered.

▎ ***ANALYSIS***

The legal requirement of delivery is not an empty formality, as the *Rosengrant* court emphasizes. Even though Harold and Mildred obviously intended to reward Jay (D) for his and his wife's kindness, the totality of the evidence just as clearly demonstrates in Harold and Mildred a hesitation, an indecision that contradicted a legally binding intent, to deliver.

■■■

Quicknotes

CONVEYANCE OF TITLE Any transfer or conveyance having an effect on title to an interest in real property.

NULLITY An act having no legal effect.

STATUTE OF WILLS An English law stating the requirements for a valid testamentary disposition.

TESTAMENTARY INSTRUMENT An instrument that takes effect upon the death of the maker.

■■■

Murphy v. Fin. Dev. Corp.

Defaulting mortgagor (P) v. Foreclosing mortgagee (D)

N.H. Sup. Ct., 495 A.2d 1245 (1985).

NATURE OF CASE: Appeal from order setting aside a foreclosure.

FACT SUMMARY: Murphy (P) contended that Financial Development Corporation (Financial) (D) failed to use due diligence in attempting to get a reasonable price for his property in a foreclosure sale.

🏛 RULE OF LAW
Mere compliance with statutory requirements may not discharge a mortgagee's duty to exercise good faith and due diligence in selling the property at foreclosure.

FACTS: Murphy (P) was the mortgagor of his residence, the mortgagee being Financial (D). Murphy (P) defaulted on loan payments and attempted several times to renegotiate and refinance the debt. Financial (D) cooperated by postponing the foreclosure sale at least once, but subsequently held the sale after proper notice. No one other than Murphy (P) appeared at the sale, at which Financial (D) pledged its mortgage and obtained title to the property. Murphy (P) sued to set aside the sale on the basis that Financial (D) failed to use due diligence in obtaining a fair price for the property. A special master was appointed who held for Murphy (P) and awarded attorney fees. Financial (D) appealed.

ISSUE: Does compliance with foreclosure sale statutes fulfill the mortgagee's duties to the mortgagor?

HOLDING AND DECISION: (Douglas, J.) No. Mere compliance with statutory requirements may not discharge a mortgagee's duty to exercise good faith and due diligence in selling the property at foreclosure. A mortgagee has an affirmative duty to act as a fiduciary toward the mortgagor's equity in the home. In this case, $27,000 was pledged for property worth twice that. No other bids were affirmatively solicited. Thus the base notice requirements did not discharge the mortgagee's duties. However, no bad faith was present, and thus no attorney fees were recoverable. Affirmed in part, reversed in part, and remanded.

▶ ANALYSIS

The property was sold soon after the foreclosure sale, but before any controversy had arisen. The buyer clearly was a bona fide purchaser; thus title to the property was not at issue here. Damages were set at the difference between a fair price for the property and the price obtained at foreclosure. This differed from the master's ruling which used the fair market value as a starting point.

■=■

Quicknotes

BONA FIDE PURCHASER A party who purchases property in good faith and for valuable consideration without notice of a defect in title.

DUE DILIGENCE The standard of care as would be taken by a reasonable person in accordance with the attendant facts and circumstances.

FAIR MARKET VALUE The price of particular property or goods that a buyer would offer and a seller accept in the open market, following full disclosure.

FORECLOSURE An action to recover the amount due on a mortgage of real property where the owner has failed to pay their debt, terminating the owner's interest in the property which must then be sold to satisfy the debt.

POWER OF SALE MORTGAGE A clause contained in a mortgage granting the mortgagee the authority to sell the property that is the subject of the mortgage upon default of the mortgage payments.

PROMISSORY NOTE A written promise to tender a stated amount of money at a designated time and to a designated person.

■=■

Commonwealth v. Fremont Investment & Loan

Massachusetts (P) v. Industrial bank (D)

Mass. Sup. Jud. Ct., 897 N.E.2d 548 (2008).

NATURE OF CASE: Appeal from trial court's granting of preliminary injunction to state.

FACT SUMMARY: Fremont (D) was selling subprime, adjustable rate mortgages to thousands of Massachusetts residents. The Commonwealth's Attorney General's office brought suit alleging the sale of such mortgages was a violation of the state's consumer protection statute.

🏛 RULE OF LAW
Mortgage loans with the following four characteristics would likely be "unfair" under the Massachusetts' Consumer Protection Act: (1) the loans were adjustable with a preliminary rate for three years; (2) the initial rate was typically three points lower than the usual mortgage rate on 30-year loans; (3) the debt to income ratio would exceed 50 percent after the introductory period expired; and (4) the loan-to-value ratio was 100 percent.

FACTS: Fremont (D) was selling loans to thousands of residents in Massachusetts. There is no dispute the loans in question had the four characteristics mentioned in the Rule of Law. In March 2007, Fremont (D) entered into an agreement with the Federal Deposit Insurance Corporation (FDIC) to cease granting subprime loans to customers without considering whether the customer would be able to pay the monthly loan amounts after the rate increased. Subsequently, Massachusetts entered into a similar agreement with Fremont. (D). Accordingly, Fremont (D) had to give the Attorney General's (P) office 90 days notice before any foreclosures. If the Attorney General (P) objected, Fremont (D) would attempt to resolve the matter short of foreclosure. As it turned out, the Attorney General (P) objected to all foreclosure requests. The Attorney General then filed this action to enjoin Fremont (D) from foreclosing on such loans because the loans were "unfair" under G.L. c. 93A, the Massachusetts consumer protection statute. The judge granted the preliminary injunction. The court ordered Fremont (D) to give notice to the Attorney General (P) prior to foreclosures and ordered Freemont (D) to resolve any foreclosure issues with the Attorney General (P). If there was no resolution, Fremont (D) was required to go to court for an order of foreclosure. Fremont (D) appealed on the grounds that its loans were customary in the industry and, therefore, the loans were not unfair.

ISSUE: Are mortgage loans with the following four characteristics likely to be "unfair" under the state's consumer protection statute: (1) the loans were adjustable with a preliminary rate for three years; (2) the initial rate was typically three points lower than the usual mortgage rate on 30-year loans; (3) the debt to income ratio would exceed 50 percent after the introductory period expired; and (4) the loan-to-value ratio was 100 percent?

HOLDING AND DECISION: (Botsford, J.) Yes. Mortgage loans with the following four characteristics would likely be "unfair" under the state's consumer protection statute: (1) the loans were adjustable with a preliminary rate for three years; (2) the initial rate was typically three points lower than the usual mortgage rate on 30-year loans; (3) the debt to income ratio would exceed 50 percent after the introductory period expired; and (4) the loan-to-value ratio was 100 percent. First, Fremont's (D) argument that the adjustable rate mortgage (ARM) loans were not unfair because they were standard practice in the industry is without merit. The record at the preliminary injunction stage revealed that Fremont (D) knew or should have known that loans that had the four characteristics stated above would most likely be difficult to repay. In addition, the record below reveals that Fremont (D) did not attempt to determine if borrowers would be able to pay the monthly loan amounts after the rate increased. FDIC's actions in this matter underscored its belief that these loans constitute unsafe and unsound banking practices. Regarding the Massachusetts Predatory Home Loan Practices Act, Fremont (D) is correct that the statute technically does not apply because that statute only applies to high-cost home mortgage loans. However, the trial court judge used the statute for policy support to conclude that loans are unfair where the lender should know the borrower will be unable to repay the loan. Lastly, that the loans in question are technically allowed by state and federal regulations does not mean they are not unfair. It has long been held that a determination of whether conduct is permitted by statute is just one aspect of the fairness analysis. It is not dispositive. The preliminary injunction is affirmed.

▶ ANALYSIS

This case is an example of a successful government action against the subprime lenders in the wake of the mortgage crisis. However, surprisingly, other states have not followed Massachusetts's tactic of using a local consumer protection statute. Rather, a handful of other states have brought actions against subprime lenders under the federal Securities Act of 1933.

Continued on next page.

Quicknotes

MORTGAGE An interest in land created by a written in-strument providing security for the payment of a debt or the performance of a duty.

PRELIMINARY INJUNCTION A judicial mandate issued to require or restrain a party from certain conduct; used to preserve a trial's subject matter or to prevent threatened injury.

U.S. Bank Natl. Assn. v. Ibanez

Purported mortgage holder (P) v. Home owner (D)

Mass. Sup. Jud. Ct., 941 N.E.2d 40 (2010).

NATURE OF CASE: Appeal from lower court decision finding that purported mortgage holders, attempting to foreclose on two properties, failed to demonstrate they actually held the mortgage on the properties at issue.

FACT SUMMARY: U.S. Bank National Association (U.S. Bank) (P) and Wells Fargo (P) foreclosed on two properties. The mortgages on each of the properties had been sold and assigned multiple times during their existence. After the foreclosure process, U.S. Bank (P) and Wells Fargo (P) brought actions in state court seeking a declaration that they were the owners in fee simple of the two properties.

🏛 RULE OF LAW
Any foreclosure proceeding initiated by a party that lacks the jurisdiction and authority to conduct the foreclosure shall be null and void.

FACTS: Antonio Ibanez (D) purchased a home in Springfield, Massachusetts, for $103,500 with a loan secured by a mortgage to the lender, Rose Mortgage, Inc. The mortgage was then assigned multiple times to different mortgage companies. In 2006, the latest holder of the mortgage pooled it with 1,200 other mortgages into a trust known as a mortgage-backed security. This process, known as a securitization, allowed these trusts to be bought and sold by investors. Eventually, U.S. Bank National Association (U.S. Bank) (P) purchased a mortgage-backed security that allegedly included Ibanez's (D) mortgage. That transaction occurred via a private placement memorandum. That document states the trust would include all mortgages placed into it and those mortgages would be reflected on an attached schedule of mortgages. A similar scenario played out with a mortgage taken out by Mark and Tammy LaRace (D). It was also pooled into a mortgage-backed security and eventually purchased by Wells Fargo (P). U.S. Bank (P) and Wells Fargo (P) foreclosed on the two properties in 2007, a process that does not require judicial approval. The foreclosure process included the properties being placed up for sale and then purchased by U.S. Bank (P) and Wells Fargo (P), respectively. (There is no dispute both homeowners defaulted on their loans.) After the foreclosure process, U.S. Bank (P) and Wells Fargo (P) brought actions in state court seeking a declaration that they were the owners in fee simple of the two properties. At the trial court level, the judge found both plaintiffs failed to prove they had the authority to foreclose on the properties. Specifically, using U.S. Bank (P) as an example, that entity did not provide the court with a schedule or any documentation that the Ibanez (D) mortgage was actually included in the mortgage-backed security that U.S. Bank (P) purchased in 2006. U.S. Bank (P) and Wells Fargo (P) appealed and the case was transferred to the Massachusetts Supreme Judicial Court.

ISSUE: Is any foreclosure proceeding initiated by a party that lacks the jurisdiction and authority to conduct the foreclosure null and void?

HOLDING AND DECISION: (Gants, J.) Yes. Any foreclosure proceeding initiated by a party that lacks the jurisdiction and authority to conduct the foreclosure shall be null and void. In these actions to quiet title to property, U.S. Bank (P) and Wells Fargo (P) have the burden of proving they were the fee simple owners of the properties. To do so, the plaintiffs need to demonstrate that they properly adhered to the statutory foreclosure process in Massachusetts. Massachusetts, like many states, does not require judicial approval before an entity forecloses on a property. The mortgagor/homeowner may petition a court to enjoin the foreclosure if he or she desires. Any mortgage includes a power of sale. However, one who sells under a power of sale must strictly follow the terms. Powers of sale have restrictions on who can actually foreclose on the property. The foreclosure can be exercised only by a mortgagee or its successors or assigns. U.S. Bank (P) claims that the private placement memorandum it received when it purchased the mortgage-backed security in 2006 made U.S. Bank (P) the holder of the Ibanez (D) mortgage. However, U.S. Bank (P) did not provide the lower court with a schedule or any documentation that the Ibanez (D) mortgage was actually included in the mortgage-backed security that U.S. Bank (P) purchased in 2006. Read closely, the private placement memorandum reveals an intent that certain mortgages would be included in the pool, but there simply was no evidence attached to that document stating which mortgages were included, if any. The last assignment on the record of Ibanez's (D) mortgage was to an entity called Option One. Accordingly, U.S. Bank (P) did not have the authority to foreclose on the mortgage. Wells Fargo (D) similarly could not demonstrate it actually held the mortgage on the LaRace (D) property. Affirmed.

CONCURRENCE: (Cordy, J.) Assignments of mortgages need not be recorded to be effective. However, the assignment or similar transaction must actually occur. In these complicated mortgage-backed security transactions, the onus is on the mortgage holders to demonstrate that

Continued on next page.

the assignment has passed to them before a foreclosure can proceed.

▶ *ANALYSIS*

This litigation and others like it were spawned after the housing crisis began in 2008. With the rate of foreclosures skyrocketing around the country, courts began to examine more closely the complicated array of transactions that occur after a homeowner takes out a mortgage. This particular decision resulted in a large number of foreclosures being placed into legal limbo until the foreclosing parties could remedy the defects in the various transactions.

■━━■

Quicknotes

FORECLOSURE An action to recover the amount due on a mortgage of real property where the owner has failed to meet the mortgage obligations, terminating the owner's interest in the property which must then be sold to satisfy the debt.

MORTGAGE An interest in land created by a written instrument providing security for the payment of a debt or the performance of a duty.

MORTGAGEE Party to whom an interest in property is given in order to secure a loan.

MORTGAGOR Party who grants an interest in property in order to secure a loan.

■━━■

Bean v. Walker

Home seller (P) v. Defaulting buyer (D)

N.Y. App. Div., 464 N.Y.S.2d 895 (1983).

NATURE OF CASE: Appeal from summary judgment granting repossession of real property branch of a land purchase contract.

FACT SUMMARY: Bean (P), a vendor, contended that Walker (D), a defaulting vendee, had no rights pursuant to their land purchase agreement, and that he should be able to repossess the premises and retain all the money paid under the contract.

RULE OF LAW
The vendee under a land sale contract acquires an interest in the property of such a nature that it must be extinguished before the vendor may resume possession.

FACTS: In January 1973, Bean (P) agreed to sell and Walker (D) agreed to buy a home for $15,000. The contract provided that this sum would be paid over a 15-year period at five percent interest, in monthly installments of $118.62. Bean (P) retained legal title to the property, which they agreed to convey upon payment in full. The contract provided that in the event Walker (D) defaulted in making payments and failed to cure the default within 30 days, Bean (P) could elect to call the remaining balance immediately due or elect to declare the contract terminated and repossess the premises. If the latter alternative was chosen, Bean (P) could retain all the money paid under the contract as "liquidated" damages. For eight years, Walker (D) paid Bean (P) as provided in their agreement. In 1981, Walker (D) came on hard times due to an injury and defaulted on the contract, having already paid over $12,000 in principal and interest and having made substantial improvement to the house. Bean (P), after the required 30-day period, commenced an action for ejectment, to be adjudged the owner in fee granted possession. From summary judgment for Bean (P), Walker (D) appealed.

ISSUE: Does the vendee under a land sale contract acquire an interest in the property of such a nature that it must be extinguished before the vendor may resume possession?

HOLDING AND DECISION: (Doerr, J.) Yes. The vendee under a land sale contract acquires an interest in the property of such a nature that it must be extinguished before the vendor may resume possession. Such an interest exists since the vendee acquires equitable title and the vendor merely holds the legal title in trust for the vendee, subject to the vendor's equitable lien for payment of the purchase price in accordance with the terms of the contract. The vendor may not enforce his rights by the simple expedient of an action in ejectment but must instead proceed to foreclose the vendee's equitable title or bring an action at law for the purchase price, neither of which remedies Bean (P) sought. The effect of the judgment granted below is that Bean (P) will have regained the property with improvements made over the years by Walker (D), along with $12,000 in principal and interest. This result would be quite inequitable. Reversed and remanded.

ANALYSIS

If the only substantive law to be applied to this case was that of contracts, the result reached by the lower court would have been correct. However, under the facts presented in the case, the law with regard to the transfer of real property must also be considered. The doctrine that equity deems as done that which ought to be done is an appropriate concept which applies to the present case. Walker (D) did not abandon the property or pay a minimal balance before he defaulted. Unfortunate circumstances prevented him from continuing what he had previously and faithfully done for over eight years. Such factors will not be taken lightly.

Quicknotes

EQUITABLE TITLE Interest in property that is not recognized in a court of law but that is protected in equity.

FIDUCIARY Person holding a legal obligation to act for the benefit of another.

LEGAL TITLE Title such that is recognized by a court of law.

LIQUIDATED DAMAGES An amount of money specified in a contract representing the damages owed in the event of breach.

MORTGAGEE Party to whom an interest in property is given in order to secure a loan.

MORTGAGOR Party who grants an interest in property in order to secure a loan.

SUMMARY JUDGMENT Judgment rendered by a court in response to a motion by one of the parties, claiming that the lack of a question of material fact in respect to an issue warrants disposition of the issue without consideration by the jury.

Title Assurance

Quick Reference Rules of Law

PAGE

1. *Luthi v. Evans.* An instrument that describes the property to be conveyed as "all of the grantor's property in a certain county" is not sufficiently specific as to be effective against subsequent purchasers and mortgagees, unless they have actual knowledge of the transfer. — 102

2. *Orr v. Byers.* A misspelled name does not give constructive notice to title searchers under the doctrine of *idem sonans*. — 103

3. *Messersmith v. Smith.* An unacknowledged deed does not qualify for recordation and therefore the recording does not give constructive notice to subsequent purchasers. — 104

4. *Board of Education of Minneapolis v. Hughes.* The recording of a deed from a grantee in an unrecorded deed to a third person is not notice of the prior unrecorded deed to a subsequent purchaser. — 105

5. *Guillette v. Daly Dry Wall, Inc.* A grantee is bound by restrictions in deeds to its neighbors from a common grantor, even if it takes without actual notice and his deed does not mention them, if the grantor has placed in writing the same restrictions on his remaining land. — 106

6. *Daniels v. Anderson.* One cannot claim bona fide purchaser status if he receives actual notice of an unrecorded interest in real estate prior to taking title. — 107

7. *Lewis v. Superior Court.* A person who records an interest in real estate after a bona fide purchaser (BFP) takes title thereto is inferior to the BFP, even if that BFP has not paid for the property. — 108

8. *Harper v. Paradise.* A deed that specifically refers to an earlier unrecorded deed puts a subsequent purchaser on notice of the existence of the earlier deed; thus, the purchaser claiming under the later deed is not entitled to priority, though the later deed was recorded first. — 109

9. *Waldorff Insurance and Bonding, Inc. v. Eglin National Bank.* Subsequent successors to legal title, after a contract to convey title has been executed, take title subject to all equitable interests of which they have notice. — 110

10. *Walker Rogge, Inc. v. Chelsea Title & Guaranty Co.* A title company's liability is limited to the policy, and the company is not liable in tort for negligence for searching records if it has not expressly contracted or implicitly agreed to do so. — 111

11. *Lick Mill Creek Apartments v. Chicago Title Insurance Co.* A title insurance company is obligated to protect the insured against defects in title but not against loss arising from physical damage to property. — 113

Luthi v. Evans

Subsequent assignee of oil and gas leases (P) v. Prior assignee (D)

Kan. Sup. Ct., 576 P.2d 1064 (1978).

NATURE OF CASE: Appeal from award of lease interest.

FACT SUMMARY: Grace V. Owens assigned her interest in all her Coffey County leases "whether or not the same are specifically enumerated above . . . ." to International Tours, Inc. (D); Owens subsequently assigned a lease, unenumerated in the first assignment, to J.R. Burris (P).

> 🏛 **RULE OF LAW**
> An instrument that describes the property to be conveyed as "all of the grantor's property in a certain county" is not sufficiently specific as to be effective against subsequent purchasers and mortgagees, unless they have actual knowledge of the transfer.

FACTS: On February 1, 1971, Grace V. Owens assigned all her interests in seven oil and gas leases located in Coffey County, Kansas, to International Tours, Inc. (D). The instrument further assigned Owens's interest in all Coffey County oil and gas leases "whether or not the same are specifically enumerated above . . . ." (This is an example of a "Mother Hubbard" clause.) The assignment was recorded on February 16, 1971. On January 30, 1975, Owens assigned a Coffey County oil and gas lease that had not been specifically enumerated in the first instrument to J.R. Burris (P). Burris's (P) personal check of the records and his abstract of title did not reveal the prior assignment. The district court found the recording of the first assignment to be insufficient notice to a subsequent innocent purchaser of a lease not specifically enumerated therein. The court of appeals reversed, and this appeal followed.

ISSUE: Does the recording of an instrument that uses a "Mother Hubbard" clause to describe the property conveyed constitute constructive notice to a subsequent purchaser?

HOLDING AND DECISION: (Prager, J.) No. The purpose of statutes authorizing the recording of conveyances is to provide notice to subsequent purchasers of instruments affecting specific tracts of land. Thus, the land conveyed must be described with sufficient specificity, either in the instrument itself or by specific reference to other recorded conveyances. Instruments containing a "Mother Hubbard" clause, while valid as between parties, thereto, are not sufficient description of the land conveyed to be effective against subsequent purchasers and mortgagees, unless they have actual knowledge of the transfer. Here, the conveying instrument used a "Mother Hubbard" clause to describe the oil and gas lease in question. This was an insufficient description; further, Burris (P) had no actual knowledge of the transfer. Reversed.

▶ **ANALYSIS**

Generally, the description in a recorded instrument must be sufficient to point out the property to one examining the record. If the property cannot be located and identified, as would be the case, for example, where the description is no more than "all other lands owned by the vendor in this state," then the sale is void as to third persons who deal upon the faith of the public records.

Quicknotes

ABSTRACT OF TITLE A summary of the history of title to a certain parcel of real property, including and transfers of, or liens against, such property.

CONVEYANCE The transfer of property, or title to property, from one party to another party.

RECORD AN INSTRUMENT The recording of a document in the public record.

Orr v. Byers

Lienholder (P) v. Subsequent purchaser (D)

Cal. Ct. App., 244 Cal. Rptr. 13 (1988).

NATURE OF CASE: Appeal of denial of declaration of rights and duties of the parties.

FACT SUMMARY: Because Orr (P) had misspelled Elliott's (D) name when recording a judgment against him, when Elliott (D) sold property that was subject to the judgment, the title search did not reveal the cloud on title.

🏛 RULE OF LAW
A misspelled name does not give constructive notice to title searchers under the doctrine of *idem sonans*.

FACTS: Orr (P) obtained a judgment for more than $50,000 against Elliott (D). Orr's (P) attorney recorded the judgment in Orange County, California, but misspelled Elliott's (D) name as "Elliot" and "Eliot." Elliott (D) then sold property to Byers (D) that should have been subject to Orr's (P) lien. However, the title search failed to disclose the judgment because of the misspelling of Elliott's name. Orr (P) filed suit against Byers (D), Elliott (D), and the bank (D) which conducted the search, seeking a declaration of the rights and duties of the parties (and, in essence, judicial foreclosure of his judgment lien). He claimed that the name was constructive notice of alternate spellings and hence the search should have included alternate spellings, based on the doctrine of *idem sonans* (identity is presumed from the similarity of sounds). The trial court ruled against Orr (P), who appealed and was granted review.

ISSUE: Does the doctrine of *idem sonans* give constructive notice to title searchers where a judgment has been recorded under a misspelled, yet similar sounding, name?

HOLDING AND DECISION: (Sonenshine, J.) No. The rule of *idem sonans* does not give constructive notice to title searchers and good faith purchasers. The *idem sonans* doctrine allows for the identity of a person to be presumed where there is an inaccurately spelled name, but the misspelling would be pronounced similarly. The rule will not be applied where the burden to track down alternate spellings is unreasonable. It is unjustifiable to insist that Byers (D), the good faith purchaser, and the bank (D) which conducted the title search comb the judgment records for other spellings of the name. The burden is better placed on the party recording the judgment to take steps to ensure the name is spelled correctly. Affirmed.

▶ ANALYSIS

The court was unpersuaded by the arguments put forth in *Green v. Myers*, 72 S.W. 128 (1903), which applied the rule of *idem sonans* to judgment records. The California court rejected the reasoning in *Green* because its effect was, essentially, to dispense with the formalities of record notice. While it was suggested that computer technology would reduce the burden of extensive title searches of multiple spellings, it was concluded that title searches should not require purchasers to hire highly trained specialists with expensive equipment to make certain that the seller of real property did not make a mistake when he recorded his deed. The decision is also in conflict with 4 American Law of Property, § 17.18 (1952), which states that similarly pronounced names beginning with the same letter give constructive notice to title searchers.

Quicknotes

ABSTRACT OF JUDGMENT Summary of the history of an action.

CONSTRUCTIVE NOTICE Knowledge of a fact that is imputed to an individual who was under a duty to inquire and who could have learned of the fact through the exercise of reasonable prudence.

GOOD FAITH PURCHASER FOR VALUE A party who purchases property in good faith and for valuable consideration without notice of a defect in title.

IDEM SONANS The doctrine that a name stated in a legal document need not be its exact spelling if the name as pronounced sounds sufficiently identical to the name in the document.

JUDGMENT LIEN Lien filed by a judgment creditor against the property of a judgment debtor pursuant to a judgment rendered in a civil case.

Messersmith v. Smith

Prior grantee (P) v. Subsequent purchaser (D)

N.D. Sup. Ct., 60 N.W.2d 276 (1953).

NATURE OF CASE: Action to quiet title.

FACT SUMMARY: In a race-notice recording statute jurisdiction, subsequent bona fide purchasers failed to record their deeds properly before a prior purchaser properly recorded.

🏛 RULE OF LAW
An unacknowledged deed does not qualify for recordation and therefore the recording does not give constructive notice to subsequent purchasers.

FACTS: Caroline Messersmith and her nephew, Frederick Messersmith (P), each owned an undivided one-half interest in land. On April 23, 1951, Smith (D) negotiated an oil and gas lease with Caroline Messersmith which was recorded on May 14, 1951. On May 7, 1951, Caroline Messersmith executed a mineral deed to the land, which was recorded on May 26, 1951. On its face, the deed indicated that it had been acknowledged, but Caroline Messersmith had not, in fact, acknowledged it. On May 7, 1946, Caroline Messersmith delivered a quit-claim deed to Frederick Messersmith (P) for the land, and the deed was recorded on July 9, 1951. On May 9, 1951, Smith (D) executed the mineral deed he had received from Caroline Messersmith to Seale, which was recorded on May 26, 1951. Seale asserted this deed which Smith (D) got from Caroline Messersmith and which was recorded on May 26, 1951, as cutting off Frederick Messersmith's (P) prior deed which was not recorded until July 9, 1951. The jurisdiction had a race-notice recording statute.

ISSUE: Does a deed that is unacknowledged, though recorded, impart constructive notice to the world so as to prevent a subsequent purchaser from being a bona fide purchaser without notice?

HOLDING AND DECISION: (Morris, C.J.) No. The recording of an instrument affecting title that does not meet the statutory requirements of the recording laws affords no constructive notice. The deed from Caroline to Smith (D) contained a certificate of acknowledgment on its face, but that is not conclusive as to its actual acknowledgment. Here, the grantor, Caroline, did not appear before an officer to acknowledge the execution of the instrument. Caroline did not acknowledge the deed to Smith (D) and, therefore, the deed was not properly recorded by Smith (D), and Seale (D) could not be a subsequent purchaser in good faith. Seale (D) must rely wholly upon his position as an innocent purchaser in compliance with the recording statutes. Therefore, Frederick Messersmith's (P) title was

not cut off by the conveyance to Smith (D) and Seale. Reversed. Rehearing denied.

▶ ANALYSIS

An unacknowledged deed does not give constructive notice because it does not qualify for recordation. Therefore, Smith's (D) deed and Seale's deed were not properly recorded. They did not prevail over Messersmith (P) because the jurisdiction had a race-notice statute, which means that the first to record a deed without actual or constructive notice of a prior deed will prevail.

■━■

Quicknotes

BONA FIDE PURCHASER A party who purchases property in good faith and for valuable consideration without notice of a defect in title.

CONSTRUCTIVE NOTICE Knowledge of a fact that is imputed to an individual who was under a duty to inquire and whom could have learned of the fact through the exercise of reasonable prudence.

RACE-NOTICE RECORDING STATUTE Statute determining priority of interests in real property whereby a person who records first has a preference over others receiving an interest in the property from the same source only if the party received no notice of the prior unrecorded conveyance.

■━■

Board of Education of Minneapolis v. Hughes

Subsequent purchaser (P) v. Prior grantee (D)

Minn. Sup. Ct., 136 N.W. 1095 (1912).

NATURE OF CASE: Action to determine adverse claims to certain real property.

FACT SUMMARY: Hughes (D) and Duryea & Wilson purchased the same lot from Hoerger. Hughes's (D) deed did not contain his name. He inserted it later. Duryea & Wilson sold to Board of Education of Minneapolis (P). Hughes's (D) deed was recorded before Duryea & Wilson's, but Board of Education of Minneapolis's (P) was recorded before either Hughes's (D) or Duryea & Wilson's.

> ## ⬛ RULE OF LAW
> The recording of a deed from a grantee in an unrecorded deed to a third person is not notice of the prior unrecorded deed to a subsequent purchaser.

FACTS: On May 17, 1906, Hoerger executed and delivered a deed to convey certain land to Hughes (D). Hughes's (D) name was not inserted as grantee. He filled it in shortly before recording the deed on December 16, 1910. On April 27, 1909, Duryea & Wilson were delivered a deed by Hoerger for the same lot. This deed was recorded on December 21, 1910. On November 19, 1909, Duryea & Wilson delivered a deed to the Board of Education of Minneapolis (P) for the lot. This deed was recorded on January 27, 1910.

ISSUE: Where a grantor has made a prior deed which has not been recorded, does the recording of a deed from the grantee to a third person constitute notice of the unrecorded deed to a subsequent purchaser?

HOLDING AND DECISION: (Bunn, J.) No. There are two questions which must be decided here. The first is whether Hughes's (D) deed became operative, since his name was not inserted. A deed that does not name a grantee is inoperative as a conveyance until the grantee's name is legally inserted. Such a deed becomes operative without a new execution or acknowledgment if the grantee, with express or implied authority from the grantor, inserts his name in the blank space for the grantee. The authority may be parole and implied from the circumstances. In this case Hughes's (D) had such authority, in the absence of evidence showing the lack of it. Hence, Hughes's (D) deed became operative when he inserted his name. The second question to be decided is whether Hughes (D) is a subsequent purchaser whose deed was duly recorded. Hughes's (D) conveyance dates from the time he filled in the blank space, which was after the deed from Hoerger to Duryea & Wilson. Hence, Hughes (D) was a subsequent purchaser. Record of a deed from a prior grantee is not notice to a subsequent purchaser of a prior unrecorded conveyance by the grantor to the prior grantee. In this case the recording of Duryea's deed to Board of Education (P) did not act as notice to Hughes (D). It was necessary that the deed to Board of Education (P) be recorded before the deed to Hughes (D); it was also necessary that the deed to Duryea & Wilson be recorded first. Order reversed and new trial granted.

▶ ANALYSIS

As between the parties, at least, a blank paper signed, sealed, and delivered and which is subsequently filled in without authority from the grantor will not pass title to any property. However, although blank when signed and sealed, if the deed is written with the grantor's authority and so delivered, it will be operative as a deed.

Quicknotes

CONVEYANCE The transfer of property, or title to property, from one party to another party.

ESTOPPEL An equitable doctrine precluding a party from asserting a right to the detriment of another whom justifiably relied on the conduct.

IMPLIED AUTHORITY Inferred power granted to an agent to act on behalf of the principal in order to effectuate the principal's objective.

NULLITY An act having no legal effect.

RECORDATION The recording of a document in the public record.

Guillette v. Daly Dry Wall, Inc.

Subdivision neighbors (P) v. Subsequent purchaser of unrestricted lot (D)

Mass. Sup. Jud. Ct., 325 N.E.2d 572 (1975).

NATURE OF CASE: Appeal from injunction in suit to enforce restrictive covenants.

FACT SUMMARY: Daly Dry Wall (Daly) (D), a grantee who took without knowledge of restrictions binding neighboring lots that had been deeded by a common grantor, proceeded to ignore the restrictions.

🏛 RULE OF LAW
A grantee is bound by restrictions in deeds to its neighbors from a common grantor, even if it takes without actual notice and his deed does not mention them, if the grantor has placed in writing the same restrictions on his remaining land.

FACTS: In 1967 and 1968, Guillette (P), the Walcotts (P), and the Paraskivas (P) bought individual lots in the same subdivision. Each of these three deeds either set out restrictions maintaining the subdivision as a residential area for single family dwellings, or incorporated such restrictions by reference. Additionally, the Guillette (P) deed provided that the lots retained by the seller were similarly restricted. Daly (D) purchased a lot in 1972 and the deed contained no restrictions; though the deed referred to the same recorded plan, this plan was also silent as to restrictions. After Daly (D) learned of the restrictions, it obtained a building permit for 36 apartment type units. Guillette (P) and the others sought to enjoin the construction. Daly (D) appealed the injunction and the case was transferred to this court.

ISSUE: Is a grantee bound by restrictions contained in deeds to its neighbors from a common grantor, even though he has no actual notice and his deed is silent as to restrictions, if the grantor has, in writing, placed the same restrictions on his remaining land?

HOLDING AND DECISION: (Braucher, J.) Yes. Although the Statute of Frauds prevents enforcement of restrictions against the grantor or subsequent purchasers of a lot not expressly restricted, where the common grantor has not bound his remaining land in writing, reciprocity of restriction between the grantor and grantee can be enforced. Therefore, if a grantor similarly restricts his remaining land by writing, a subsequent purchaser from the common grantor acquires title subject to the restrictions in the deed to the earlier purchaser. Further, each grantee within the scope of the common scheme may enforce the restrictions against other such grantees. Here, the Guillette (P) deed similarly restricted the grantor's remaining land. The deed was properly recorded. As a subsequent purchaser, Daly (D) took subject to these restrictions. Affirmed.

▶ ANALYSIS

Cases are equally divided between the position illustrated by *Guillette v. Daly Dry Wall* and the position that restrictions on neighboring property deeded by a common grantor are not in the subsequent purchaser's chain of title.

■≡■

Quicknotes

CHAIN OF TITLE Successive transfers of particular property.

COMMON GRANTOR Mutual conveyor of property.

RESTRICTIVE COVENANT A promise contained in a deed to limit the uses to which the property will be made.

STATUTE OF FRAUDS A statute that requires specified types of contracts to be in writing in order to be binding.

■≡■

Daniels v. Anderson

Purchase option holder (P) v. Subsequent purchaser (D) and seller (D)

Ill. Sup. Ct., 642 N.E.2d 128 (1994).

NATURE OF CASE: Appeal from judgment granting specific performance of a real estate purchase option.

FACT SUMMARY: Daniels (P) claimed that Zografos (D) could not claim bona fide purchaser status as to certain real estate because he had actual notice of Daniels's (P) interest therein prior to conveyance of title.

🏛 RULE OF LAW
One cannot claim bona fide purchaser status if he receives actual notice of an unrecorded interest in real estate prior to taking title.

FACTS: Daniels (P), besides purchasing two lots from Jacula (D), purchased a right of first refusal as to purchase of an adjacent parcel. This interest was not recorded. Jacula (D) later contracted with Zografos (D) to purchase the parcel. Daniels (P) was not notified of Zografos's (D) offer. The contract called for installment payments, with title to pass upon completion of payments. After Zografos (D) had paid several installments, but before title passed, Daniels (P) became aware of Zografos's purchase contract. He sued for specific performance of his purchase option. The trial court ordered Zografos (D) to convey the land to Daniels (P), and ordered Daniels (P) to reimburse Zografos (D) for the installments paid. The appellate court affirmed, and the Illinois Supreme Court granted review.

ISSUE: Can one claim bona fide purchaser status if he receives actual notice of an unrecorded interest in real estate prior to taking title?

HOLDING AND DECISION: (Freeman, J.) No. One cannot claim bona fide purchaser status if he receives actual notice of an unrecorded interest in real estate prior to taking title. A bona fide purchaser, by definition, is one who takes title to property without actual or constructive notice of another's rights therein. When one has not taken title, one is not a bona fide purchaser (BFP). That the putative BFP has made installment payments pursuant to a land sales contract is not sufficient to elevate him to BFP status. Here, Zografos (D) was given actual notice of Daniels's interest prior to title passing, so he was not a bona fide purchaser. His remedy was return of the monies paid, which is what the lower court ordered. Affirmed.

▌ *ANALYSIS*

Zografos (D) argued, on appeal, that he had taken equitable title to the property upon payment of the first installment, so he actually did fit the definition of a BFP. The court refused to consider the argument because it had not been raised at trial. It is quite clear from the tone of the court's opinion that, even if it had considered the defense, it would have rejected it.

■══■

Quicknotes

ACTUAL NOTICE Direct communication of information that would cause an ordinary person of average prudence to inquire as to its truth.

BONA FIDE PURCHASER A party who purchases property in good faith and for valuable consideration without notice of a defect in title.

EQUITABLE TITLE Interest in property that is not recognized in a court of law but that is protected in equity.

SPECIFIC PERFORMANCE An equitable remedy whereby the court requires the parties to perform their obligations pursuant to a contract.

■══■

Lewis v. Superior Court

Purchasers (P) v. *Lis pendens* recorder (D)

Cal. Ct. App, 37 Cal. Rptr. 2d 63 (1994).

NATURE OF CASE: Petition for writ of mandate following denial of motion for summary judgment in action seeking to quiet title.

FACT SUMMARY: Fontana Films (D) recorded a *lis pendens* on property before the Lewises (P), purchasers of real estate, took title thereto, but the *lis pendens* was not indexed until after the Lewises (P) acquired title.

🏛 RULE OF LAW
A person who records an interest in real estate after a bona fide purchaser (BFP) takes title thereto is inferior to the BFP, even if that BFP has not paid for the property.

FACTS: Fontana Films (D) sought to record a *lis pendens* (notice of lawsuit affecting title) on certain property. However, the Lewises (P) purchased the property, and took title thereto, the day before the *lis pendens* was indexed. At the time they took title, the Lewises (P) had not paid for the property, as they were obligated under the land sale contract to make installments. The Lewises (P) filed an action to quiet title. They moved for summary judgment. The trial court denied the motion. The Lewises (P) petitioned for a writ seeking reversal of the denial.

ISSUE: Is a person who records an interest in real estate after a BFP takes title thereto inferior to the BFP, even if that BFP has not paid for the property?

HOLDING AND DECISION: (Woods, J.) Yes. A person who records an interest in real estate after a BFP takes title thereto is inferior to the BFP, even if that BFP has not paid for the property. Fontana Films (D) argues that a BFP who has not yet paid for property is not actually injured if he has not made a payment for property prior to recordation of an interest, and therefore the mere fact that title has passed should not make one in the Lewises' (P) position superior to the *lis pendens* recorder. While some old authority arguably supports this position, it is totally contrary to current practice in the real estate market. One who engages a title search, pays a down payment, and receives title to property has every right to expect that his right to the property is secure. The logical conclusion of Fontana's (D) position is that a person buying real estate under a typical 30-year mortgage would have to do a title search prior to each payment, a total of 360 searches over the life of the note. This is a ludicrous result that cannot be supported in any realistic view of real estate law. Therefore, the rule must be that, to defeat a claim of BFP status, the party challenging the BFP's status must have recorded his interest before the BFP took legal title, irrespective of when payments are made. Here, the *lis pendens* was not properly recorded until it was indexed, the day after title passed to the Lewises (P). Since the Lewises (P) took legal title before Fontana Films (D) recorded its interest, the Lewises (P) had superior title and entitled to summary judgment on this issue. Petition granted.

▶ *ANALYSIS*

The generally accepted definition of a BFP is a person who takes title for value without actual or constructive notice of another's claim thereto. In this instance, the Lewises (P) had made a down payment. It is possible that if title were to pass without payment, BFP status could be defeated. (It is also unusual that this would happen in a normal real estate transaction.)

■━■

Quicknotes

BONA FIDE PURCHASER A party who purchases property in good faith and for valuable consideration without notice of a defect in title.

LEGAL TITLE Title such that is recognized by a court of law.

LIS PENDENS A pending action.

QUIET TITLE Equitable action to resolve conflicting claims to an interest in real property.

RECORDATION The recording of a document in the public record.

SUMMARY JUDGMENT Judgment rendered by a court in response to a motion by one of the parties, claiming that the lack of a question of material fact in respect to an issue warrants disposition of the issue without consideration by the jury.

WRIT OF MANDAMUS A court order issued commanding a public or private entity, or an official thereof, to perform a duty required by law.

■━■

Harper v. Paradise

Remaindermen (P) v. Subsequent grantees (D)

Ga. Sup. Ct., 210 S.E.2d 710 (1974).

NATURE OF CASE: Appeal from directed verdict in title dispute.

FACT SUMMARY: After Maude Harper's death, her children (P) claimed some land under a deed that had named Maude as life tenant and her children (P) as remaindermen, and the Paradises (D) claimed title to the same land, through a security deed executed by Maude to secure a loan which became in default.

🏛 RULE OF LAW
A deed that specifically refers to an earlier unrecorded deed puts a subsequent purchaser on notice of the existence of the earlier deed; thus, the purchaser claiming under the later deed is not entitled to priority, though the later deed was recorded first.

FACTS: Susan Harper conveyed a farm in 1922 to Maude Harper, her daughter-in-law, for life with remainder in fee to Maude's children (P). The deed was misplaced and so not recorded until 1957. While the deed was presumed lost, Susan Harper died, and her heirs gave Maude a quitclaim deed in 1928 "to take the place of the deed made . . . by Mrs. Susan Harper . . . ." On February 27, 1933, Maude executed a security deed, recorded the same day, which purported to convey the entire fee to Ella Thornton to secure a loan. When the loan became in default, Thornton foreclosed. Lincoln and William Paradise (D) were grantees in an unbroken chain of record title tracing back to Thornton. They also claim as adverse possessors. When Maude died in 1972, her children (P) brought an action to recover the land. They appealed from the trial court's finding that the Paradises (D) had superior title.

ISSUE: Does a deed that refers to an earlier unrecorded deed put a subsequent purchaser on inquiry notice regarding the existence of the earlier deed?

HOLDING AND DECISION: (Ingram, J.) Yes. If the Paradises (D) relied on the 1922 deed, they could have no interest except in the life estate, for a life tenant cannot sell anything more. As for the 1928 deed, heirs might join in a deed to an innocent person acting without notice of an earlier deed, and thereby convey a fee simple. But here the grantee of the quitclaim was Maude Harper, who surely had notice of the earlier deed. Furthermore, the 1928 deed stated it was intended to replace the earlier, missing deed. A deed that specifically refers to an earlier unrecorded deed puts a subsequent purchaser on notice of the existence of the earlier deed; thus, the purchaser claiming under the later deed is not entitled to priority, though the later deed was recorded first. Here, the recital in the 1928 deed put the Paradises (D) on inquiry notice, so they are not entitled to priority. Finally, the Paradises (D) have not gained title by adverse possession, as prescription did not start to run until the life estate ended in 1972. Reversed with direction.

▶ ANALYSIS

The majority rule is that the record affords notice not only of those facts recited therein, but also material matters suggested thereby, which might be disclosed by reasonable inquiry. Compare this to the uniform simplification of Land Transfers Act, which states that, unless a document refers to another document by its record location, a grantee is not charged with knowledge of the document or an adverse claim founded upon it.

Quicknotes

ADVERSE POSSESSION A means of acquiring title to real property by remaining in actual, open, continuous, exclusive possession of property for the statutory period.

DIRECTED VERDICT A verdict ordered by the court in a jury trial.

INQUIRY NOTICE The communication of information that would cause an ordinary person of average prudence to inquire as to its truth.

PRIORITY The relative preference of different claims to specific property.

QUITCLAIM A deed whereby the grantor conveys whatever interest he or she may have in the property without any warranties or covenants as to title.

REMAINDERMAN A person who has an interest in property to commence upon the termination of a present possessory interest.

Waldorff Insurance and Bonding, Inc. v. Eglin National Bank

Condo owner (P) v. Foreclosing-manager (D)

Fla. Dist. Ct. App., 453 So. 2d 1383 (1984).

NATURE OF CASE: Appeal from foreclosure judgment.

FACT SUMMARY: Eglin National Bank (Eglin) (D) contended it had no notice of Waldorff Insurance and Bonding, Inc.'s (Waldorff's) (P) ownership of the condominium unit, and thus it obtained good title upon foreclosure.

🏛 RULE OF LAW
Subsequent successors to legal title, after a contract to convey title has been executed, take title subject to all equitable interests of which they have notice.

FACTS: Choctaw Partnership (Chocktaw) mortgaged a condominium project to Eglin (D). It sold a single unit to Waldorff (P), which occupied the unit and paid all expenses and rent. Choctaw executed a second mortgage in favor of Eglin (D) on which it defaulted. Eglin (D) foreclosed on the project, including the unit occupied by Waldorff (P). Waldorff (P) sued, contending it had better title. The trial court held Eglin (D) had no notice of Waldorff's (P) ownership merely because of possession. Waldorff (P) appealed.

ISSUE: Do subsequent successors to legal title take subject to all equitable interests, of which they have notice?

HOLDING AND DECISION: (Shivers, J.) Yes. Subsequent successors to legal title take subject to all equitable interests of which they have notice. A contract to convey legal title on payment of the purchase price creates an equitable interest in the purchaser. Beneficial ownership passes to the purchaser while the seller retains mere naked title. The occupancy of the unit placed Eglin (D) on notice of Waldorff's (P) interest. Thus Waldorff (P) retained greater title. Reversed and remanded.

▶ ANALYSIS

Choctaw owed Waldorff (P) $35,000 in insurance premiums on the project. The parties agreed that Waldorff (P) would receive full title to the unit in return for a cancellation of the debt. The court rejected Eglin's (D) argument that because Waldorff (P) wrote the Choctaw debt off for tax purposes, no consideration supported the purchase. Choctaw's receipt of cancellation of a debt constituted sufficient consideration.

Quicknotes

BENEFICIAL OWNERSHIP A party holding equitable but not legal title to property that is held by a third party for his benefit.

CONSIDERATION Value given by one party in exchange for performance, or a promise to perform, by another party.

EQUITABLE INTEREST A beneficiary's interest in a trust.

Walker Rogge, Inc. v. Chelsea Title & Guaranty Co.

Tract purchaser (P) v. Title-company (D)

N.J. Sup. Ct., 562 A.2d 208 (1989).

NATURE OF CASE: Appeal from award of damages for negligence.

FACT SUMMARY: When Walker Rogge, Inc. (Rogge) (P) discovered by survey that its property contained 5.5 less acres than the seller had represented, it sued Chelsea Title & Guaranty Co. (Chelsea Title) (D) for failing to discover and disclose the correct acreage contained in Chelsea Title's (D) files.

🏛 RULE OF LAW
A title company's liability is limited to the policy, and the company is not liable in tort for negligence for searching records if it has not expressly contracted or implicitly agreed to do so.

FACTS: While negotiating to sell a tract of land, Kosa, the seller, showed Rogge (P), the prospective buyer, a Price Walker survey indicating that the tract was 18.33 acres. Rogge (P) ordered a title policy, but not a title search, from Chelsea Title (D). Chelsea Title (D) had issued two prior title policies on the same property and had a deed in its files that showed that the tract actually consisted of only 12.48 acres. Neither the Kosa-to-Rogge (P) deed nor the title policy issued by Chelsea Title (D) included an acreage count, but both referenced the Price Walker survey. The title policy stated that Chelsea Title (D) insured against loss or damage from defects in title or unmarketability of title. It also stated that Chelsea Title (D) did not insure against any matters that could be disclosed by an accurate survey and inspection of the property. Six years after closing, in preparation for subdividing the land, Rogge (P) hired a new surveyor, who concluded that the actual quantity of acreage in the property was 12.43 acres. Rogge (P) filed suit against Chelsea Title (D), alleging that the 5.5-acre shortage was an insurable loss under the policy, and that Chelsea Title (D) was liable in negligence for failing to disclose documents in its files revealing that the property contained fewer than 18 acres. The trial court concluded that the shortage constituted a defect in title, rendering it unmarketable, and assessed damages at $88,000. Finding that Rogge (P) did not contract for a title search, however, the court dismissed the negligence charge against Chelsea Title (D). The appeals court affirmed, and Chelsea Title (D) appealed.

ISSUE: Is a title company liable in tort for negligence for searching records if it has not expressly contracted or implicitly agreed to do so?

HOLDING AND DECISION: (Pollock, J.) No. A title company is not liable in tort for negligence for searching records if it has not expressly contracted or implicitly

agreed to do so. A title company's liability is limited to the policy, and a company is not liable in contract for an acreage shortage, if no acreage is stated in a deed, or in tort for failure to search records, if it has not agreed to do so. A title insurance policy is a contract of indemnity under which the insurer agrees to indemnify the insured against loss through defects of title to or liens or encumbrances upon realty owned by the insured. However, title insurance is no substitute for a survey. If no acreage is stated on a deed, a title company does not insure the quantity of land. In this case, Chelsea Title's (D) insurance policy contained an enforceable survey exception that placed the risk of paying for nonexistent acres on Rogge (P). Had Rogge (P) obtained the survey prior to closing, rather than six years later, he could have eliminated the survey exception from the policy, and transferred the risk of an acreage shortage to Chelsea Title (D). Since he did not, Chelsea Title (D) is not liable in contract. It may, however, be subject to a negligence action if the failure to assure the quantity of acreage was the direct result of duties voluntarily assumed by it in addition to the mere contract to insure title. A title company is not liable in tort for negligence in searching records unless it agreed to conduct a search and to provide the insured with an abstract of title in addition to the title policy. Although Rogge (P) did not order a separate abstract of title, Chelsea Title (D) had insured the property before and had the correct amount of acreage in its files. On remand, the trial court must determine whether, under the circumstances, Chelsea Title (D) assumed an independent duty to assure the quantity of acreage, whether it breached that duty, or whether the breach caused any damage to Rogge (P). Affirmed in part; reversed in part; and remanded.

▶ ANALYSIS

In some jurisdictions, statutes require a title search to be performed prior to the issuance of any policies regardless of whether the insurance company has contracted to conduct such a search. In the absence of a statute, the majority rule holds that the title insurance company owes a duty to its insured to search the records. This rule assumes that the issuance of a policy is predicated upon a careful examination of the title and an exhaustive study of the applicable law. It also assumes that a person seeking title insurance expects to obtain a professional title search as well as an opinion as the condition of that title. *Rogge*, on the other hand, represents the minority rule that any duty on the part of the insurance company to search

Continued on next page.

the records must be expressed in or implied from the policy.

■══■

Quicknotes

DEFEAT IN TITLE Termination or annulment of a title.

INDEMNIFY Securing against potential injury; compensation for injury suffered.

TITLE POLICY A policy insuring against loss incurred as the result of a defective title.

TITLE SEARCH An examination of records of title documents in order to ascertain whether title to a particular property is defective.

■══■

Lick Mill Creek Apartments v. Chicago Title Insurance Co.

Developer (P) v. Title insurance company (D)

Cal. Ct. App., 283 Cal. Rptr. 231 (1991).

NATURE OF CASE: Appeal from dismissal of action for indemnification for hazardous waste cleanup costs.

FACT SUMMARY: After paying for removal and cleanup of hazardous substances existing but unknown at the time a title insurance policy was issued on its property, Lick Mill Creek Apartments (Lick Mill) (P) sued Chicago Title Insurance Co. (Chicago Title) (D) for reimbursement, contending that the presence of hazardous waste rendered the title unmarketable and constituted an encumbrance on title.

> ## 🏛 RULE OF LAW
> A title insurance company is obligated to protect the insured against defects in title but not against loss arising from physical damage to property.

FACTS: While acquiring lots for development, Lick Mill (P) purchased title insurance from Chicago Title (D). Before issuing the policy, Chicago Title (D) commissioned a survey and inspection of the entire site. Unbeknownst to Chicago Title (D) or Lick Mill (P), the government had been keeping records documenting the presence of hazardous substances in the soil, subsoil, and groundwater of the property. After Lick Mill (P) purchased the property, it incurred costs for removal and cleanup of the hazardous materials. It then sought indemnity from Chicago Title (D) for the cost of the cleanup, arguing that the presence of hazardous substances rendered the title defective or unmarketable within the terms of the title insurance policy. Lick Mill (P) also contended that liability for the costs of the cleanup constituted an encumbrance on title. The trial court concluded that Chicago Title's (D) insurance policy did not cover the costs of removing hazardous substances. Lick Mill (P) appealed.

ISSUE: Is a title insurance company obligated to protect the insured against defects in title but not against loss arising from physical damage to property?

HOLDING AND DECISION: (Agliano, J.) Yes. A title insurance company is obligated to protect the insured against defects in title but not against loss arising from physical damage to property. Title insurance covers title marketability, which relates to defects affecting legally recognized rights and incidents of ownership. Title insurance does not cover market value. It is possible to hold perfectly marketable title to valueless, unmarketable land. Here, the presence of hazardous material may affect the market value of Lick Mill's (P) land, but it does not affect the title to the land. Chicago Title (D) was obligated, under its policy, to insure Lick Mill (P) against unmarketability of title. But since marketability of title and the market value of the land itself are separate and distinct, Lick Mill (P) could not claim coverage, under the policy, for the property's physical condition. Furthermore, it could not claim coverage for an encumbrance where no lien has been filed against the property. "Encumbrances" include only liens, easements, restrictive covenants, and other such interests in or rights to the land that are held by third persons. The mere possibility that the state may attach a lien in the future to secure payment of cleanup costs is not sufficient to create an encumbrance on title. Affirmed.

▌ANALYSIS

Title insurance reflects the faith of the insurer in the validity of title, not the physical condition of the property. Title insurance policies are contractual devices. Most courts will construe policies to insure only what they say they insure. This will be true even if the court subscribes to the presumption that policies are to be strictly construed in favor of the insured and against the title insurance company.

▬▬■

Quicknotes

ENCUMBRANCE An interest in property that operates as a claim or lien against its title making it potentially unmarketable.

INDEMNITY The duty of a party to compensate another for damages sustained.

LIEN A claim against the property of another in order to secure the payment of a debt.

TITLE INSURANCE A policy insuring against loss incurred as the result of a defective title.

TITLE MARKETABILITY Title that, although not perfect, would be acceptable to a reasonably well-informed buyer exercising ordinary business prudence.

▬▬■

Judicial Land Use Controls: The Law of Nuisance

Quick Reference Rules of Law

PAGE

1. *Morgan v. High Penn Oil Co.* Lawful conduct that is non-negligent may constitute a nuisance if it is intentional and unreasonable under the circumstances.   *116*

2. *Estancias Dallas Corp. v. Schultz.* Even though a jury finds facts constituting a nuisance, equities must be balanced in order to determine if an injunction should be granted.   *117*

3. *Boomer v. Atlantic Cement Co.* Although the rule in New York is that a nuisance will be enjoined even when there is a marked disparity shown in economic consequence between the effect of the injunction and the effect of the nuisance, an injunction should not be applied if the result is to close down a plant. Permanent damages may be awarded as an alternative.   *118*

4. *Spur Industries, Inc. v. Del E. Webb Development Co.* The doctrine of coming to the nuisance does not prohibit granting injunctive relief against the nuisance.   *119*

Morgan v. High Penn Oil Co.

Homeowners (P) v. Polluting-refinery (D)

N.C. Sup. Ct., 77 S.E.2d 682 (1953).

NATURE OF CASE: Appeal from award of damages and injunction in nuisance suit.

FACT SUMMARY: The Morgans (P) sought to enjoin High Penn Oil Co. (High Penn) (D) from emitting gas and odors from its refinery, and to recover damages for past impairment of the use and enjoyment of their property due to refinery emissions.

> ## 🏛 RULE OF LAW
> Lawful conduct that is non-negligent may constitute a nuisance if it is intentional and unreasonable under the circumstances.

FACTS: The Morgans (P) had resided on their property since August 1945 and had since established a trailer park and restaurant thereon, which supplemented their income. High Penn (D) had operated its oil refinery, located approximately 1,000 feet from the Morgans' (P) dwelling, since October 1950. The Morgans (P) offered evidence to show that the refinery regularly emitted nauseating gases and odors in large quantities, which invaded neighboring property and made people sick. Further, High Penn (D) disregarded the Morgans' (P) demand to abate the nuisance. The trial court awarded damages and an injunction, and High Penn (D) appealed.

ISSUE: If one conducts a lawful enterprise on one's own property may that enterprise only constitute a nuisance if it is operated or constructed negligently?

HOLDING AND DECISION: (Ervin, J.) No. Private nuisances may be nuisances per se, that is, at all times and under any circumstances, or they may be nuisances per accidens, that is, nuisances by reason of their location or manner of construction or operation. A lawful enterprise cannot be a nuisance per se, but may be one per accidens, and this is so even if it is constructed and operated non-negligently. A private nuisance exists whenever one uses one's own property in a way that substantially interferes with another's interest in the private use and enjoyment of that other's land. Liability arises, if the conduct was unintentional, when the actions are negligent, reckless, or ultrahazardous. But if the conduct was intentional, a person is liable if his actions were unreasonable under the circumstances. This is the case where the person acts for the purpose of causing the nuisance, or where he knows it is resulting or substantially certain to result from his conduct. In this case, the evidence supports a finding that High Penn (D) intentionally and unreasonably caused noxious gas and odors to escape the refinery, and that an injunction

was required to avoid irreparable injury to the Morgans (P). Affirmed.

▶ ANALYSIS

Great confusion exists regarding the legal basis of liability in the law of nuisance. *Morgan v. High Penn Oil Co.* states the Restatement rule: An interference with the use and enjoyment of another's land gives rise to liability if it is substantial and either intentional and unreasonable, or the unintentional result of negligence, recklessness or abnormally dangerous activity. But the application of this rule is difficult because, as Professor Prosser notes, the courts work in an ad hoc fashion to resolve land-use conflicts in a way that makes compatible dissimilar needs and desires. 10 Prosser, *The Law of Torts 571* (4th ed. 1971).

Quicknotes

INJUNCTION A remedy imposed by the court ordering a party to cease the conduct of a specific activity.

NUISANCE PER ACCIDENS An action, occupation or building that becomes a nuisance due to its location or method of operation.

NUISANCE PER SE An action, occupation or building that is a nuisance at any time and under any condition.

PRIVATE NUISANCE An unlawful use of property interfering with the enjoyment of the private rights of an individual or a small number of persons.

Estancias Dallas Corp. v. Schultz

Apartment complex (D) v. Homeowners (P)

Tex. Civ. App., 500 S.W.2d 217 (1973).

NATURE OF CASE: Appeal from grant injunction in nuisance suit.

FACT SUMMARY: The Schultzes (P) sought to enjoin Estancias Dallas Corp. (D) from operating air conditioning equipment on the property adjoining the Schultzes' (P) residence.

🏛 RULE OF LAW
Even though a jury finds facts constituting a nuisance, equities must be balanced in order to determine if an injunction should be granted.

FACTS: Estancias Dallas Corp. (D) completed construction of an apartment complex in 1969. An air conditioning unit, which serviced the entire complex, was located about five feet from the Schultzes' (P) property line. The Schultzes (P) testified that the neighborhood was a quiet one prior to the construction of these apartments, that they could not converse or sleep due to the tremendous noise of the unit, and that it had decreased the value of their property from $25,000 to about $10,000. The jury found that a continuous and permanent nuisance existed, although it failed to find that the nuisance proximately caused material personal discomfort, inconvenience, annoyance, and impairment of health to the Schultzes (P). When the trial court granted a permanent injunction, Estancias Dallas Corp. (D) appealed.

ISSUE: Do nuisance cases require a balancing of equities by the court, even though a jury finds facts constituting a nuisance?

HOLDING AND DECISION: (Stephenson, J.) Yes. Texas law requires a balancing of equities in nuisance cases, even if the jury has found that a nuisance exists. *Storey v. Central Hide & Rendering Co.*, 148 Tex. 509, 226 S.W.2d 615 (1950). The *Storey* court noted that if the injury to the public in enjoining the nuisance would be great, the nuisance might be permitted to exist "of necessity." Here, it is implied by the entering of the judgment granting the injunction that the court balanced the equities in favor of the Schultzes (P). Furthermore, the existence of the unit is of no public benefit, and so the enjoining of its operation would cause no public injury. Affirmed.

▶ ANALYSIS

An owner of real property is entitled to the full beneficial use of that property, provided that he does not invade the corresponding property rights of others. When determining liability for the use of one's own property, the test is one of reasonableness. It follows that an owner is liable only for injury to others resulting from his "unreasonable" use, and this must be determined as a question of fact in light of the particular circumstances of the case. Hence, balancing is required in every nuisance case.

■━■

Quicknotes

BALANCING TEST Court's balancing of an individual's constitutional rights against the state's right to protect its citizens.

INJUNCTION A court order requiring a person to do or prohibiting that person from doing a specific act.

NECESSITY A defense to liability for unlawful activity where the conduct is unavoidable and is justified by preventing the injury to life or health.

NUISANCE An unlawful use of property that interferes with the lawful use of another's property.

PROXIMATE CAUSE Something that causes a result in the natural sequence of events without which an injury would not have been sustained.

■━■

Boomer v. Atlantic Cement Company

Landowners (P) v. Cement plant (D)

N.Y. Ct. App., 257 N.E.2d 870 (1970).

NATURE OF CASE: Action to enjoin maintenance of nuisance and for damages.

FACT SUMMARY: Trial court refused to issue injunction that would close down plant, but awarded permanent damages instead.

🏛 RULE OF LAW
Although the rule in New York is that a nuisance will be enjoined even when there is a marked disparity shown in economic consequence between the effect of the injunction and the effect of the nuisance, an injunction should not be applied if the result is to close down a plant. Permanent damages may be awarded as an alternative.

FACTS: A group of landowners (P), complaining of injury to their property from dirt, smoke, and vibration emanating from a neighboring cement plant (D), brought an action to enjoin the continued operation of the plant and for damages. The trial court held that the plant constituted a nuisance, found substantial damage but, because an injunction would shut down the plant's operation, refused to issue one. Permanent damages of $185,000 were awarded the group of landowners (P) instead.

ISSUE: Where the issuance of an injunction to enjoin the maintenance of a business would shut down a business, may permanent damages be issued as an alternative?

HOLDING AND DECISION: (Bergan, J.) Yes. Damages may be awarded as an alternative to an injunction in nuisance cases. Another alternative would be to grant the injunction but postpone its effect to a specified future date to give opportunity for technical advances to permit the company (D) to eliminate the nuisance. However, there is no assurance that any significant technical improvement would occur. Moreover, the problem is universal, and can only be solved by an industry-wide effort. Permanent damages would themselves be a spur to conduct more research. Future owners of this land would not be able to recover additional damages, since the award is to the land. Reversed and remanded.

DISSENT: (Jasen, J.) The majority approach is licensing a continuing wrong. Furthermore, permanent damages alleviate the need for more research and decrease incentive.

▌ *ANALYSIS*

The reasoning advanced here has been carried one step further by other courts. In *Pennsylvania Coal Co. v. Sanderson*, 113 Pa. St. 126, 6 A. 453 (1886), a suit for damages was frowned upon by the Supreme Court which said, "To encourage the development of the great natural resources of a country, trifling inconveniences to particular persons must sometimes give way to the necessities of a great community."

Quicknotes

INJUNCTION A court order requiring a person to do or prohibiting that person from doing a specific act.

NUISANCE An unlawful use of property that interferes with the lawful use of another's property.

TEMPORARY DAMAGES Monetary compensation awarded by the court to a party for injuries sustained as the result of another party's occasional wrongful actions.

Spur Industries, Inc. v. Del E. Webb Development Co.

Developer (P) v. Feedlot operator (D)

Ariz. Sup. Ct., 494 P.2d 700 (1972).

NATURE OF CASE: Appeal from permanent injunction.

FACT SUMMARY: Del E. Webb Development Co. (Webb) (P) sought to enjoin Spur Industries, Inc. (Spur) (D) from running a cattle feedlot near its Sun City retirement community.

> ## 🏛 RULE OF LAW
> The doctrine of coming to the nuisance does not prohibit granting injunctive relief against the nuisance.

FACTS: In 1956, Spur's (D) predecessors in interest developed feedlots in an area some 15 miles west of the urban area of Phoenix, Arizona. In May 1959, Webb (P) began to plan the development of an urban retirement area to be known as Sun City, by purchasing 20,000 acres of farmland near Spur's (D) feedlots. In 1960, Spur (D) purchased the property in question and began a rebuilding and expansion program extending to the north and south of the original feedlot facilities. Homes were first offered for sale by Webb (P) in 1960, when odors from the Spur (D) feedlot were not considered to be a problem. In December 1967, Webb (P) filed suit, complaining that in excess of 1,000 lots in its development were unfit for sale because of the operation of the Spur (D) feedlot. Webb (P) alleged that the Spur (D) feeding operation was a public nuisance because of the flies and odor, which were drifting over Sun City. The trial court permanently enjoined Spur (D) from operating a cattle feedlot near Sun City, and Spur (D) appealed.

ISSUE: Does the doctrine of coming to the nuisance prohibit granting injunctive relief against the nuisance?

HOLDING AND DECISION: (Cameron, J.) No. Spur's (D) operation was an enjoinable public nuisance as far as the people in the southern portion of Webb's (P) Sun City were concerned. Spur's (D) operation, which constituted a breeding place for flies, was a public nuisance dangerous to the public health, and Webb (P), having shown a special injury in the loss of sales, has standing to bring suit to enjoin the nuisance. However, there was no indication here at the time Spur (D) and its predecessors located in Maricopa County that a new city would spring up, full-blown, alongside the feeding operation, and that the developer of that city would ask the court to order Spur (D) to move because of the new city. Spur (D) is required to move not because of any wrongdoing on the part of Spur (D), but because of a proper and legitimate regard of the courts for the rights and interests of the public. Having brought people to the nuisance to the foreseeable detriment of Spur (D), Webb (P) must indemnify Spur (D) for a reasonable amount of the cost of moving or shutting down. Affirmed in part, reversed in part, and remanded for further proceedings.

▶ ANALYSIS

The majority view is that coming to a nuisance does not completely bar a suit for damages or injunctive relief, but is a factor to be considered in adjudicating the action. The position taken by the court in this case attempts to promote both ideas of fairness to the parties, and a concern over the most efficient use of the property in question. The court's remedy, abating the nuisance accompanied by compensatory damages to Spur (D), attempts to effectuate these concerns.

■━■

Quicknotes

"COMING TO THE NUISANCE" A claim may be weakened when a plaintiff moves to the defendant's established locale.

COMPENSATORY DAMAGES Measure of damages necessary to compensate victim for actual injuries suffered.

INJUNCTION A court order requiring a person to do or prohibiting that person from doing a specific act.

NUISANCE An unlawful use of property that interferes with the lawful use of another's property.

■━■

Private Land Use Controls: The Law of Servitudes

Quick Reference Rules of Law

PAGE

1. *Willard v. First Church of Christ, Scientist.* Contrary to the ancient common-law rule, modernly, a grantor, in deeding property to one person, may effectively reserve and vest an interest in the same property in a third party. — 123

2. *Kienzle v. Myers.* An easement by estoppel arises when the owner of property has allowed another to use her land under circumstances where it was reasonably foreseeable that the user would substantially change position in the belief that the permission would not be revoked, and the user did actually change position in reasonable reliance on that belief. — 124

3. *Holbrook v. Taylor.* A right to the use of a roadway over the land of another may be established by estoppel. — 125

4. *Van Sandt v. Royster.* Whether there is an implied easement on certain property will be inferred from the intentions of the parties, and such inference will be drawn from the circumstances under which the conveyance was made. Parties to a conveyance will be assumed to know and to contemplate the continuance of reasonably necessary uses that have so altered the premises as to make them apparent upon reasonably prudent investigation. — 126

5. *Othen v. Rosier.* In order to create an easement by necessity, the necessity must have existed at the time that the estate was created. — 128

6. *Matthews v. Bay Head Improvement Association.* The public must be given access to and use of privately owned land as reasonably necessary for the enjoyment of adjacent public lands. — 129

7. *Miller v. Lutheran Conference & Camp Association.* An easement in gross may arise by prescription and is assignable if the parties to its creation so intend. — 130

8. *Brown v. Voss.* If an easement is appurtenant to a particular parcel of land, any extension thereof to other parcels is a misuse of the easement, unless the servient estate does not overburden it. — 131

9. *Preseault v. United States.* A change in use of an easement from a rail line to a recreational path constitutes a taking. — 132

10. *Tulk v. Moxhay.* Privity of estate notwithstanding, a person who acquires real property with notice of a restriction placed upon it will not be allowed, in equity, to violate its terms. — 133

11. *River Heights Associates L.P. v. Batten.* A restrictive covenant can be nullified by changed conditions only when the changes are so radical as to destroy the essential objectives and purposes of the covenant. — 134

12. *Sanborn v. McLean.* (1) If the owner of two or more lots, which are situated so as to bear a relation to each other, sells one with restrictions that are of benefit to the land retained, during the period of restraint, the owner of the lot or lots retained can do nothing forbidden to the owner of the lot sold. This is the doctrine of reciprocal negative easements. (2) A reciprocal negative easement is not personal to owners but is operatve upon use of the land by any owner having actual or constructive notice thereof. — 135

CHAPTER 10

13. *Neponsit Property Owners' Association, Inc. v. Emigrant Industrial Savings Bank.* A covenant in deed subjecting land to an annual charge for improvements to the surrounding residential tract is enforceable by the property owners' association against subsequent purchasers if: (1) grantor and grantee so intended; (2) it appears that the covenant is one touching or concerning the land; and (3) privity of estate is shown between the party claiming benefit of the covenant and the party under the burden of such covenant.   136

14. *Shelley v. Kraemer.* State court enforcement of private, discriminatory restrictive covenants constitutes state action under the Fourteenth Amendment.   138

15. *Western Land Co. v. Truskolaski.* A restrictive covenant is enforceable so long as its provisions remain of substantial value.   139

16. *Rick v. West.* Courts will not engage in a balancing of equities but will enforce restrictive covenants unless there is a substantial change of conditions in the general neighborhood.   140

17. *Nahrstedt v. Lakeside Village Condominium Association, Inc.* A recorded use restriction imposed by a common interest development in California must be enforced uniformly against all residents of the development unless the restriction is unreasonable.   141

18. *40 West 67th Street Corp. v. Pullman.* Under the business judgment rule, courts will defer to the residential cooperative's vote and findings as competent evidence that the tenant is objectionable and subject to eviction.   143

Quicknotes

IMPLIED EASEMENT An easement that is not expressly stated in a deed, but which is inferred upon conveyance, that a portion of one parcel had been used to benefit the other parcel and that upon sale the buyer of the benefited parcel could reasonably expect such benefits to continue.

QUASI-DOMINANT TENEMENT Property whose owners benefit from the use of another's property.

QUASI-SERVIENT TENEMENT Property that is burdened in some aspect for the benefit of a dominant estate.

Othen v. Rosier

Road user (P) v. Property owner (D)

Tex. Sup. Ct., 226 S.W.2d 622 (1950).

NATURE OF CASE: Appeal from judgment denying the existence of an easement by either prescription or necessity.

FACT SUMMARY: Othen (P) alleged that he had acquired an easement across the land of Rosier (D), after Rosier (D) erected a levee on the land.

🏛 RULE OF LAW
In order to create an easement by necessity, the necessity must have existed at the time that the estate was created.

FACTS: Othen (P) and Rosier (D) own tracts of land that were formerly part of one larger parcel. In order to reach any public highways, Othen (P) must cross over someone else's property. Othen (P) had used a road that ran across Rosier's (D) property, which Rosier (D) kept in repair. As a result of encroaching surface waters, Rosier (D) erected a levee on his property, which made the road so muddy that for weeks at a time it was impassable except by horseback. Othen (P) filed suit for injunctive and declaratory relief, and for damages. The trial court found that Othen (P) had acquired an easement by necessity. However, the appellate court reversed, holding that Othen (P) had acquired neither an easement by necessity nor one by prescription.

ISSUE: In order to create an easement by necessity, must the necessity have existed at the time that the estate was created?

HOLDING AND DECISION: (Brewster, J.) Yes. Before an implied easement by necessity can be held to be created, it must be shown that there was a unity of ownership of the alleged dominant and servient estates; that the roadway is a necessity and not a mere convenience; and that the necessity existed at the time of severance of the two estates. Here, there was unity of ownership of the lands now owned by Othen (P) and Rosier (D). However, no easement may be implied for the road because the original owner did not reserve such an easement when he first sold the property now owned by Rosier (D). The record does not indicate that the roadway was a necessity as of the date of the original grant deed, rather than a mere convenience. Othen (P) has additionally not acquired an easement by prescription, because his use of the road was not under claim of right. Othen's (P) use of the roadway was merely permissive and therefore constituted only a license, which could not and did not ripen into a prescriptive right. Affirmed.

▶ ANALYSIS

Several states have attempted to solve the problems posed by landlocked property through statutory provisions providing for condemnation of private ways. While the statutory provisions vary from state to state, all jurisdictions require payment to be made for the land taken by the owner of the benefited property. The degree of necessity required for condemnation also varies; some states require a showing of strict necessity; while others only require that the necessity be reasonable under all the circumstances.

■■■

Quicknotes

CLAIM OF RIGHT Person claiming a right in property is in possession and intends to claim ownership of that property without regard to the record title owner.

CONDEMNATION The taking of private property for public use so long as just compensation is paid therefor.

DOMINANT ESTATE Property whose owners benefit from the use of another's property.

EASEMENT BY NECESSITY An easement that arises by operation of law without which the owner of the benefited property is deprived of the use and enjoyment of his property.

EASEMENT BY PRESCRIPTION A manner of acquiring an easement in another's property by continuous and uninterrupted use in satisfaction of the statutory requirements of adverse possession.

LICENSE A right that is granted to a person allowing him or her to conduct an activity that without such permission he or she could not lawfully do, and which is unassignable and revocable at the will of the licensor.

PRESCRIPTIVE RIGHTS Rights to an easement in another's property acquired by continuous and uninterrupted use in satisfaction of the statutory requirements of adverse possession.

SERVIENT ESTATE Property that is burdened in some aspect for the benefit of a dominant estate.

■■■

Matthews v. Bay Head Improvement Association

Resident (P) v. Beach association (D)

N.J. Sup. Ct., 471 A.2d 355, *cert. denied*, 469 U.S. 821 (1984).

NATURE OF CASE: Appeal from judgment in favor of the defendant in a case alleging violation of public access rights to shoreline areas.

FACT SUMMARY: Matthews (P) alleged that her right to use the beach was violated when Bay Head (D) residents formed an association denying her access to land held as a public trust.

🏛 RULE OF LAW
The public must be given access to and use of privately owned land as reasonably necessary for the enjoyment of adjacent public lands.

FACTS: The Bay Head Improvement Association (BHIS) (D) was formed as a privately owned nonprofit corporation in order to own and operate bathing beaches along the ocean. Membership was generally limited to residents of Bay Head, who paid for badges to wear in order to gain access to the beach. Matthews (P), a Point Pleasant inhabitant, sued the Borough of Bay Head and BHIS (D) because they prevented her from gaining access to the Atlantic Ocean and the public beachfront in Bay Head. The Public Advocate later intervened as a plaintiff and asserted that BHIS (D) had denied the general public its right of access to public trust lands along the beaches and its right to use private property fronting on the ocean incidental to the public's right under the public trust doctrine. The trial court held that the Association (D) was not an arm of the Borough of Bay Head, that the Association (D) was not a municipal agency, and that nothing in the record justified a finding that public privileges could attach to the private properties owned or leased by the Association (D). A divided appellate division affirmed. Matthews (P) appealed.

ISSUE: Must the public be given access to and use of privately owned land as reasonably necessary for the enjoyment of adjacent public lands?

HOLDING AND DECISION: (Schreiber, J.) Yes. The public must be given access to and use of privately-owned land as reasonably necessary for the enjoyment of adjacent public lands. Where a municipal beach is dedicated to public use, the public use doctrine dictates that the beach and the ocean waters must be open to all on equal terms and without preference. Where use of dry sand is essential or reasonably necessary for enjoyment of the ocean, the public trust doctrine warrants the public's use of the upland dry sand area subject to an accommodation of the interests of the owner. The Bay Head residents (D) may not frustrate the public's right to enjoy the foreshore.

By limiting membership only to residents and foreclosing the public, the Association (D) was acting in conflict with the public good and contrary to the strong public policy in favor of encouraging and expanding public access to and use of shoreline areas. Membership in the Association (D) must be open to the public at large and fees charged must be reasonable and may not discriminate between residents and nonresidents. Reversed in part and affirmed in part.

▶ ANALYSIS

The public trust doctrine acknowledges that the ownership, domination and sovereignty over land flowed by tidal waters is vested in the State in trust for the people. In order to exercise those rights guaranteed by the public trust doctrine, the public must have access to municipally owned dry sand areas as well as the foreshore. Municipal ordinances requiring nonresidents to pay a higher fee than residents for the use of the beach have also been struck down in New Jersey.

■■■

Quicknotes

PUBLIC TRUST DOCTRINE The government holds lands that are submerged beneath the water, or that are capable of being submerged, in trust for the public's benefit.

PUBLIC USE Basis for governmental taking of property pursuant to its power of eminent domain so that property taken may be utilized for the benefit of the public at large.

SOVEREIGNTY The absolute power conferred to the state to govern and regulate all persons located and activities conducted therein.

■■■

Miller v. Lutheran Conference & Camp Association

Easement-in-gross owners (P) v. Easement assignees (D)

Pa. Sup. Ct., 200 A. 646 (1938).

NATURE OF CASE: Appeal from issuance of injunction.

FACT SUMMARY: Miller (P) sought to prevent the Lutheran Conference & Camp Association (the Association) (D) from using a lake for swimming or boating.

🏛 RULE OF LAW
An easement in gross may arise by prescription and is assignable if the parties to its creation so intend.

FACTS: In September 1895, Frank C. Miller and his brother Rufus W. Miller formed the Pocono Spring Water Ice Company in order to have the exclusive use of the waters of Lake Naomi, a man-made lake. By deed dated March 20, 1899, the Company granted to "Frank C. Miller, his heirs and assigns forever, the exclusive right to fish and boat in all the waters" of Lake Naomi. On February 17, 1900, Frank C. Miller (his wife Katherine (P) not joining) granted to Rufus W. Miller, his heirs and assigns forever, a one-fourth interest in the "fishing, boating and bathing rights" of Lake Naomi. On July 13, 1929, the executors of Rufus W. Miller's estate granted a one-year license to the Association (D) to boat, bathe, and fish in the lake. Frank C. Miller and his wife, Katherine D. Miller (P), then filed suit to enjoin the Association (D) from using the lake, on the grounds that the rights to use the lake were easements in gross and therefore inalienable and indivisible. The trial court issued the injunction, and the Association (D) appealed.

ISSUE: May an easement in gross arise by prescription, and is it assignable if the parties to its creation so intend?

HOLDING AND DECISION: (Stern, J.) Yes. The deed of 1899 from the Pocono Springs Water Ice Company to Frank C. Miller clearly did not convey any bathing rights. However, Frank C. Miller did establish title to the bathing rights by prescription because the rights were used systematically for commercial purposes. An adverse enjoyment of an easement in gross may ripen into title thereto by prescription; and therefore Frank C. Miller and Rufus W. Miller acquired title to the bathing rights by prescription. Further, Frank C. Miller made a valid assignment of a one-fourth interest in all rights to Rufus W. Miller. The rights of fishing and boating were conveyed to Frank C. Miller, his heirs and assigns, thus showing that the grantor, the Pocono Spring Water Ice Company, intended to attach the attribute of assignability to the privilege granted. However, even though the easements may be divided amongst different title holders, the easements must be used or exercised as an entirety. They cannot be commercially used and licenses, thereunder, cannot be granted without the common consent and joinder of the Millers (P), who own a portion of the easements. It follows that the executors of the estate of Rufus W. Miller did not have the right, in and by themselves, to grant a license to the Association (D). Affirmed.

▶ ANALYSIS

The modern trend rejects the old notion that the benefit of an easement in gross was not assignable. The Restatement view is that "easements in gross, if of a commercial character, are, alienable property interests." Commercial character is defined as "when the use authorized by it results in economic benefit rather than personal satisfaction." See, 5 Restatement of Property, § 489; and § 489, Comment C (1944).

Quicknotes

ASSIGNABLE Capable of being transferred or conveyed.

EASEMENT IN GROSS A right to use the land of another that is specific to a particular individual and which expires upon the death of that person.

INJUNCTION A court order requiring a person to do or prohibiting that person from doing a specific act.

LICENSE A right that is granted to a person allowing him or her to conduct an activity that without such permission he or she could not lawfully do, and which is unassignable and revocable at the will of the licensor.

PRESCRIPTION The acquisition of an easement in or on another's property as a result of continuous use for the statutory period.

Brown v. Voss

Easement grantee (P) v. Easement grantor (D)

Wash. Sup. Ct., 715 P.2d 514 (1986).

NATURE OF CASE: Appeal from denial of injunctive relief.

FACT SUMMARY: The court of appeals held that an easement granted for the benefit of one dominant estate could be used for two dominant estates where no increased burden to the servient estate is shown.

🏛 RULE OF LAW
If an easement is appurtenant to a particular parcel of land, any extension thereof to other parcels is a misuse of the easement, unless the servient estate does not overburden it.

FACTS: In 1952, Voss (D) granted an easement to Brown (P) to allow ingress and egress to Voss's (D) property. Brown (P) subsequently obtained title to a third parcel and attempted to use the easement to gain access thereto. Brown (P) sued to establish the right to so use the easement, yet Voss (D) sought an injunction to forbid such use. The trial court denied the injunction, the court of appeals reversed, and Voss (D) appealed.

ISSUE: If an easement is appurtenant to a particular parcel of land, is any extension thereof to other parcels a misuse of the easement, unless the easement is not overburdened?

HOLDING AND DECISION: (Brachtenbach, J.) Yes. If an easement is appurtenant to a particular parcel of land, any extension thereof to other parcels is a misuse of the easement, unless the use does not overburden the easement. The easement received no greater use as a result of Brown's (P) acquisition of the second parcel. Brown (P) reasonably developed his property, and thus the injunction was correctly denied. Reversed.

DISSENT: (Dore, J.) Any extension of this easement is a misuse. Thus, injunctive relief should have been granted.

▶ *ANALYSIS*

This case illustrates that while the law of easements can be traced back to common law, it is subject to judicial interpretation. Here, the reasonableness of the development, in the eyes of the court, served as the basis for denying the injunction.

■=■

Quicknotes

APPURTENANT A burden attached to real property that either benefits or burdens the owner's right to utilize that property.

DOMINANT ESTATE Property whose owners benefit from the use of another's property.

EASEMENT The right to utilize a portion of another's real property for a specific use.

INJUNCTIVE RELIEF A court order issued as a remedy, requiring a person to do, or prohibiting that person from doing, a specific act.

SERVIENT ESTATE Property that is burdened in some aspect for the benefit of a dominant estate.

Preseault v. United States

Right-of-way owners (P) v. Federal government (D)

100 F.3d 1525 (Fed. Cir. 1996).

NATURE OF CASE: Appeal from judgment rejecting claim for compensation due to exercise of eminent domain.

FACT SUMMARY: The Preseaults (P) contended that the federal Government (D) took their property when it authorized the conversion of a former railroad right-of-way over their property to public trail use.

⚖ RULE OF LAW
A change in use of an easement from a rail line to a recreational path constitutes a taking.

FACTS: An agreement executed in 1899 gave the federal government an easement across three parcels of land owned by the Preseaults' (P) predecessor for use as a rail line. The line began operating not long thereafter, but by 1970, rail operations had ceased. In 1975, the switches and tracks were removed. In 1986, under the Federal Rails-to-Trails Act, the land on which the rail line had once run was converted into a recreational trail. The Preseaults (P) filed suit in the Court of Federal Claims, contending that the new use constituted a taking for which they were entitled to compensation. The Court of Federal Claims rejected this contention, and they appealed.

ISSUE: Does a change in use of an easement from a rail line to a recreational path constitute a taking?

HOLDING AND DECISION: (Plager, J.) Yes. A change in use of an easement from a rail line to a recreational path constitutes a taking. Typically, an easement does not contain a specific termination date, but usually ends by way of abandonment. Abandonment is not effected merely by nonuse, but rather by acts that are inconsistent with the use for which the easement exists. Here, in 1975, the railroad took out the rail hardware, an act inconsistent with use as a rail line. At that point, then, abandonment was effected. At this point, the interest the Government (D) had in the Preseaults' (P) property was extinguished. The creation of the recreational path, therefore, was not a legitimate expansion of the original easement, but, rather, a taking of the Preseaults' (P) property, which, under the Fifth Amendment, required compensation. Reversed and remanded.

▶ ANALYSIS

It is not uncommon for strips of land to be deeded for transport purposes. The drafters of these documents are not always careful in the language utilized, and the question often arises as to whether it was an easement or fee simple that was conveyed. As a rule, courts tend to view "right-of-way" language in such instruments as conveying easements, not fees.

Quicknotes

ABANDONMENT The voluntary relinquishment of a right without the intent of reclaiming it.

EASEMENT The right to utilize a portion of another's real property for a specific use.

EMINENT DOMAIN The governmental power to take private property for public use so long as just compensation is paid therefor.

FEE SIMPLE An estate in land characterized by ownership of the entire property for an unlimited duration and by absolute power over distribution.

RIGHT-OF-WAY The right of a party to pass over the property of another.

TAKING A governmental action that substantially deprives an owner of the use and enjoyment of his or her property, requiring compensation.

Tulk v. Moxhay

Original covenantor (P) v. Subsequent purchaser (D)

Ct. Ch., 2 Phillips 774, 41 Eng. Rep. 1143 (1848).

NATURE OF CASE: Bill for injunction to enforce covenant in deed.

FACT SUMMARY: Moxhay (D) indicated an intention to build upon a park-like piece of land, even though he was aware of an original, prohibitive covenant passed on by Tulk (P), 40 years earlier, which forbade any construction on the ground.

🏛 RULE OF LAW
Privity of estate notwithstanding, a person who acquires real property with notice of a restriction placed upon it will not be allowed, in equity, to violate its terms.

FACTS: Tulk (P), owner in fee of a square garden containing a statue, as well as adjacent houses, sold the property to Elms. A covenant in the deed of conveyance prohibited Elms and his assigns from ever constructing upon the ground. The piece of land eventually came into the hands of Moxhay (D), whose purchase deed contained no similar covenant, yet Moxhay (D) admitted he knew of the original covenant. When Moxhay (D) indicated he wanted to build on the piece of ground, Tulk (P) successfully obtained an injunction.

ISSUE: Can the purchaser of a deed of conveyance containing a restriction violate the restriction if he has notice of the original covenant?

HOLDING AND DECISION: (Cottenham, Lord Chan.) No. To hold otherwise would make it impossible for an owner of land to sell part of it without running the risk of seeing the part he retained rendered worthless. At issue is not whether the covenant "runs" with the land, but whether a party may violate a contract entered into by his vendor by using the land in an inconsistent manner. If there was mere agreement and no covenant, a court would enforce it against a party purchasing with notice; so long as equity is attached by an owner, no one purchasing with notice can stand in a different situation than the original purchaser.

▶ ANALYSIS

Notice is the key element of the principle, commonly referred to as "the doctrine of *Tulk v. Moxhay*," enunciated in this case. Notice of the restriction may be either actual, inquiry, or record. The rights and obligations recognized here are variously named, but are generally known as "equitable servitudes." The restriction in the transfer of land need not be embodied in covenant—an informal contract or agreement is sufficient. A party intended to receive the benefit, as well as the original covenantor, can bring the suit in equity. However, proof of notice is essential to the doctrine.

◼▬◼

Quicknotes

CONVEYANCE The transfer of property, or title to property, from one party to another party.

COVENANT A written promise to do, or to refrain from doing, a particular activity.

DIVERS MESNE CONVEYANCE A conveyance falling between the original owner and the present owner in the chain of title.

EQUITABLE SERVITUDE Land use restriction enforceable in equity.

EQUITY Fairness; justice; the determination of a matter consistent with principles of fairness and not in strict compliance with rules of law.

INJUNCTION A court order requiring a person to do or prohibiting that person from doing a specific act.

OWNER IN FEE An owner of an absolute and unlimited interest in property.

PRIVITY OF ESTATE Common or successive relation to the same right in property.

◼▬◼

River Heights Associates L.P. v. Batten

Owner of undeveloped lots (P) v. Residential property owner (D)

Va. Sup. Ct., 591 S.E.2d 683 (2004).

NATURE OF CASE: Appeal from lower court decision finding that subdivision's restrictive covenant prohibiting commercial use was enforceable.

FACT SUMMARY: Alice Batten (P), a residential property owner in a subdivision, sought to prevent commercial development of four undeveloped lots within the subdivision. The subdivision was created in 1959 with a restrictive covenant that all lots would only be used for residential homes.

🏛 RULE OF LAW
A restrictive covenant can be nullified by changed conditions only when the changes are so radical as to destroy the essential objectives and purposes of the covenant.

FACTS: Alice Batten (P), a residential property owner in the Carrsbrook Subdivision in Virginia, sought to prevent commercial development of four undeveloped lots within the subdivision. Wendell Wood (D) had an ownership interest in the four different entities that owned the four undeveloped lots. The subdivision was created in 1959 with a restrictive covenant that all lots would be used only for residential homes. The four lots in question had frontage on Route 29. When the subdivision was created, Route 29 was a two-lane road. Both residential homes and small businesses existed along the road. Currently, Route 29 is a bustling eight-lane thoroughfare lined with hotels, shopping centers, and restaurants. No residential properties have been built on Route 29 near the subdivision in over 30 years. The trial court found that the subdivision itself had not undergone any radical changes and found the restrictive covenant to be enforceable. Wood (D) and the four entities appealed.

ISSUE: Can a restrictive covenant be nullified by changed conditions only when the changes are so radical as to destroy the essential objectives and purposes of the covenant?

HOLDING AND DECISION: (Carrico, J.) Yes. A restrictive covenant can be nullified by changed conditions only when the changes are so radical as to destroy the essential objectives and purposes of the covenant. The initial inquiry is a determination of the area that must be examined to determine whether or not changed conditions exist. Wells (D) argues the trial court improperly examined only the subdivision itself and not the surrounding areas. In particular, Wells (D) argues that Route 29 has changed from a small road to a major commercial district. Wells (D) is incorrect. He seeks a rule that would ignore the

changes, or lack thereof, within the subdivision itself. The subdivision at issue remains an entirely residential area. To ignore the subdivision would deny the lot owners the protection of the covenant to which they are entitled. The court agrees the analysis to determine if the covenant still serves its intended purposes should include a review of the subdivision as well as the surrounding areas. Based on this court's review, particularly the fact that the subdivision itself has not changed at all in 30 years, the changes are not so radical as to defeat the original purposes of the covenant. Affirmed.

▶ ANALYSIS

The changed condition doctrine varies from jurisdiction to jurisdiction. This case provides the common-law interpretation as it applies to restrictive covenants. The doctrine can also be used to attack easements or other types of servitudes, although not in all jurisdictions.

∎═∎

Quicknotes

RESTRICTIVE COVENANT A promise contained in a deed to limit the uses to which the property will be made.

∎═∎

Sanborn v. McLean

Neighbor (P) v. Gas station owner (D)

Mich. Sup. Ct., 206 N.W. 496 (1925).

NATURE OF CASE: Action to enjoin erection of gasoline filling station.

FACT SUMMARY: Sanborn (P) and McLean (D) trace the titles to their adjoining lots to the proprietor of the subdivision. Residences are built on all the surrounding lots. Sanborn (P) objected to McLean's (D) erection of a gas station on her lot.

RULE OF LAW
(1) If the owner of two or more lots, which are situated so as to bear a relation to each other, sells one with restrictions that are of benefit to the land retained, during the period of restraint, the owner of the lot or lots retained can do nothing forbidden to the owner of the lot sold. This is the doctrine of reciprocal negative easements.
(2) A reciprocal negative easement is not personal to owners but is operative upon use of the land by any owner having actual or constructive notice thereof.

FACTS: On December 28, 1892, McLaughlin, who was then owner of the lots on Collingwood Avenue, deeded four of the lots with the restriction that only residences would be built on the lots. On July 24, 1893, McLaughlin conveyed several more lots with the same restriction. Sanborn (P) traces title to McLaughlin. McLean's (D) title runs back to a deed dated September 7, 1893, which does not contain the restrictions. No buildings other than residences have been erected on any of the lots of the subdivision.
(1) If the owner of two or more lots, which are situated so as to bear a relation to each other, sells one with restrictions that are of benefit to the land retained, during the period of restraint, can the owner of the lot or lots retained do anything forbidden to the owner of the lot sold?
(2) Is a reciprocal negative easement personal to owners?

HOLDING AND DECISION: (Wiest, J.)
(1) No. The doctrine of reciprocal negative easements makes restrictions that are of benefit to the land retained mutual so that the owner can do nothing upon the land he has retained that is forbidden to the owner of the lot sold. In this case McLaughlin deeded lots with the restriction that only residences may be built on them. Such restrictions were imposed for the benefit of the lands retained by McLaughlin to carry out the scheme of a residential district, and a restrictive negative easement attached to the lots retained. Since his was one of the lots retained in the December 1892 and July 1893 deeds, a reciprocal negative easement attached to the lot which later became McLean's (D).
(2) No. A reciprocal negative easements is not personal to owners but is operative upon use of the land by any owner having actual or constructive notice thereof. In this case the reciprocal negative easement attached to McLean's (D) lot may now be enforced by Sanborn (P) provided McLean (D) had constructive knowledge of the easement at the time of purchase. At the time of purchase, McLean (D) had an abstract of title showing the subdivision and the 97 companion lots adjacent to his lot. He could not avoid noticing the strictly uniform residence character of the companion lots, and the least inquiry would have revealed the fact that his lot was subject to a reciprocal negative easement. The injunction is granted and the decree in the Circuit is affirmed.

ANALYSIS

Reciprocal negative easements must start with common owners. They cannot arise and fasten upon one lot by reason of other lot owners conforming to a general plan. Such easements are never retroactive, and as demonstrated here, they pass their benefits and carry their obligations to all purchasers of land provided the purchaser has constructive notice of the easement.

■=■

Quicknotes

CONSTRUCTIVE NOTICE Knowledge of a fact that is imputed to an individual who was under a duty to inquire and who could have learned of the fact through the exercise of reasonable prudence.

INJUNCTION A court order requiring a person to do or prohibiting that person from doing a specific act.

RECIPROCAL NEGATIVE EASEMENTS An implied covenant that arises when a common grantor conveys property and fails to contain a restriction placed on prior conveyances, pursuant to a general development scheme, to the present one and the grantee has either actual or constructive notice of such restrictions.

TITLE ABSTRACT Summary of the history of a title to property.

■=■

Neponsit Property Owners' Association, Inc. v. Emigrant Industrial Savings Bank

Covenantor's assignees (P) v. Subsequent purchaser (D)

N.Y. Ct. App., 15 N.E.2d 793 (1938).

NATURE OF CASE: Action to foreclose a lien upon land.

FACT SUMMARY: Neponsit Property Owners (P) claim that Emigrant Bank's (D) deed to certain property conveyed such property subject to a covenant contained in the original deed which provided for the payment by all subsequent purchasers of an annual improvements charge.

🏛 RULE OF LAW
A covenant in deed subjecting land to an annual charge for improvements to the surrounding residential tract is enforceable by the property owners' association against subsequent purchasers if: (1) grantor and grantee so intended; (2) it appears that the covenant is one touching or concerning the land; and (3) privity of estate is shown between the party claiming benefit of the covenant and the party under the burden of such covenant.

FACTS: Neponsit Property Owners' (P) assignor, Neponsit Realty Company, conveyed the land now owned by Emigrant Bank (D) to R. Deyer and wife by deed. That original deed contained a covenant providing: (1) that the conveyed land should be subject to an annual charge for improvements upon the entire residential tract then being developed; (2) that such charge should be a lien; (3) such charge should be payable by all subsequent purchasers to the company or its assigns, including a property owners' association which might thereafter be organized; and (4) such covenant runs with the land. Neponsit Property Owners (P) brought action based upon the above covenant to foreclose a lien upon the land which Emigrant Bank (D) now owns, having purchased it at a judicial sale. Emigrant Bank (D) appealed from an order denying their motion for judgment on the pleadings.

ISSUE: Does a covenant in the original deed subjecting land to an annual charge for improvements run with the land and create a lien that is enforceable against subsequent owners by Neponsit Property Owners (P)?

HOLDING AND DECISION: (Lehman, J.) Yes. A covenant will run with the land and will be enforceable against a subsequent purchaser if: (1) the grantor and grantee intend that the covenant run with the land; (2) the covenant touches or concerns the land with which it runs; (3) there is privity of estate between the party claiming benefit of the covenant and the party who rests under the burden of the covenant. In the instant case the grantor and grantee manifested their intent that the covenant run

with the land by so stating in the original deed. The covenant touches or concerns the land in substance if not in form, i.e., the covenant alters the legal rights of ownership of the land, by providing that the burden of paying the cost of maintaining public improvements is inseparably attached to the land which enjoys the benefits of such improvements. The concept of privity of estate between parties usually requires that the party claiming benefit from the enforcement of a covenant own the property that benefits from such enforcement. Although Neponsit Property Owners (P), the corporation, does not own the property that would benefit from enforcement, the corporation is acting as the agent of property owners and should therefore be considered in privity in substance if not in form. Since the covenant complies with the legal requirements for one that runs with the land and is enforceable against subsequent purchasers, the order that denied Emigrant Bank's (D) motion for judgment on the pleadings is affirmed.

▶ ANALYSIS

It has been suggested that the technical requirements that determine the enforceability of covenants as to future parties, e.g., *Neponsit*, might well be abandoned and that the intention of the covenanting parties be the sole criterion. This suggestion is supported by the following developments: (1) the benefit of a contract may now be assigned, or even created, initially for the benefit of a third person; (2) recording systems, though imperfect, afford much protection to the purchaser of land against outstanding burdens of which he may be unaware. It should be noted, however, that the unrestricted enforcement of covenants may seriously impair the usefulness of land. A student reading this case should keep in mind that *Neponsit* is not concerned with the enforcement of covenants between original covenanting parties. That question of enforceability is left to the contracts course.

■=■

Quicknotes

COVENANT A written promise to do, or to refrain from doing, a particular activity.

FORECLOSURE An action to recover the amount due on a mortgage of real property where the owner has failed to pay their debt, terminating the owner's interest in the property which must then be sold to satisfy the debt.

Continued on next page.

JUDICIAL SALE   A sale of property by a sheriff pursuant to a judgment.

LIEN   A claim against the property of another in order to secure the payment of a debt.

PRIVITY OF ESTATE   Common or successive relation to the same right in property.

"RUN WITH THE LAND"   Covenants that are binding on successor in interest to the property to which they are attached.

Shelley v. Kraemer

Home buyer (D) v. Neighbors (P)

334 U.S. 1 (1948).

NATURE OF CASE: Appeal from state high court decision in favor of defendants.

FACT SUMMARY: Shelley (D), an African-American, sought to purchase a home. A group of neighbors sought to uphold a restrictive covenant that prohibited the sale of any neighborhood homes to any person "not of the Caucasian race."

🏛 RULE OF LAW
State court enforcement of private, discriminatory restrictive covenants constitutes state action under the Fourteenth Amendment.

FACTS: On February 16, 1911, 30 of 39 owners of property in a neighborhood of St. Louis executed an agreement prohibiting the sale of any of the homes to any person "not of the Caucasian race." In 1945, Shelley (D), an African-American, sought to buy one of the homes covered by the agreement. Other homeowners led by Kraemer (P), brought suit to uphold the restrictive covenant and to prevent the sale. The Missouri Supreme court upheld the validity of the restrictive covenant. Shelley (D) appealed to the United States Supreme Court.

ISSUE: Does state court enforcement of private, discriminatory restrictive covenants constitute state action under the Fourteenth Amendment?

HOLDING AND DECISION: (Vinson, C.J.) Yes. State court enforcement of private, discriminatory restrictive covenants constitutes state action under the Fourteenth Amendment. First, the Fourteenth Amendment requires equality in the enjoyment of property rights. Moreover, if the prohibition in the private agreement was contained in a state statute or local ordinance, the Fourteenth Amendment would bar such prohibition because state action would be present. Here, the restrictive covenant is contained in an agreement between private individuals. We therefore conclude that without any state court intervention, private, restrictive covenants, even if discriminatory, do not run afoul of the Fourteenth Amendment because no state action is present. However, in the instant case, state courts have entered the fray and upheld the validity of the clearly discriminatory, private agreement. We have long held that "state action" includes action of the state courts and judicial officials. Therefore, the state court's intervention to uphold the covenants constitutes state action. That action is a violation of Shelley's (D) right to equal protection under the laws. Reversed.

▶ ANALYSIS

Shelley was the first case to strike down private, race-based restrictive covenants. The Civil Rights Act, plus a host of other state and local ordinances now outlaw discrimination in the private, residential housing market.

■=■

Quicknotes

FOURTEENTH AMENDMENT Declares that no state shall make or enforce any law that shall abridge the privileges and immunities of citizens of the United States. No state shall deny to any person within its jurisdiction the equal protection of the laws.

RESTRICTIVE COVENANT A promise contained in a deed to limit the uses to which the property will be made.

■=■

Western Land Co. v. Truskolaski

Subdivision homeowners (P) v. Subdivision developer (D)

Nev. Sup. Ct., 495 P.2d 624 (1972).

NATURE OF CASE: Appeal from order enjoining construction.

FACT SUMMARY: Western Land Co. (D) wanted to build a shopping center near property owned by Truskolaski (P), who argued that such construction would violate a restrictive covenant.

🏛 RULE OF LAW
A restrictive covenant is enforceable so long as its provisions remain of substantial value.

FACTS: In 1941, Western Land Co. (D) subdivided and developed a 40-acre parcel in Reno, Nevada. At that time, Western Land Co. (D) subjected the individual lots to certain restrictive covenants which specifically restricted the entire 40 acres of the subdivision to single family dwellings and further prohibited any stores, butcher shops, grocery, or mercantile business of any kind. In 1969, Truskolaski (P) and other homeowners in the subdivision sued to enjoin Western Land Co. (D) from constructing a shopping center on a parcel of land located within the subdivision. In holding for Truskolaski (P), the trial court found that the restrictive covenants remained of substantial value to the homeowners in the subdivision, despite the growth of commercial development in the area.

ISSUE: Is a restrictive covenant enforceable so long as its provisions remain of substantial value?

HOLDING AND DECISION: (Batjer, J.) Yes. So long as the original purpose of restrictive covenants can be accomplished and substantial benefit inure to the restricted area by their enforcement, the covenants will stand even though the subject property has a greater value if used for other purposes. Even though nearby streets have become heavily traveled, restrictive covenants are still enforceable if the single-family residential character of the neighborhood has not been adversely affected, and the purpose of the restrictions has not been thwarted. Here, Western Land Co. (D) has not carried its burden of showing that the subdivision is not now suitable for residential purposes because of the growth of commercial activities. Further, even though the Reno City Council considered rezoning the area around the subdivision, a zoning ordinance cannot override privately placed restrictive covenants. Affirmed.

▌ *ANALYSIS*

Several states have now enacted statutes which terminate restrictive covenants or limit their application by requiring that they be re-recorded after a specified period of time. Perhaps typical of the duration to be accorded these cove-

nants are provisions contained in the statutes of Georgia (20 years) and Massachusetts (30 years). In a few states, restrictive covenants will not be enforced if the covenant carries no substantial benefit, or where there has been substantial compliance for a reasonable period of time.

■=■

Quicknotes

RESTRICTIVE COVENANT   A promise contained in a deed to limit the uses to which the property will be made.

■=■

Rick v. West

Subsequent purchaser (P) v. Servitude proponent (D)

N.Y. Sup. Ct., Westchester County, 228 N.Y.S.2d 195 (1962).

NATURE OF CASE: Appeal from judgment enforcing restrictive covenant.

FACT SUMMARY: West (D), owner of a half-acre lot in a residential subdivision, refused to consent to a release of a covenant in her favor restricting the lots to single-family dwellings, thereby frustrating Rick's (P) plans to construct a hospital in the subdivision.

🏛 RULE OF LAW
Courts will not engage in a balancing of equities but will enforce restrictive covenants unless there is a substantial change of conditions in the general neighborhood.

FACTS: When Rick's (P) predecessor in title, the owner of 62 acres of vacant land, first subdivided the land, he filed a declaration of covenants, restricting the land to single-family dwellings. West (D) purchased a half-acre lot and built her house on it. Rick's predecessor (P) attempted to sell 45 acres for industrial use, but West (D) refused to release the covenant in her favor. After purchasing the remaining acreage, Rick (D) attempted to sell a 15-acre tract for construction of a hospital. Again West (D) refused to release the covenant. Rick (P) sued to have the covenant declared unenforceable, claiming changed conditions. The trial court held for West (D), and Rick (P) appealed.

ISSUE: Will courts enforce restrictive covenants, notwithstanding the parties' relative equities, so long as there is no substantial change of conditions in the general neighborhood?

HOLDING AND DECISION: (Hoyt, J.) Yes. Courts will enforce restrictive covenants, notwithstanding the parties' relative equities, so long as there is no substantial change of conditions in the general neighborhood. In this case, Rick's (P) predecessor in title chose to promote a residential development, imposing the residential restriction, upon which West (D) relied. She has a right to continue to rely on the restrictive covenant. The court will not engage in a balancing of equities, regardless of the location's suitability for a hospital. Because the restriction is not outmoded and affords real benefit to West (D), West (D) may not be awarded damages in lieu of enforcement. Affirmed.

▶ ANALYSIS

If this case had been litigated in Massachusetts, the outcome might have been different. Massachusetts has a statute that requires that the person seeking to enforce the servitude show that the restriction actually benefits her.

However, damages are the only remedy and will be awarded if there have been changes in the neighborhood that reduce the need for the restriction, or if continuation of the restriction would impede reasonable use of the land for purposes for which it is most suitable or would impair the growth of the neighborhood. Therefore, if Massachusetts law had been applied in the case above, even if West (D) could have demonstrated such a benefit, she probably could not have actually enforced the restriction but would have instead received an award of money damages.

Quicknotes

CHANGED CONDITIONS A defense to a claim of ameliorative waste, based on the theory that a change in the surrounding area warranted the alterations to the property.

RESTRICTIVE COVENANT A promise contained in a deed to limit the uses to which the property will be made.

SERVITUDE Land use restriction enforceable in equity.

Nahrstedt v. Lakeside Village Condominium Association, Inc.

Cat lover (P) v. Homeowners association (D)

Cal. Sup. Ct., 878 P.2d 1275 (1994).

NATURE OF CASE: Suit challenging the validity of a provision in a common interest development's Covenants, Conditions and Restrictions (CC&Rs) that prohibited the keeping of pets in the development.

FACT SUMMARY: A resident of a common interest development in California kept three cats in her condominium in violation of the development's governing CC&Rs. The homeowners association therefore assessed continuing penalties against her for the violations.

🏛 RULE OF LAW
A recorded use restriction imposed by a common interest development in California must be enforced uniformly against all residents of the development unless the restriction is unreasonable.

FACTS: Nahrstedt (P) owned and lived in a condominium in Lakeside Village, a 530-unit common interest development in Los Angeles County overseen by the Lakeside Village Condominium Association ("the homeowners association") (D). Nahrstedt's (P) ownership of her condominium gave her membership in the homeowners association (D). One of the homeowners association's (D) duties was to enforce Lakeside Village's governing, duly recorded CC&Rs. One clause of the CC&Rs provided that "[n]o animals (which shall include dogs and cats) . . . shall be kept in any unit." Nahrstedt (P), who alleged that she did not know of the pet restriction when she bought her condominium, lived in her unit with her three cats, but she did not let her cats have free run of Lakeside Village's common areas. When the homeowners association (D) learned that Nahrstedt (P) was keeping the cats in her home, it started assessing monthly fines against her for violating the CC&Rs. Nahrstedt (P) sued the homeowners association (D), asking the trial court to invalidate the assessments already imposed against her, to enjoin the homeowners association (D) from making such assessments against her in the future, and to declare the pet restriction in the CC&Rs "unreasonable" as applied to situations involving non-disturbing, essentially entirely in-home pet ownership like hers. The homeowners association (D) filed a demurrer to Nahrstedt's (P) complaint [i.e., the homeowners association (D) moved to dismiss her complaint for failing to state a claim upon which relief could be granted]. The trial court agreed with the homeowners association (D) and dismissed Nahrstedt's (P) complaint. On Nahrstedt's (P) appeal, the intermediate appellate court reversed the trial court's judgment, agreeing with Nahrstedt (P) that the reasonableness of a recorded use restriction in a common interest development must be determined on a case-by-case basis. The homeowners association (D) petitioned the California Supreme Court for further review.

ISSUE: Must a recorded use restriction imposed by a common interest development in California be enforced uniformly against all residents of the development unless the restriction is unreasonable?

HOLDING AND DECISION: (Kennard, J.) Yes. A recorded use restriction imposed by a common interest development in California must be enforced uniformly against all residents of the development unless the restriction is unreasonable. Homeowners in a common interest development sacrifice certain freedoms in exchange for, among other things, their ability to enforce restrictive covenants against other homeowners in the development. These restrictions are enforceable, though, only if they qualify as equitable servitudes or as covenants running with the land. In Section 1354(a) of the California Civil Code, California's legislature has established the test for determining whether a common interest development's use restrictions are enforceable: under Section 1354(a), a recorded declaration's use restrictions are "enforceable . . . unless unreasonable." Some states have reached similar conclusions through the courts. For example, in *Hidden Harbour Estates v. Basso*, 393 So. 2d 637 (Fla. Ct. App. 1981), a Florida appellate court held that a recorded declaration's stated use restrictions are entitled to a heavy presumption of validity, so much so that even somewhat unreasonable restrictions should nevertheless be enforced. The *Hidden Harbour Estates* court concluded further that arbitrary restrictions or those that violate public policy or a fundamental constitutional right should not be enforced. In a case involving a pet restriction, *Noble v. Murphy*, 612 N.E.2d 266 (Mass. App. Ct. 1993), the court agreed with the *Hidden Harbour Estates* rationale that otherwise-valid use restrictions should be enforced unless they violate constitutional rights or public policy. This court concludes, then, that recorded restrictive covenants should not be enforced when they violate public policy, as in *Shelley v. Kramer*, 334 U.S. 1 (1948) (racial restriction), or when they are arbitrary and bear no rational relation to a purpose involving the land. In such cases, the harm resulting from enforcement of arbitrary use restrictions or restrictions that violate fundamental public policy always outweighs any benefit that such restrictions might confer. Such principles also inform Section 1354(a) of the California Civil Code, which this court interprets as requiring enforcement of use restrictions unless they are arbitrary, violate public policy, or impose burdens outweighing any benefit. This presump-

Continued on next page.

tion of validity for recorded restrictive covenants means that homeowners associations can enforce their covenants without fear of instigating litigation. The presumption also relieves the judicial system from making case-by-case determinations of whether covenants are reasonable as applied to a particular homeowner. The presumption thus in turn means that homeowners in common interest developments will have the assurance that their covenants will be enforced uniformly and predictably. In this particular case, the appellate court failed to apply the pertinent rules governing equitable servitudes and erroneously relied on two opinions, *Portola Hills Community Assn. v. James*, 5 Cal. Rptr. 2d 580 (Cal. Ct. App. 1993), and *Bernardo Villas Management Corp. v. Black*, 235 Cal. Rptr. 509 (Cal. Ct. App. 1987), both of which are hereby disapproved because those courts did not use appropriately deferential review of the covenants at issue in those cases. Whether a use restriction is reasonable or unreasonable must be determined by referring to the entire common interest development, not by referring to the particular facts of a specific complaining homeowner. More specifically, the court holds that the Lakeside Village pet restriction is not arbitrary because it rationally promotes the other owners' legitimate concerns about health, sanitation, and noise; Nahrstedt (P) has failed to allege that the restriction's burden is so disproportionate to the legitimate benefits that the pet restriction is unreasonable. Moreover, no fundamental public policy requires that pets be kept in a condominium development, and no constitutional provision or California statute grants the right to keep pets in such a situation, either. Reversed and remanded.

DISSENT: (Arabian, J.) The majority's reasoning has technical merit, but the application of that analysis to these facts reveals a narrow understanding of the relationship between the law and the human spirit. The pet restriction at issue here violates Section 1354(a). It is arbitrary and unreasonable, within the meaning of Section 1354(a), because it imposes an undue burden on owners who keep their pets within their units and do not permit their pets to disturb the use of other homeowners' properties. The restriction's burden on such homeowners outweighs those homeowners' quality of life in the common interest development, and indeed the restriction only worsens the breakdown of our social fabric. All that the majority has done today is to accept, uncritically, the homeowners association's (D) assurances that uniform enforcement will promote all owners' "health and happiness." The first question in an appropriately probing inquiry should be to recognize that the burden on the particular use at issue here goes well beyond the impersonal and mundane issues normally covered by restrictive covenants. The majority instead asks only whether the use restriction at issue was stated in the original recorded declaration. If it was, it now shall be presumed valid unless it violates public policy. Such a standard means that almost all recorded use restrictions are valid, a status that only the commandments issued by Moses have enjoyed before today. Further, the proscribed activity here, pet ownership that is wholly confined to one's own home, deprives homeowners of the American dream, a notion that has always included the ownership and full enjoyment of one's home. Courts should rule with more humanity and strive to create harmony, not division, within the populace.

▌ *ANALYSIS*

Despite the emotionalism of Justice Arabian's dissent, and despite the intermediate appellate court's contrary ruling (relying on two now-invalidated opinions), today this case seems relatively easy for all the reasons cited by the majority. Public policy argues heavily against Nahrstedt's (P) position because that position would create great instability within homeowners associations, and because the burden of deciding enforceability of use restrictions on a case-by-case basis would substantially increase the caseloads of a judicial system that is already over-burdened. Under the rationale of *Nahrstedt* and cases like it, homeowners now can know that, when they sign a development's recorded covenants and use restrictions, those covenants and restrictions will almost certainly be enforced.

■=■

Quicknotes

CC&Rs Covenants, conditions, and restrictions that residents of a condominium development agree to abide by when they take ownership of a unit in that development.

DECLARATORY RELIEF A judgment of the court establishing the rights of the parties.

■=■

40 West 67th Street Corp. v. Pullman

Residential cooperative (P) v. Tenant (D)

N.Y. Ct. App., 790 N.E.2d 1174 (2003).

NATURE OF CASE: Appeal from intermediate appellate court decision in favor of plaintiff.

FACT SUMMARY: Pullman (D) engaged in a series of acts objectionable to the residential cooperative corporation (P), of which Pullman (D) was a member tenant. The cooperative (P) voted to evict him from his apartment.

🏛 RULE OF LAW
Under the business judgment rule, courts will defer to the residential cooperative's vote and findings as competent evidence that the tenant is objectionable and subject to eviction.

FACTS: The cooperative (P) owns the building at 40 West 67th Street in Manhattan. Pullman (D) rented one of the apartments in the building and signed a lease subjecting him to the rules and regulations of the cooperative (P). After moving in, Pullman (D) began complaining, without merit, about the loud noise from the television of the tenants above him, an elderly couple that had lived there for twenty years. After a physical altercation with the husband from that apartment, Pullman (D) also distributed flyers in the building stating that there was a "psychopath in our midst." In a separate flyer, Pullman (D) accused the same gentleman as having an affair with the wife of the cooperative's board president. Lastly, Pullman (D) made physical alterations to his apartment without proper approval. The cooperative called for a vote to evict Pullman (D) based on his "objectionable conduct." The cooperative (P), with 75 percent of the tenants present, voted unanimously to evict Pullman (D). After Pullman (D) refused to leave, the cooperative (P) brought this action to evict him. The trial court held that the business judgment rule did not apply. It held that the cooperative (P) had to prove its claim of objectionable conduct by competent evidence in a court of law. The intermediate appellate court reversed and held that the business judgment rule did apply here. Pullman (D) appealed.

ISSUE: Under the business judgment rule, will courts defer to the residential cooperative's vote and findings as competent evidence that the tenant is objectionable and subject to eviction?

HOLDING AND DECISION: (Rosenblatt, J.) Yes. Under the business judgment rule, courts will defer to the residential cooperative's vote and findings as competent evidence that the tenant is objectionable and subject to eviction. The parties disagree on the standard to be applied to the cooperative's (P) vote to evict Pullman (D). Pullman (D) believes Real Property Actions and Proceedings Law 711 (RPAPL 711) requires a court to make its own evaluation of the cooperative's conduct using a reasonableness standard. The cooperative (P) believes the business judgment rule applies, where courts defer to the good faith decisions made by boards of directors in business settings. We hold the business judgment rule applies. The rule balances the competing interests of the cooperative in governing itself while providing a limited judicial review in the case of abuses. Moreover, application of the business judgment rule does not conflict with RPAPL 711's requirement of a finding of competent evidence that a tenant is objectionable before facing eviction. We hold that the cooperative's own determination whether a tenant is objectionable constitutes competent evidence under the statute. Accordingly, in these contexts, courts must defer to the cooperative's determination pursuant to the business judgment rule. However, there are certain instances when courts may inquire further into a cooperative's actions. Those instances are when the cooperative acts: (1) outside the scope of its authority; (2) in a manner that does not further the cooperative's purpose; and (3) in bad faith. In this matter, we find that none of these circumstances are present. Affirmed.

▶ ANALYSIS

Only a small handful of states apply the business judgment rule to decisions by residential cooperatives or similar homeowner's associations. The majority of states use a less deferential reasonableness standard based on the court's independent review of the cooperative's actions. This case only applies to eviction actions by residential cooperatives. Different standards apply in other forms of housing, most notably in the public housing sector.

■=■

Quicknotes

BUSINESS JUDGMENT RULE Doctrine relieving corporate directors and/or officers from liability for decisions honestly and rationally made in the corporation's best interests.

■=■

CHAPTER 1

Legislative Land Use Controls: The Law of Zoning

Quick Reference Rules of Law

PAGE

1. *Village of Euclid v. Ambler Realty Co.* A zoning ordinance, as a valid exercise of the police power, will only be declared unconstitutional where its provisions are clearly arbitrary and unreasonable, having no substantial relation to the public health, safety, morals, or general welfare.   *146*

2. *PA Northwestern Distributors, Inc. v. Zoning Hearing Board.* A zoning ordinance that requires the amortization and discontinuance of a lawful preexisting nonconforming use is confiscatory and violative of the state constitution as a taking of property without just compensation.   *148*

3. *State ex rel. Stoyanoff v. Berkeley.* The protection of property values is a legitimate objective of zoning ordinances.   *150*

4. *Anderson v. City of Issaquah.* A building code cannot consist of design criteria that are strictly subjective in nature.   *151*

5. *City of Ladue v. Gilleo.* A municipality may not enact a blanket prohibition against signs on residential property.   *152*

6. *Guru Nanak Sikh Society of Yuba City v. County of Sutter.* Under the Religious Land Use and Institutionalized Persons Act of 2000 (RLUIPA), no government shall apply a land-use regulation in a manner that imposes a substantial burden on a person or a religious assembly or institution.   *153*

7. *Fisher v. Giuliani.* A court will not overturn an agency determination regarding the requirement of an environmental impact statement unless the decision was affected by an error of law or was arbitrary, capricious or constituted an abuse of discretion.   *154*

8. *Village of Belle Terre v. Boraas.* A city may pass an ordinance that prohibits unrelated individuals from living in one location.   *156*

9. *City of Edmonds v. Oxford House, Inc.* A family-composition zoning rule is not exempt from Fair Housing Act scrutiny.   *157*

10. *Southern Burlington County NAACP v. Township of Mount Laurel.* Municipal land-use regulations must provide a realistic opportunity for low- and moderate-income housing.   *158*

Village of Euclid v. Ambler Realty Co.

Municipal corporation (D) v. Tract owner (P)

272 U.S. 365 (1926).

NATURE OF CASE: Action to enjoin enforcement of a zoning ordinance.

FACT SUMMARY: Euclid (D) zoned property of Ambler Realty (P) in a manner which materially reduced its potential value.

🏛 RULE OF LAW
A zoning ordinance, as a valid exercise of the police power, will only be declared unconstitutional where its provisions are clearly arbitrary and unreasonable, having no substantial relation to the public health, safety, morals, or general welfare.

FACTS: Ambler Realty (P) was the owner of 68 acres in the village of Euclid (D). Though surrounded primarily by residential neighborhoods, the 68 acres also is bounded by a major thoroughfare to the south and a railroad to the north. Euclid (D) instituted zoning ordinances placing use, height, and area restrictions. Restrictions were placed on Ambler Realty's (P) property prohibiting (1) apartment houses, hotels, churches, schools, or any other public or semi-public buildings for the first 620 feet from Euclid Avenue, the above-described major thoroughfare, and (2) industry, theatres, banks, shops, etc., for the next 130 feet after that. As a result of this zoning, the value of Ambler Realty's (P) property has declined from $10,000 per acre to $2,500 per acre. Ambler Realty (P) brought an action to enjoin Euclid (D) from enforcing the ordinance on the ground that it constitutes a violation of Fourteenth Amendment due process. From a decree in favor of Amber Realty (P), Euclid (D) appeals, contending that the ordinance was a valid exercise of the police power of the state.

ISSUE: Is a zoning ordinance unconstitutional as a deprivation of property without due process because it results in a diminution of value in the property zoned?

HOLDING AND DECISION: (Sutherland, J.) No. A zoning ordinance, as a valid exercise of the police power, will only be declared unconstitutional where its provisions are clearly arbitrary and unreasonable, having no substantial relation to the public health, safety, morals, or general welfare. Zoning ordinances, and all similar laws and regulations, must find their justification in some aspect of the police power, asserted for the public welfare. Until recent years, urban life was comparatively simple; but with the great increase and concentration of population, problems have developed which require new restrictions on the use and occupation of private lands in urban communities. There is no serious difference of opinion on the state

power to avoid the nuisances which industry may cause in a residential area. As for residential regulation, many considerations point toward their validity. Segregation of residential business and industrial buildings makes it easier to provide appropriate fire apparatus, for example. Further, it is often observed that the construction of one type of building destroys an area for other types. In light of these considerations, the court is not prepared to say that the end of public welfare here is not sufficient to justify the imposition of this ordinance. It clearly cannot be said that it ". . . passes the bounds of reason and assumes the character of a merely arbitrary fiat." The decree must be reversed.

▶ ANALYSIS

Village of Euclid v. Ambler Realty is the landmark United States Supreme Court decision on zoning ordinances as valid exercises of the police power. Essentially, any zoning ordinance which is tied to public health, safety, morals, or welfare will be upheld unless clearly arbitrary and unreasonable. So-called *Euclidian* Zoning, which resulted from this decision, usually consists in the division of areas into zones, in which building use, height, and area are regulated in a manner designed to guarantee homogeneity of building patterns. All too often, however, zoning operates not so much to protect the public interest as to protect the vested interests in a community. Building restrictions may all too easily be used as an economic sanction by which social segregation is perpetuated. (Barring low-cost housing keeps out economically deprived segment of the population.) Note, however, that *Euclid* did not foreclose the possibility that government land-use regulations may constitute a "taking" which requires compensation. In *Pennsylvania Coal Co. v. Mahon*, 260 U.S. 393 (1922), the United States Supreme Court held that an anti-mining restriction, which totally destroyed the interest of the party who owned only the mineral rights, constituted a taking as to that person for which compensation had to be paid. In the *Mahon* case, the diminution in value of the party's property was total, and was thus clearly a "taking."

■==■

Quicknotes

INJUNCTION A court order requiring a person to do or prohibiting that person from doing a specific act.

POLICE POWER The power of a government to impose restrictions on the rights of private persons, as long as

Continued on next page.

those restrictions are reasonably related to the promotion and protection of public health, safety, morals, and the general welfare.

PUBLIC WELFARE The well-being of the general community.

TAKING A governmental action that substantially deprives an owner of the use and enjoyment of his or her property, requiring compensation.

ZONING ORDINANCE A statute that divides land into defined areas and which regulates the form and use of buildings and structures within those areas.

PA Northwestern Distributors, Inc. v. Zoning Hearing Board

Adult bookstore owner (P) v. Zoning board (D)

Pa. Sup. Ct., 584 A.2d 1372 (1991).

NATURE OF CASE: Appeal from dismissal of action challenging constitutionality of amortization ordinance.

FACT SUMMARY: Three weeks after PA Northwestern Distributors, Inc. (PA Northwestern) (P) opened an adult book store in Moon Township, Pennsylvania, the Board of Supervisors adopted an ordinance restricting permissible locations for bookstores and allowing only 90 days for nonconforming uses to either comply or shut down.

🏛 RULE OF LAW
A zoning ordinance that requires the amortization and discontinuance of a lawful preexisting nonconforming use is confiscatory and violative of the state constitution as a taking of property without just compensation.

FACTS: After obtaining the necessary permits, PA Northwestern (P) opened an adult book store in Moon Township. Three weeks later, following a public meeting, the Moon Township Board of Supervisors amended the zoning ordinances to impose extensive restrictions on the location and operation of "adult commercial enterprises." Any preexisting use in conflict with the new amendments was given 90-days' grace period, designed as a period of amortization, to either come into compliance with the ordinance or discontinue business. PA Northwestern (P) could not meet the place restrictions set forth in the ordinance because it was not located in an area designated for adult commercial enterprises. It filed an appeal with the Zoning Hearing Board (D), challenging the validity of the amortization provision, but the Hearing Board (D) validated the provision. PA Northwestern (P) appealed to the Court of Common Pleas, which dismissed the appeal. The Commonwealth Court affirmed applying the criteria set forth in *Sullivan v. Zoning Bd.*, 83 Pa. Commw. 228, 478 A.2d 912 (1984), comparing the impact of the provision on the property to the beneficial effects that would accrue to the community as a result of a discontinuance of the use. PA Northwestern (P) appealed.

ISSUE: Is a zoning ordinance that requires the amortization and discontinuance of a lawful preexisting nonconforming use confiscatory and violative of the state constitution as a taking of property without just compensation?

HOLDING AND DECISION: (Larsen, J.) Yes. A zoning ordinance that requires the amortization and discontinuance of a lawful preexisting nonconforming use is confiscatory and violative of the state constitution as a

taking of property without just compensation. Contrary to the appellate court's interpretation, Sullivan is not a correct statement of Pennsylvania law regarding amortization provisions. The usual presumption of a zoning ordinance's validity must be tempered by the fact that zoning involves governmental restrictions on a property owner's constitutionally guaranteed right to use his property, except where the use violates a law or creates a nuisance. Municipalities lack the power to compel a change in the nature of an existing lawful use of property. A lawful nonconforming use establishes in the property owner a vested property right which cannot be abrogated or destroyed. A "taking" under the Pennsylvania Constitution is not limited to actual physical possession or seizure of property. If the effect of the zoning law is to deprive an owner of the lawful use of his property, it amounts to a taking for which he must be compensated. In this case, the amortization ordinance deprived PA Northwestern (P) of the lawful use of its property because it forced it to cease using its property as an adult book store within 90 days. Therefore, the amortization provision was unconstitutional on its face because it effected a taking of PA Northwestern's (P) property without just compensation. Reversed.

CONCURRENCE AND DISSENT: (Nix, C.J.) Although the amortization provision in this case is unreasonable and must be struck down because it failed to provide adequate time for elimination of the nonconforming use, the per se prohibition against amortization provisions advanced by the majority is too restrictive. Amortization provisions that provide adequate notice to the property owner so that he is not deprived of the property or its use are an effective way to reconcile community interests with business needs.

▶ ANALYSIS

Pennsylvania is part of a small minority of states that forbid amortization ordinances altogether. In most states, a requirement that a nonconforming use cease within a certain time period does not constitute a taking, so long as the time period is reasonable. If the time period gives the owner adequate time to make new plans, any loss he suffers may be offset by the monopoly position he occupies for as long as the nonconforming business remains in place.

Continued on next page.

CASENOTE® LEGAL BRIEFS **149**
Property

Quicknotes

AMORTIZATION The satisfaction of a debt by the tendering of regular, equal payments over a period of time.

TAKING A governmental action that substantially deprives an owner of the use and enjoyment of his or her property, requiring compensation.

■■■

State ex rel. Stoyanoff v. Berkeley

Landowner (P) v. Architectural board (D)

Mo. Sup. Ct., 458 S.W.2d 305 (1970).

NATURE OF CASE: Appeal from finding of property deprivation without due process.

FACT SUMMARY: Stoyanoff (P) desired to build a house of unusual shape in a St. Louis, Missouri, suburb.

🏛 **RULE OF LAW**
The protection of property values is a legitimate objective of zoning ordinances.

FACTS: Stoyanoff (P) desired to build a home in the City of Ladue, which is one of the finer suburbs in the St. Louis area. The plans called for the home to be of pyramid shape, with a flat top, and with triangular-shaped windows or doors at one or more corners. A city ordinance established an architectural board to ensure that new residences "conform to certain minimum architectural standards of appearance and conformity with surrounding structures, and that unsightly, grotesque and unsuitable structures detrimental to the ... welfare of surrounding property ... be avoided." The homes surrounding Stoyanoff's (P) lot were virtually all two-story houses of conventional architectural design. After the architectural board (D) denied Stoyanoff's (P) application for a building permit, a trial court issued a peremptory writ of mandamus to compel the City of Ladue to issue Stoyanoff (P) a residential building permit.

ISSUE: Is the protection of property values a legitimate objective of zoning ordinances?

HOLDING AND DECISION: (Pritchard, Commr.) Yes. The stabilizing of property values and giving some assurance to the public that, if property is purchased in a residential district, its value will be preserved, is a legitimate objective for zoning ordinances. Property use that offends sensibilities and decreases property values affects not only the adjoining property owners in that vicinity, but the general public as well. When property values are destroyed or seriously impaired, the tax base of the community is affected, and the public suffers economically as a result. Here, the denial of a building permit for Stoyanoff's (P) highly modernistic residence in an area where traditional Colonial, French Provincial, and English Tudor styles of architecture are erected does not appear to be arbitrary and unreasonable when the basic purpose to be served is that of the general welfare of persons in the entire community. Reversed.

▶ *ANALYSIS*

The court in this case rested its decision on the objective of protecting property values. This is because many early cases held that aesthetic concerns were insufficient to support restrictive zoning regulations. The modern trend, though, shows that many courts are inclined to accept the legitimacy of zoning based exclusively on aesthetic considerations.

■═■

Quicknotes

WRIT OF MANDAMUS A court order issued commanding a public or private entity, or an official thereof, to perform a duty required by law.

ZONING ORDINANCE A statute that divides land into defined areas and which regulates the form and use of buildings and structures within those areas.

■═■

Anderson v. City of Issaquah

Developer (P) v. Municipality (D)

Wash. Ct. App., 851 P.2d 744 (1993).

NATURE OF CASE: Appeal from denial of building permit.

FACT SUMMARY: The building code of the City of Issaquah, Washington (the City) (D) included criteria with respect to building design that were strictly subjective in nature.

🏛 RULE OF LAW
A building code cannot consist of design criteria that are strictly subjective in nature.

FACTS: The City (D) included, as part of its municipal building code, certain design criteria to be followed in new building developments. The code mandated, inter alia, that buildings be "harmonious" with surrounding architecture and that building proportions be "appropriate." Anderson (P), intending to develop certain commercial property, submitted his building design to the Development Commission. During several hearings, the members expressed dissatisfaction with the design, although the members themselves did not seem to agree on what could be done to make the design more acceptable. After several revisions, Anderson (P) submitted his final plans, which were not approved. He appealed to the city council, which also denied approval. He filed suit seeking an injunction mandating approval. The trial court dismissed the complaint, and Anderson (P) appealed.

ISSUE: Can a building code consist of design criteria that are strictly subjective in nature?

HOLDING AND DECISION: (Kennedy, J.) No. A building code cannot consist of design criteria that are strictly subjective in nature. A statute that either forbids or requires the doing of an act in terms so vague that persons of common intelligence must necessarily guess at its meaning and differ as to its application violates due process. It is inherent in due process that laws be crafted in such a fashion that a person can reasonably be able to understand them. Terms that are totally subjective cannot meet this standard. The ordinance at issue here is an example of this. It mandates that design be "harmonious" and "appropriate." Obviously, what might or might not meet these standards is strictly in the eye of the beholder. This is borne out by the fact that the individual Commission members seemed to have had differing ideas as to what Anderson (P) had to do to bring his design into compliance, which left him in a totally impossible situation. Since the ordinance was clearly unconstitutionally vague, the City (D) should have issued the building permit. So ordered.

▶ ANALYSIS

Private developments, such as condominium complexes, often have similar design criteria and their own architectural committees. Courts, as a general rule, have been much more deferential to decisions of private developments. Of course, the state constitution applies to state actions only, so the Due Process Clause is generally inapplicable in such situations.

■═■

Quicknotes

BUILDING CODE Local ordinances that govern requirements for residential housing.

DUE PROCESS CLAUSE Clauses found in the Fifth and Fourteenth Amendments to the United States Constitution providing that no person shall be deprived of "life, liberty, or property, without due process of law."

INJUNCTION A court order requiring a person to do or prohibiting that person from doing a specific act.

STATE ACTION Actions brought pursuant to the Fourteenth Amendment claiming that the government violated the plaintiff's civil rights.

■═■

City of Ladue v. Gilleo

Municipality (D) v. Antiwar homeowner (P)

512 U.S. 43 (1994).

NATURE OF CASE: Review of order striking down municipal land-use regulation.

FACT SUMMARY: The City of Ladue (the City) (D) enacted a zoning ordinance that prohibited all signs on residential property, with the exception of "for sale"-type placards.

> ## 🏛 RULE OF LAW
> A municipality may not enact a blanket prohibition against signs on residential property.

FACTS: The City (D) enacted an ordinance that prohibited all signs on residential property, with a few narrow exceptions, the main one being "for sale"-type signs of no greater than a specified size. Gilleo (P) had erected a sign protesting the Gulf War. When City (D) authorities cited her for violation of the ordinance, she filed an action in district court challenging the constitutionality of the ordinance. The district court held the ordinance unconstitutional, and the court of appeals affirmed. The United States Supreme Court granted review.

ISSUE: May a municipality enact a blanket prohibition against signs on residential property?

HOLDING AND DECISION: (Stevens, J.) No. A municipality may not enact a blanket prohibition against signs on residential property. Signs are clearly a form of expression protected by the First Amendment. However, they do implicate the rights of local government police power, as they take up space and may obstruct views. Therefore, local government does have some regulatory power over sign placement. Any regulation of this nature, however, will have to walk a fine line between legitimate health and safety concerns and freedom of expression. The regulation at issue here, however, clearly does not. The ordinance forecloses a venerable means of communication that is both unique and important. Residential signs often play an important role in political campaigns. They are also a low-cost means of expression, and may be the only practical mode of expression for persons of modest means. While municipalities can regulate the time, place, and manner of speech, they cannot cut off an entire mode without leaving reasonable alternative means. A blanket prohibition at issue here does not do so, and as such, runs afoul of the First Amendment. Affirmed.

▌ *ANALYSIS*

This case is almost the mirror image of an earlier case, *Linmark Associates, Inc. v. City of Willingboro*, 431 U.S. 85 (1977). In that case, a city had forbade "for sale" signs on the theory that such signs lowered property values and encouraged "white flight." The Court there found the ordinance unconstitutional. Given this precedent, it would have been hard for the Court to have ruled otherwise in the present case, which involved a much more severe restriction on signs.

■══■

Quicknotes

BLANKET PROHIBITION A prohibition that is absolute.

FIRST AMENDMENT Prohibits Congress from enacting any law respecting an establishment of religion, prohibiting the free exercise of religion, abridging freedom of speech or the press, the right of peaceful assembly, and the right to petition for a redress of grievances.

ZONING ORDINANCE A statute that divides land into defined areas and which regulates the form and use of buildings and structures within those areas.

■══■

Guru Nanak Sikh Society of Yuba City v. County of Sutter

Non-profit (P) v. State county (D)

456 F.3d 978 (9th Cir. 2006).

NATURE OF CASE: Appeal from granting of summary judgment to the plaintiff.

FACT SUMMARY: Guru Nanak Sikh Society of Yuba City (Nanak) (P) applied twice in Sutter County for a permit to build a Sikh temple. The County (D) denied both applications.

🏛 RULE OF LAW

Under the Religious Land Use and Institutionalized Persons Act of 2000 (RLUIPA), no government shall apply a land-use regulation in a manner that imposes a substantial burden on a person or a religious assembly or institution.

FACTS: Nanak (P), a non-profit organization set up to teach the practices of the Sikh religion, first applied for a permit in Sutter County (D) in 2001. The Planning Commission denied the conditional use permit because of concerns over increased noise and traffic in the residential area. In 2002, Nanak (P) applied for a second permit in an area of the same county zoned for agricultural use. This site was much larger, and Nanak (P) also agreed to a 25-foot no-development buffer, to a requirement that all ceremonies be held indoors, and to landscaping requirements. After an initial approval, the County's (D) board of supervisors denied the application. One supervisor found the property was for agricultural uses only. Another supervisor suggested the temple was too far removed from the city and would not promote orderly growth. Another supervisor agreed, calling it "leapfrog development." Nanak (P) filed suit under RLUIPA, and the federal district court granted summary judgment to Nanak (P). The County (D) appealed.

ISSUE: Under RLUIPA, may a government apply a land-use regulation in a manner that imposes a substantial burden on a person or a religious assembly or institution?

HOLDING AND DECISION: (Bea, J.) No. Under RLUIPA, no government shall apply a land-use regulation in a manner that imposes a substantial burden on a person or a religious assembly or institution. RLUIPA is the most recent attempt by Congress to craft a constitutionally valid mechanism to protect rights of discrete religions. The statute applies if a government entity imposes a substantial burden on the free exercise of religion by making an individualized assessment of the proposed use of the property at issue. The requirement of an individualized assessment is significant. It distinguishes those permit or zoning procedures that are neutral laws of general applicability. If there is no individualized assess-

ment present, a plaintiff may not avail itself of the statute's protections. The County (D) made an individualized assessment of Nanak's (P) second application. The County's (D) own zoning code requires a comprehensive review for conditional use permits, which should be reviewed "under the circumstances of the particular case." Turning to the substantial burden analysis, Nanak (P) bears the burden of proof. For a land-use regulation to constitute a substantial burden, it must be "oppressive to a significantly great extent." We agree with the lower court that the County (D) imposed a substantial burden upon Nanak (P). In this matter, the parcel in the agricultural zone left a great deal of space between the proposed temple and neighbors. Moreover, the County's (D) concern with leapfrog development could apply to all future permit requests by religious organizations. In addition, other churches already exist in the same area, including another Sikh temple one mile away in the same agricultural zone. The County's (D) permitting is simply not consistent. Lastly, Nanak (P) agreed to all of the county planning board's conditions, including the set back provisions. All of these facts support the lower court's conclusion that the County's (D) denial constituted a substantial burden upon Nanak's (P) free exercise of religion. Summary judgment affirmed.

▶ ANALYSIS

Several circuit courts of appeals have agreed with the Ninth Circuit's definition of "substantial burden," that the regulation at issue must be "oppressive to a great extent."

■=■

Quicknotes

FREE EXERCISE CLAUSE The guarantee of the First Amendment to the United States Constitution prohibiting Congress from enacting laws regarding the establishment of religion or prohibiting the free exercise thereof.

SUMMARY JUDGMENT Judgment rendered by a court in response to a motion made by one of the parties, claiming that the lack of a question of material fact in respect to an issue warrants disposition of the issue without consideration by the jury.

■=■

Fisher v. Giuliani

City residents (P) v. New York City (D)

N.Y. App. Div., 720 N.Y.S.2d 50 (2001).

NATURE OF CASE: Appeal from trial court's decision in favor of plaintiffs.

FACT SUMMARY: In 1998, New York City (D) amended its zoning laws for the Theater District to allow transfer of development rights to any possible site within the district, not just nearby parcels. Residents of an adjoining district brought suit, alleging the City (D) was obligated to prepare an environmental impact statement before modifying the zoning laws.

🏛 RULE OF LAW
A court will not overturn an agency determination regarding the requirement of an environmental impact statement unless the decision was affected by an error of law or was arbitrary, capricious or constituted an abuse of discretion.

FACTS: New York City (D) amended its zoning laws for the Theater District, including Broadway, in 1998 to allow certain theaters to transfer development rights to any sites within the theater subdistrict. Previously, such transfers could only be made to nearby parcels, not to anywhere within the district. The transfer of the development rights included a 20 percent increase in the floor-to-area ratio (FAR) of the receiving site. In addition, the new amendments created a discretionary mechanism where a developer could obtain the same 20 percent increase of the FAR amount. Prior to submitting the amendments for public review, the city conducted an environmental assessment of the transfer of rights amendment required by the State Environmental Quality Review Act (SEQRA). This Environmental Assessment Statement would state whether or not the zoning amendment would have a significant effect on the environment. If the answer was in the affirmative, the local zoning agency would have to then prepare a separate Environmental Impact Statement. Accordingly, at the preliminary stage, the City (D) reviewed the development trends for a ten-year period into the future and concluded that zoning capacity would accommodate demand twice over. Also, the City (D) reviewed the amendment's effect on traffic, transit, and air quality and determined the amendment would not have a significant effect. The City (D) therefore decided, in a 75-page single-spaced report, that no additional Environmental Impact Statement was necessary. There was no separate environmental review conducted for the other zoning amendment regarding the discretionary review mechanism. The plaintiffs, a group of city residents in a nearby district, brought suit, alleging the City's (D) preparation of the preliminary Environmental Assessment Statement was deficient in sev-

eral respects. The trial court agreed with the plaintiffs and invalidated the new zoning amendments due to the deficient Environmental Assessment Statement.

ISSUE: May a court overturn an agency determination regarding the requirement of an environmental impact statement if the decision was not affected by an error of law or was not arbitrary, capricious, or an abuse of discretion?

HOLDING AND DECISION: (Friedman, J.) No. A court may not overturn an agency determination regarding the requirement of an environmental impact statement unless the decision was affected by an error of law or was arbitrary, capricious, or constituted an abuse of discretion. It is not a court's role to weigh desirability of the proposed rules or competing considerations. Instead, in regards to environmental decisions of city or state agencies, courts should review whether the agency identifies the relevant areas of environmental concern and takes a "hard look" at them. The petitioners' claim that the City (D) did not thoroughly review the environmental impact is without merit. First, the City's (D) determination that market demand and consequent development will remain constant is rational and based upon reasonable forecasting methods of future development. Second, the City's (D) use of a ten-year future projection was "hardly an irrational examination" of the future development prospects. Therefore, the City (D) was correct that a further Environmental Impact Statement was not required. Separately, however, the amendment's discretionary mechanism for approval of FAR increases for individual theaters is invalid. The City (D) erroneously believed that because environmental impact reviews would occur when individual owners applied for the FAR permit, the City (D) did not need to conduct an environmental assessment prior to the adoption of that amendment. Under SEQRA, there must be an environmental assessment completed prior to adoption of the zoning amendments in all respects. Accordingly, that portion of the amendments is hereby severed and annulled. Reversed in part and affirmed in part.

▶ ANALYSIS

Fisher is an example of judicial deference to the expertise of a particular agency. In several different areas of the law, courts often decline to overturn agency decisions, particularly when the agency is interpreting its own governing regulations. Here, the facts supported the finding that the

Continued on next page.

City (D) had addressed the relevant environmental concerns present in the case.

■═■

Quicknotes

ARBITRARY AND CAPRICIOUS STANDARD Standard imposed in reviewing the decision of an agency or court when the decision may have been made in disregard of the facts or law.

■═■

Village of Belle Terre v. Boraas

Municipality (D) v. Unrelated tenants (P)

416 U.S. 1 (1974).

NATURE OF CASE: Appeal from judgment invalidating zoning ordinance.

FACT SUMMARY: Belle Terre (D) passed an ordinance restricting land use to one-family dwellings.

🏛 RULE OF LAW
A city may pass an ordinance that prohibits unrelated individuals from living in one location.

FACTS: Belle Terre (D) is a village on Long Island's north shore of about 220 homes inhabited by 700 people. Its total land area is less than one square mile. It has restricted land use to one family dwellings excluding, lodging houses, boarding houses, fraternity houses, or multiple-dwelling houses. Boraas (P) and five other students at State University at Stony Brook, who were not related to each other by blood, adoption, or marriage, rented a home in Belle Terre (D) in December 1971. When Belle Terre (D) served the owners of the home with an "Order to Remedy Violations" of the ordinance, the owners plus three tenants brought an action under the Civil Rights Act for an injunction and a judgment declaring the ordinance unconstitutional. The court of appeals held that the law was unconstitutional, and Belle Terre (D) appealed.

ISSUE: May a city pass an ordinance that prohibits unrelated individuals from living in one location?

HOLDING AND DECISION: (Douglas, J.) Yes. The concept of the public welfare is broad and inclusive. The ordinance here does not burden any fundamental rights guaranteed by the Constitution, nor does it inflict procedural disparities on some but not on others. Rather, this ordinance is in the field of economic and social legislation and will be upheld if it bears a rational relationship to a permissible state objective. A quiet place where yards are wide, people few, and motor vehicles restricted are legitimate guidelines in a land-use project addressed to family needs. The police power is not confined to elimination of filth, stench, and unhealthy places. It is ample to lay out zones where family values, youth values, and the blessings of quiet seclusion and clean air make the area a sanctuary for people. Reversed.

DISSENT: (Marshall, J.) The ordinance in this case unnecessarily burdens the First Amendment freedom of association and the right to privacy. The First and Fourteenth Amendments protect the freedom to choose one's associates. Constitutional protection is extended, not only to modes of association that are political in the usual sense, but also to those that pertain to the social and economic benefit of the members. The choice of household compan-

ions involves deeply personal considerations as to the kind and quality of intimate relationships within the home. That decision surely falls within the ambit of the right to privacy protected by the Constitution.

▶ ANALYSIS

The United States Supreme Court, in a later decision invalidating an ordinance that defined "family" to include no more than one set of grandchildren, limited the holding of this case. "The ordinance (in *Belle Terre*) affected only unrelated individuals . . . East Cleveland, in contrast, has chosen to regulate the occupancy of its housing by slicing deeply into the family itself . . . (The) freedom of personal choice in matters of marriage and family life is one of the liberties protected by the Due Process Clause of the Fourteenth Amendment . . . ." *Moore v. City of East Cleveland*, 431 U.S. 494 (1977).

Quicknotes

EUCLIDEAN ZONING A zoning scheme whereby zoning districts are established based on the uses permitted pursuant to local ordinance.

FIRST AMENDMENT Prohibits Congress from enacting any law respecting an establishment of religion, prohibiting the free exercise of religion, abridging freedom of speech or the press, the right of peaceful assembly, and the right to petition for a redress of grievances.

POLICE POWER The power of a state or local government to regulate private conduct for the health, safety, and welfare of the general public.

PUBLIC WELFARE The well-being of the general community.

ZONING ORDINANCE A statute that divides land into defined areas and which regulates the form and use of buildings and structures within those areas.

City of Edmonds v. Oxford House, Inc.

Municipality (P) v. Halfway house (D)

514 U.S. 725 (1995).

NATURE OF CASE: Review of order striking down municipal land-use regulation.

FACT SUMMARY: The City of Edmonds (the City) (P) contended that its limitation of residences to single-family use was exempt from the ambit of the Fair Housing Act.

🏛 RULE OF LAW
A family-composition zoning rule is not exempt from Fair Housing Act scrutiny.

FACTS: The City (P) had enacted a zoning ordinance that, among other things, limited occupancy of certain areas of resident property to "single family" use. "Single family" was defined as a group of people related by blood, marriage, or adoption, or any group of five or fewer unrelated persons living in the same household. Oxford House, Inc. (Oxford) (D), instituted at a dwelling covered by the ordinance a halfway house for recovering alcoholics and drug addicts. The City (P) cited Oxford (D) for violating the regulation. It then sued in federal court, seeking a declaration that the Fair Housing Act did not constrain its family definition rule. Oxford (D) counterclaimed, contending that the City (P) had not made a reasonable accommodation for its group home as required by the Fair Housing Act. The district court ruled that the ordinance was a reasonable restriction on the maximum number of occupants, which was exempt from the Fair Housing Act per § 3607(b)(1) of the Act. The Ninth Circuit reversed, and held the ordinance to violate the Fair Housing Act. The United States Supreme Court granted review.

ISSUE: Is a family-composition zoning rule exempt from the Fair Housing Act?

HOLDING AND DECISION: (Ginsburg, J.) No. A family-composition zoning rule is not exempt from the Fair Housing Act. Section 3607(b)(1) of the Fair Housing Act exempts from its ambit laws or ordinances that limit the number of persons living in a household. This exemption was inserted into the Act as recognition that localities have an interest in preventing overcrowding. Here, the district court, apparently looking at the portion of the ordinance defining a "family" as, among other things, "five or fewer individuals," concluded that the ordinance fell within the exemption. This was an incorrect analysis. "Family" is also defined in the ordinance as persons related by blood, marriage, or adoption, without regard to number of persons. Consequently, the rule at issue here is not in any real sense a limitation on the number of persons living

in a dwelling. The district court therefore erred in so holding. Affirmed.

▶ ANALYSIS

The Court's decision here was a rather narrow one. It did not decide whether or not the City's (P) ordinance actually violated the Fair Housing Act; rather, it simply decided that § 3607's exemption did not apply. The present decision will most likely be of little import in future Fair Housing Act cases.

Quicknotes

FAIR HOUSING ACT 42 U.S.C. § 3601 Prohibits housing discrimination on the basis of familial status.

LAND-USE REGULATION Regulation governing the development and/or zoning of real estate.

SINGLE-FAMILY USE With respect to zoning refers to area restricted to single-family housing.

ZONING ORDINANCE A statute that divides land into defined areas and which regulates the form and use of buildings and structures within those areas.

Southern Burlington County NAACP v. Township of Mount Laurel

Civil rights organization (P) v. Municipality (D)

N.J. Sup. Ct., 336 A.2d 713, *appeal dismissed and cert. denied*, 423 U.S. 808 (1975).

NATURE OF CASE: Appeal from invalidation of zoning ordinance.

FACT SUMMARY: The trial court held that a bona fide attempt by a municipality to provide zoned land for low-cost housing fulfilled its constitutional obligations.

🏛 RULE OF LAW
Municipal land-use regulations must provide a realistic opportunity for low- and moderate-income housing.

FACTS: The NAACP (P) sued Mount Laurel (D), contending the municipality's zoning scheme violated the New Jersey constitution by failing to provide for low-income housing outside of depressed areas. The New Jersey Supreme Court invalidated the ordinances and remanded for further proceedings. The trial court held that it was sufficient that Mount Laurel (D) had made a bona fide attempt to comply with the Supreme Court decision and upheld the new ordinance enacted in response. The NAACP (P) appealed, contending a mere attempt to provide such zoning did not discharge Mt. Laurel's (D) constitutional obligations.

ISSUE: Must municipal land-use regulations provide a realistic opportunity for low- and moderate-income housing?

HOLDING AND DECISION: (Hall, J.) Yes. Municipal land-use regulations must provide a realistic opportunity for low- and moderate-income housing. Such obligation extends beyond attempting to provide for such housing. The housing must be in direct proportion to the percentage of lower income residents in the city. To reach this goal, affirmative governmental action may be required. The elimination of some obstacles and the creation of a new zoning scheme may be frustrated by other restrictions that effectively deprive the poor of adequate housing. Therefore, the zoning scheme, which merely manifested intent to abide by the original Supreme Court, holding was insufficient to discharge Mount Laurel's (D) constitutional obligations. Reversed and judgment of the Law Division modified.

▌ ANALYSIS

The rationale behind the *Mount Laurel* case is that the use of all land is controlled by the state. The state has constitutional obligations to all its residents whether rich or poor. Municipalities, as state subjects, must set aside a fair share of its land for lower income housing. They cannot allocate only dilapidated land for the poor and retain valuable land for the rich exclusively. While this rationale appears clear in theory, in execution it has proven very difficult. The main difficulty is in developing an equitable formula for determining "fair share." Until a definitive formula is developed, this will prevent widespread application of this rule.

■━■

Quicknotes

AFFIRMATIVE ACTION A form of benign discrimination designed to remedy existing discrimination by favoring one group over another.

LAND-USE REGULATION Regulation governing the development and/or zoning of real estate.

ZONING ORDINANCE A statute that divides land into defined areas and which regulates the form and use of buildings and structures within those areas.

■━■

Eminent Domain and the Problem of Regulatory Takings

Quick Reference Rules of Law

PAGE

1. *Kelo v. City of New London*. A city's proposed taking of private property for general economic development qualifies as a public use consistent with the Takings Clause of the Fifth Amendment to the United States Constitution. 160

2. *Loretto v. Teleprompter Manhattan CATV Corp*. Any permanent physical occupation of an owner's property that is governmentally authorized constitutes a taking of property for which just compensation must be paid. 162

3. *Hadacheck v. Sebastian*. A municipality may regulate business operations to prevent harm to the public. 163

4. *Pennsylvania Coal Co. v. Mahon*. Private property may be regulated pursuant to the police power of the state to protect public health, safety, or morals; but if such regulation goes so far as to destroy or appropriate a property right, it becomes a "taking" under the Fifth and Fourteenth Amendments, requiring just compensation therefor. 164

5. *Penn Central Transportation Company v. City of New York*. A city may place restrictions on the development of individual historic landmarks without effecting a taking requiring just compensation. 165

6. *Lucas v. South Carolina Coastal Council*. The state must compensate a landowner when a regulatory action denies an owner economically viable use of his land, unless the prohibited use of the land constitutes a nuisance under state common law. 166

7. *Palazzolo v. Rhode Island*. A purchaser or successive title holder is not barred from bringing a takings claim by the mere fact that the title was acquired after the effective date of the state regulation. 168

8. *Tahoe-Sierra Preservation Council, Inc. v. Tahoe Regional Planning Agency*. A moratorium on development imposed during the process of devising a comprehensive land-use plan does not constitute a per se taking of property requiring compensation under the Takings Clause. 170

9. *Stop the Beach Renourishment, Inc. v. Florida Department of Environmental Protection*. (1) In upholding the state's legislation to restore beaches, a process that modifies private property boundary lines, the court's decision does not constitute a judicial taking or violate the due process clause. (2) Beachfront property owners do not have a right of accretion superior to the state's right to fill in reclaimed land. 172

10. *Nollan v. California Coastal Commission*. A state may not condition a property use permit on an act not addressing the problem caused by the permitted use. 175

11. *Dolan v. City of Tigard*. A city may condition a land-use permit upon dedication of the land to a public use if such dedication is roughly proportional to the impact upon the community caused by the proposed land use. 176

12. *Koontz v. St. Johns River Water Management District*. Under the unconstitutional conditions doctrine, a government agency may condition the approval of a permit on the landowner's dedication of property to the public only if there is a nexus or rough proportionality between the property the government agency demands and the social costs of the permit applicant's development plans. 178

Kelo v. City of New London

Landowners (P) v. Municipality (D)

545 U.S. 469 (2005).

NATURE OF CASE: Suit for orders enjoining a city from taking private properties to promote the city's planned economic revitalization.

FACT SUMMARY: A city adopted a development plan designed to revitalize the local economy. To implement its plan, the city sought to condemn 15 properties owned by nine private landowners who refused to sell their properties to the city.

🏛 RULE OF LAW
A city's proposed taking of private property for general economic development qualifies as a public use consistent with the Takings Clause of the Fifth Amendment to the United States Constitution.

FACTS: In 1990, a Connecticut state agency officially designated the City of New London ("the City" or "New London") (D) as a "distressed municipality." New London's (D) economy worsened in 1996 when the federal government closed a facility that employed 1,500 people. The City's (D) unemployment rate almost doubled that for the rest of the state, and its population had dwindled to its lowest level in almost 80 years. State and local officials therefore targeted the City (D) for economic revitalization. Eventually a development plan focused on a 90-acre area known as Fort Trumbull as the center of the City's (D) revitalization efforts. The drafters designed the development plan to coincide with the expected arrival of a major company, Pfizer Inc., and to rejuvenate the local economy with jobs, tax revenue, and a generalized momentum for future growth and recreational activities. Most landowners in the Fort Trumbull area agreed to sell their properties to the City (D). Nine owners, however, refused to sell their 15 properties, and the City (D) initiated condemnation proceedings for the 15 properties. The City (D) condemned the properties purely because they were within the area designated for development; the City (D) never alleged that the properties were in any degree of substandard condition. Susette Kelo (P) and the other eight resisting owners sued the City (D) in state court, where the trial judge permanently enjoined the City (D) from taking 11 of the contested properties but permitted the taking of the other four properties. Both sides appealed to the Connecticut Supreme Court, which held that all 15 properties could properly be taken by New London (D). Applying state statute, that court held that the proposed taking was for a public use that satisfied both state and federal constitutional requirements. Kelo (P) and her fellow landowners petitioned the United States Supreme Court for further review.

ISSUE: Does a city's proposed taking of private property for general economic development qualify as a public use consistent with the Takings Clause of the Fifth Amendment to the United States Constitution?

HOLDING AND DECISION: (Stevens, J.) Yes. A city's proposed taking of private property for general economic development qualifies as a public use consistent with the Takings Clause of the Fifth Amendment to the United States Constitution. A government may not take private property merely to transfer it to another private owner; conversely, private property may be taken, if the taking is legitimately for "use by the public." Neither of these general propositions controls this case, though, because the question here narrows to whether a proposed taking for general economic development serves a "public purpose," which is the broader reading of "public use" that this Court has consistently used for more than a century. The Court upheld the redevelopment plan at issue in *Berman v. Parker*, 348 U.S. 26 (1954), because creating a "better balanced, more attractive community" was a valid public purpose. Similarly, in *Hawaii Housing Authority v. Midkiff*, 467 U.S. 229 (1984), the Court upheld a state statute that took fee title from lessors and vested title in lessees to eliminate the "social and economic evils of land oligopoly." These cases show that the determinative question is the proposed taking's purpose, not the specific means by which the government proposes to achieve its purpose. Under this appropriately deferential standard of review, New London's (D) proposed takings here do meet the public-use requirement imposed by the Takings Clause. Kelo's (P) request that the Court reject economic development as an acceptable public use contradicts not only precedent but also logic because no principled distinction exists between economic development and other accepted public uses. Further, her objection that economic development confuses the distinction between public and private use also contradicts precedent; public use often benefits specific private owners, too. Finally, Kelo's (P) objection that nothing would stop a city from transferring land from one private owner to another specific private owner for a public purpose presents issues that are not before the Court in this case. Accordingly, this Court's takings jurisprudence provides no basis for enjoining the City of New London (D) from taking the 15 properties in the Fort Trumbull area. Affirmed.

Continued on next page.

CONCURRENCE: (Kennedy, J.) Deferential review should not become so deferential that it ignores a taking designed primarily to favor another private party. Furthermore, a more stringent standard of review might apply in cases where economic development is the asserted public use.

DISSENT: (O'Connor, J.) Past cases have recognized three kinds of takings that meet the public-use requirement: transferring private property to public ownership, to private ownership for common public use, and to private ownership within a program serving a public purpose. The third category, represented by *Midkiff* and *Berman*, raises the most questions. The takings in those two cases addressed identifiable public harms (oligopoly and blight, respectively), but this case goes beyond curing a public harm—and it goes too far.

DISSENT: (Thomas, J.) The proper reading of the public use clause is that it allows the government to take property only if the government owns, or the public has a right to use, the property, as opposed to "taking" it for any purpose whatsoever. Extending the public purpose doctrine to encompass any economic development guarantees that the losses of property will fall disproportionately on poor communities who are the least politically powerful. Urban renewal projects have long been associated with the displacement of minorities and today's holding will further exacerbate these effects.

▶ *ANALYSIS*

Despite the firestorm of criticism that greeted the *Kelo* decision, the majority opinion fits only the most naive definitions of judicial activism. Indeed, at least in the casebook excerpts, it is Justice O'Connor's reasoning in dissent that seems the more ill-considered: If New London's (D) chronic and deepening economic demise does not qualify as a public harm, what does?

■══■

Quicknotes

EMINENT DOMAIN The governmental power to take private property for public use so long as just compensation is paid therefore.

FIFTH AMENDMENT Provides that no person shall be compelled to serve as a witness against himself, or be subject to trial for the same offense twice, or be deprived of life, liberty, or property without due process of law.

PUBLIC USE Basis for governmental taking of property pursuant to its power of eminent domain so that property taken may be utilized for the benefit of the public at large.

TAKING A governmental action that substantially deprives an owner of the use and enjoyment of his property, requiring compensation.

TAKINGS CLAUSE Provision of the Fifth Amendment to the United States Constitution prohibiting the government from taking private property for public use without providing just compensation therefor.

■══■

Loretto v. Teleprompter Manhattan CATV Corp.

Fee owners (P) v. State (D)

458 U.S. 419 (1982).

NATURE OF CASE: Appeal from enforcement of state statute.

FACT SUMMARY: Loretto (P) contended that a New York law requiring apartment house owners to allow for the installation of cable television equipment allowed a taking of property without just compensation.

🏛 RULE OF LAW
Any permanent physical occupation of an owner's property that is governmentally authorized constitutes a taking of property for which just compensation must be paid.

FACTS: New York enacted a statute that required apartment house owners to provide tenants with access to cable television reception. Loretto (P) brought a class action against Teleprompter Manhattan CATV Corp. (Teleprompter) (D), contending its placement of its cable television installation equipment constituted trespass and that the statute allowed for a taking of her property without just compensation. The trial court granted summary judgment for Teleprompter (D), upholding the constitutionality of the statute. The appellate court affirmed, and Loretto (P) appealed to the United States Supreme Court.

ISSUE: Is any permanent physical occupation of an owner's property that is authorized by the government a taking of property that requires the payment of just compensation?

HOLDING AND DECISION: (Marshall, J.) Yes. Any permanent physical occupation of an owner's property that is authorized by the government constitutes a taking of property that requires a payment of just compensation. Any occupation, no matter how slight, impacts on the owner's right to exclusive possession of his property. In this case, the equipment occupied a very small area of the property. Yet its presence constituted a physical occupation and thus necessarily must be classified as a taking of property within the meaning of the Fifth Amendment. Therefore, just compensation must be paid. Reversed and remanded.

DISSENT: (Blackmun, J.) The Court goes against established precedent by recognizing a per se "taking" rule. It has previously been held on many occasions that each taking case must be considered on its peculiar facts. A rigid per se rule finding a taking in every physical encroachment will require compensation in situations not justified under previous interpretations of the taking clause.

▶ ANALYSIS

The Court recognizes the fundamental inconsistency with the elements of private ownership presented by any physical invasion of the property by a stranger. When such an invasion is authorized by the government, a compensable taking occurs. The amount of money necessary to constitute just compensation will vary with the case. The Court declined to rule on whether the $1 per unit payment was sufficient in this case.

Quicknotes

CLASS ACTION A suit commenced by a representative on behalf of an ascertainable group that is too large to appear in court, who shares a commonality of interests and who will benefit from a successful result.

JUST COMPENSATION The right guaranteed by the Fifth Amendment to the United States Constitution of a person, when his property is taken for public use by the state, to receive adequate compensation in order to restore him to the position he enjoyed prior to the appropriation.

SUMMARY JUDGMENT Judgment rendered by a court in response to a motion by one of the parties, claiming that the lack of a question of material fact in respect to an issue warrants disposition of the issue without consideration by the jury.

TAKING A governmental action that substantially deprives an owner of the use and enjoyment of his or her property, requiring compensation.

TRESPASS Unlawful interference with, or damage to, the real or personal property of another.

Hadacheck v. Sebastian

Brick yard owner (P) v. Chief of police (D)

239 U.S. 394 (1915).

NATURE OF CASE: Appeal from decision upholding the validity of condemnation proceedings.

FACT SUMMARY: Hadacheck (P) was convicted of violating a municipal ordinance prohibiting the operation of a brick yard or brick kiln.

🏛 RULE OF LAW
A municipality may regulate business operations to prevent harm to the public.

FACTS: Hadacheck (P) was convicted of a misdemeanor for the violation of a Los Angeles city ordinance making it unlawful for any person to establish or operate a brick yard or brick kiln within the city limits. Hadacheck (P), whose business was established before the ordinance was enacted, asserted that his business was not a nuisance as defined under state statutes. The enforcement of the ordinance, according to Hadacheck (P), amounted to a taking of property without compensation, violating guarantees of due process. The California Supreme Court upheld the ordinance as a valid, nondiscriminatory regulatory measure.

ISSUE: May a municipality regulate business operations in order to prevent harm to the public?

HOLDING AND DECISION: (McKenna, J.) Yes. The imperative necessity of the police power precludes any limitation on its use when it is not exerted arbitrarily. There must be progress, and if in its march private interests are in the way they must yield to the good of the community. Even granting that Hadacheck's (P) business was not a nuisance per se, the municipality found that fumes and dust from Hadacheck's (P) brick-making plant had occasionally caused sickness and serious discomfort to those living in the vicinity. It may be that brick yards in other localities within the city where the same conditions exist are not regulated or prohibited, but it does not follow that they will not be. That Hadacheck's (P) business was first in time to be prohibited does not make its prohibition unlawful. Affirmed.

▌ ANALYSIS

The doctrines of eminent domain and police power are distinct and separate powers of the government. In eminent domain proceedings, land is taken by the state because it will thereby be of more use to the public. Under the police power, private property rights are impaired by the state not because they have become necessary or useful to the public, but because their free exercise is believed to be harmful to important public interests.

■=■

Quicknotes

CONDEMNATION The taking of private property for public use so long as just compensation is paid therefor.

DUE PROCESS CLAUSE Clauses found in the Fifth and Fourteenth Amendments to the United States Constitution providing that no person shall be deprived of "life, liberty, or property, without due process of law."

EMINENT DOMAIN The governmental power to take private property for public use so long as just compensation is paid therefor.

JUST COMPENSATION The right guaranteed by the Fifth Amendment to the United States Constitution of a person, when his property is taken for public use by the state, to receive adequate compensation in order to restore him to the position he enjoyed prior to the appropriation.

NUISANCE PER SE An action, occupation or building that is a nuisance at any time and under any condition.

POLICE POWER The power of a government to impose restrictions on the rights of private persons, as long as those restrictions are reasonably related to the promotion and protection of public health, safety, morals, and the general welfare.

PUBLIC INTEREST Something in which the public has either a monetary or legal interest.

TAKING A governmental action that substantially deprives an owner of the use and enjoyment of his or her property, requiring compensation.

■=■

Pennsylvania Coal Co. v. Mahon

Surface rights owner (P) v. Coal company (D)

260 U.S. 393 (1922).

NATURE OF CASE: Appeal from the granting of an injunction.

FACT SUMMARY: Mahon (P) desired to prevent the exercise of the mineral rights which the Pennsylvania Coal Co. (Coal Co.) (D) reserved in a deed transferring certain surface property to Mahon (P).

🏛 RULE OF LAW
Private property may be regulated pursuant to the police power of the state to protect public health, safety, or morals; but if such regulation goes so far as to destroy or appropriate a property right, it becomes a "taking" under the Fifth and Fourteenth Amendments, requiring just compensation therefor.

FACTS: In 1878, Coal Co. (D) transferred certain real property to Mahon (P) by a deed in which Coal Co. (D) reserved the mineral rights on the property and Mahon (P) waived all rights to object to or receive damages for the removal of such minerals. In 1921, the Pennsylvania legislature enacted the "Kohler Act," which forbade the mining of coal in such a way as to cause the subsidence of any human habitation. When Coal Co. (D) decided to exercise its mineral rights pursuant to the deed, Mahon (P) instituted an action for an injunction on the grounds that the mining would violate the Kohler Act by causing the subsidence of his home. From a decree granting the injunction, Coal Co. (D) appealed, contending that such an application of the statute would constitute a taking without compensation contrary to due process.

ISSUE: Will an exercise of the police power be upheld if it, in effect, provides for the destruction or appropriation of a private property right?

HOLDING AND DECISION: (Holmes, J.) No. Private property may be regulated pursuant to the police power of the state to protect public health, safety, or morals; but if such regulation goes so far as to destroy or appropriate a property right, it becomes a "taking" under the Fifth and Fourteenth Amendments, requiring just compensation therefor. It is well established, of course, that some property rights must yield to the public interest and the police power. Here, however, the limited public interest in protecting Mahon's (P) surface rights does not justify the total destruction of the mineral rights which Coal Co. (D) reserved in its deed to Mahon (P). As such, the Kohler Act is unconstitutional insofar as it fails to provide for compensation for the taking of Coal Co.'s (D) property rights. The decree that was based upon it is accordingly reversed.

DISSENT: (Brandeis, J.) No taking occurred here. Rather, the state merely exercised the police power to prevent a noxious use of property. The property remains in the possession of the owners.

▶ ANALYSIS

This case illustrates the minority rule. Generally, when a landowner conveys to someone else a right to take minerals underneath the surface of his land, the grantee owes the grantor-landowner the duty to support the surface in its natural state (i.e., without any buildings). Furthermore, generally, ownership of land carries with it the right to have the land supported in its natural state by adjoining land (i.e., the right to have the support of the land undisturbed by excavation on adjoining land). Under this general rule, if an adjoining landowner excavates in such a manner as to cause subsidence on one's own land, he is "absolutely liable" for such subsidence. If, however, there is a structure on the land which subsides "and the land would not have subsided but for such structure," the adjoining landowner is not liable as a matter of law (i.e., he is not "absolutely liable"), but he may be liable for negligent excavation.

━━━

Quicknotes

FIFTH AMENDMENT Provides that no person shall be compelled to serve as a witness against himself, or be subject to trial for the same offense twice, or be deprived of life, liberty, or property without due process of law.

FOURTEENTH AMENDMENT 42 U.S.C. § 1983 Defamation by state officials in connection with a discharge implies a violation of a liberty interest protected by the due process requirements of the United States Constitution.

INJUNCTION A court order requiring a person to do or prohibiting that person from doing a specific act.

KOHLER ACT Legislation passed in 1921 that prohibited the mining of coal that would cause the caving in, collapse, or subsidence of a number of specific structures or public facilities.

POLICE POWER The power of a government to impose restrictions on the rights of private persons, as long as those restrictions are reasonably related to the promotion and protection of public health, safety, morals, and the general welfare.

━━━

Penn Central Transportation Company v. City of New York

Railroad (P) v. City (D)

438 U.S. 104 (1978).

NATURE OF CASE: Appeal from denial of compensatory relief.

FACT SUMMARY: Penn Central Transportation Company (Penn Central) (P) contended that New York (D) had taken its property without just compensation when it declared its station a historical landmark.

RULE OF LAW
A city may place restrictions on the development of individual historic landmarks without effecting a taking requiring just compensation.

FACTS: In 1965, New York City (D) adopted the Landmarks Preservation Law, which was enacted to identify and preserve historic and scenic landmarks. Under the law, the Landmarks Preservation Commission would identify properties and areas to be designated as landmarks. The owner of the property in question had the right to appeal the decision at several levels, including judicial review. The law also allowed such property owners to transfer development rights to other parcels of land. On January 22, 1968, Penn Central (P) entered into a contract with UGP Properties, Inc. to construct a multistory office building above the Grand Central Terminal, which had previously been designated a landmark. After the Commission rejected its application, Penn Central (P) filed suit, alleging that the application of the law had taken its property without just compensation in violation of the Fifth and Fourteenth Amendments. The New York Court of Appeals found no denial of due process, and Penn Central (P) appealed.

ISSUE: May a city place restrictions on the development of individual historic landmarks without effecting a taking requiring just compensation?

HOLDING AND DECISION: (Brennan, J.) Yes. In deciding whether a particular governmental action has effected a taking, the focus is both on the character of the action and on the nature and extent of the interference with rights in the parcel as a whole. It is true that the Landmarks Law has a more severe impact on some landowners than on others, but that in itself does not mean that the law effects a taking. Legislation designed to promote the general welfare commonly burdens some more than others. The Landmarks Law's effect is simply to prohibit Penn Central (P) or anyone else from occupying portions of the air space above the Terminal, while permitting Penn Central (P) to use the remainder of the parcel in a gainful fashion. The New York City (D) law is not rendered invalid by its failure to provide just compensation whenever a landmark owner is restricted in the exploitation of property interests, such as air rights, to a greater extent than provided for under applicable zoning laws. The restrictions imposed are substantially related to the promotion of the general welfare and not only permit reasonable beneficial use of the landmark site but also affords Penn Central (P) opportunities further to enhance not only the Terminal site, but also other properties. Affirmed.

DISSENT: (Rehnquist, J.) The City of New York (D) has imposed a substantial cost on less than one one-tenth of one percent of the buildings in New York City for the general benefit of all its people. It is exactly this imposition of general costs on a few individuals at which the taking protection is directed.

▶ ANALYSIS

One commentary on this case, states: "The majority implied that esthetics is no less a compelling governmental interest than public health and that the relative sizes of the groups benefited and burdened are, at best, of minor importance. With the tests upon which many courts have come to rely no longer controlling, the protection of private property from governmental interference will depend more than ever on each court's subjective interpretation of 'fairness and justice.'" "The Supreme Court, 1977 Term," 92 *Harv. L. Rev.* 57, 228–232 (1978).

Quicknotes

DUE PROCESS The constitutional mandate requiring the courts to protect and enforce individuals' rights and liberties consistent with prevailing principles of fairness and justice and prohibiting the federal and state governments from such activities that deprive its citizens of life, liberty, or property interest.

TAKINGS CLAUSE Provision of the Fifth Amendment to the United States Constitution prohibiting the government from taking private property for public use without providing just compensation therefor.

Lucas v. South Carolina Coastal Council

Beachfront property owner (P) v. State (D)

505 U.S. 1003 (1992).

NATURE OF CASE: Appeal from reversal of award of damages in action for compensation under the Takings Clause.

FACT SUMMARY: After Lucas (P) invested $975,000 in two beachfront lots, South Carolina (D) enacted a statute prohibiting construction on the barrier islands where the lots were located, entitling him, he contended, to compensation under the Takings Clause.

🏛 RULE OF LAW
The state must compensate a landowner when a regulatory action denies an owner economically viable use of his land, unless the prohibited use of the land constitutes a nuisance under state common law.

FACTS: Lucas (P) purchased two residential lots for $975,000 on the Isle of Palms, a barrier island off the coast of South Carolina, on which he planned to build single-family homes. The Isle of Palms development, of which Lucas (P) was a co-owner, was located on highly unstable ground, prone to flooding and erosion. At the time of purchase, the state, county, and town had not imposed any restrictions on residential use of the property. However, two years after Lucas's (P) purchase, but before he began construction, South Carolina (D) enacted the Beachfront Management Act (the Act), in an attempt to counteract the critical erosion of South Carolina beaches. The Act prohibited, without exception, the construction of any habitable improvements seaward of a baseline connecting historical points of erosion on the Isle of Palms. Lucas's (P) lots were located within the restricted area. He filed suit against South Carolina (D), contending that the Act's ban on construction amounted to a taking of his property without just compensation. He conceded that the Act was a lawful exercise of South Carolina's (D) police power but claimed that the Act rendered his property valueless, entitling him to compensation. The trial court agreed and ordered South Carolina (D) to pay $1,232,387. The Supreme Court of South Carolina reversed, ruling that when an otherwise valid regulation respecting the use of property is designed to prevent public harm, as this Act was, no compensation was owed. Lucas (P) appealed, and the United States Supreme Court granted certiorari.

ISSUE: Must the state compensate a landowner when a regulatory action denies an owner economically viable use of his land?

HOLDING AND DECISION: (Scalia, J.) Yes. The state must compensate a landowner when a regulatory action denies an owner economically valuable use of his land, unless the prohibited use of the land constitutes a nuisance under state common law. Traditionally, compensation has been required for two separate categories of regulatory actions: (1) those that cause a physical invasion of private property and (2) those that deprive a landowner of all economically beneficial or productive use of land. However, there is also a long line of cases denying compensation to owners whose property is regulated to prevent a public harm, the seminal case being *Mugler v. Kansas*, 123 U.S. 623 (1887), in which a law prohibiting the manufacture of alcoholic beverages was sustained against a taking claim brought by a brewery owner. Under this line of cases, regulation of "harmful or noxious uses" of property was allowed to affect property values without obligating the government to pay compensation. This early focus on noxious uses later evolved into the Court's contemporary analysis that finds no taking if a land-use regulation substantially advances a legitimate state interest. Whether the regulation prevents a harmful use can no longer be the basis for an exception from the rule that total regulatory taking must be compensated; if it were, no compensation would ever be necessary, since most regulations may be described as mitigating some harm, depending on the observer's point of view. Instead, a better test is that confiscatory regulations, i.e., those that prohibit all economically beneficial use of land, may not be enacted without compensation, unless the regulation serves to prohibit a purpose that was already unlawful under existing nuisance and property law. In this case, the Act rendered Lucas's (P) lots valueless by requiring that they remain in their natural state. Therefore, South Carolina (D) must either identify the relevant common-law principles of nuisance and property that would prohibit construction on Lucas's (P) beachfront property or compensate him for the value of his property. Reversed and remanded.

CONCURRENCE: (Kennedy, J.) The majority provided the lower courts with guidance regarding the analysis on remand, but did not reach the ultimate question of whether a taking had occurred. The factual record is not complete. It is an open question whether the owner of the property actually intended to build homes on the property. The majority improperly concludes that the beach front property loses all value based on the new regulations. However, the determination of value must be considered by referring to the owner's reasonable expectations. Those reasonable expectations are shaped by what the judicial

Continued on next page.

branch says about how far legislatures can go when regulating property. Where a regulatory taking allegedly deprives the property of all value, the test is whether the deprivation is inconsistent with reasonable, investment-backed expectations of the property owner.

CONCURRENCE: (Souter, J.) This Court improperly granted a writ of certiorari to this appeal. The state trial court concluded that the state regulation deprived the owner of his entire economic interest in the property. That no longer appears to be the case, based on our prior decisions. The issue of whether a total deprivation occurred is not reviewable and was not briefed by the parties. Because the factual record is not complete, the Court should not have accepted this case for further review.

DISSENT: (Blackmun, J.) This Court has consistently upheld regulations that prohibit an owner from using his property in a way that is harmful to the public. Lucas (P) never challenged the legislature's findings that a building ban was necessary to protect property and life and, therefore, the lower court correctly found no taking. Now, with this case, the majority has created a new rule and an exception, based on the trial court's finding that the property had lost all economic value. Furthermore, the majority alters the traditional rule that the plaintiff challenge the constitutionality of an ordinance, by requiring the state to convince the courts that its legislative judgments are correct. Finally, the majority decides that it will permit a state to regulate all economic value only if the state prohibits uses that would not be permitted under state common law, notwithstanding that the Court has previously and explicitly rejected any consideration of a nuisance when evaluating a taking. There is no reason to believe the majority's claim that new interpretation of old common-law nuisance doctrine will be any more objective or value-free than reliance on legislative judgments of what constitutes harm.

DISSENT: (Stevens, J.) The majority's categorical rule that total regulatory takings must be compensated is an unsound and unwise addition to the law, unsupported by prior decisions, and its exception to that rule is too rigid and too narrow. Because the majority's new rule only applies to total regulatory takings, it arbitrarily awards compensation to a landowner whose property is diminished by 100 percent, while denying compensation to one who suffers a 95 percent diminishment. Furthermore, the Court's holding effectively freezes a state's traditional common law, making it immune to legislative revision.

▶ ANALYSIS

Note that the central debate in Lucas is actually over who should have the authority to allocate loss. Lucas allocates the authority to decide which regulations will require compensation to the state judiciary, rather than to the state legislature. Lucas implies that the state's ability to

completely extinguish the value of a parcel of land gives it too much power and potential for excessive legislative regulation, necessitating an independent judicial determination of what constitutes a nuisance. Although Lucas was the most closely watched land-use case of 1991 (over 50 amicus briefs were filed), its impact may turn out to be relatively slight since its fact pattern is relatively rare.

Quicknotes

CERTIORARI A discretionary writ issued by a superior court to an inferior court in order to review the lower court's decisions; the United States Supreme Court's writ ordering such review.

JUST COMPENSATION The right guaranteed by the Fifth Amendment to the United States Constitution of a person, when his property is taken for public use by the state, to receive adequate compensation in order to restore him to the position he enjoyed prior to the appropriation.

NUISANCE An unlawful use of property that interferes with the lawful use of another's property.

REGULATORY TAKING A governmental action that substantially deprives an owner of the use and enjoyment of his property, whereby the application of a law or regulation deprives the owner of economically viable use of his property, requiring compensation.

TAKINGS CLAUSE Provision of the Fifth Amendment to the United States Constitution prohibiting the government from taking private property for public use without providing just compensation therefor.

Palazzolo v. Rhode Island

Developer (P) v. State (D)

533 U.S. 606 (2001).

NATURE OF CASE: Inverse condemnation action.

FACT SUMMARY: Palazzolo (P) brought an inverse condemnation suit against Rhode Island (D) after his development proposals for a parcel of waterfront property were rejected.

🏛 RULE OF LAW
A purchaser or successive title holder is not barred from bringing a takings claim by the mere fact that the title was acquired after the effective date of the state regulation.

FACTS: Palazzolo (P) owned a waterfront parcel of land, almost all of which was designated as coastal wetlands. After his development proposals were rejected he filed suit in state court claiming the State's (D) application of its wetlands regulations constituted a taking in violation of the Fifth Amendment. The Rhode Island Supreme Court rejected the claim that Palazzolo (P) was denied all economically beneficial use of the property since the regulation predated his ownership of the property. Palazzolo (P) appealed.

ISSUE: Is a purchaser or successive title holder barred from bringing a takings claim by the mere fact that the title was acquired after the effective date of the state regulation?

HOLDING AND DECISION: (Kennedy, J.) No. A purchaser or successive title holder is not barred from bringing a takings claim by the mere fact that the title was acquired after the effective date of the state regulation. We agree with the court's decision that all economically viable use of the property was not deprived since the uplands portion of the property could still be developed. Reversed in part, affirmed in part, and remanded.

CONCURRENCE: (O'Connor, J.) The majority is correct that the Rhode Island Supreme Court erred when it barred all takings claims based on any use restrictions that were in place prior to the purchase of the property in question. This Court has held in the past that justice and fairness dictates compensating those members of the public that are more affected by land-use regulations than others. There is no set formula for determining when justice and fairness require compensation from the government. One significant factor is the nature and extent of permitted development under the local regulatory regime. The takings analysis is always a fact-specific inquiry.

CONCURRENCE: (Scalia, J.) The fact that a land-use regulation exists and is on the books prior to the purchase of the property at issue should have no bearing on the takings analysis. Courts should never presume that a land-use restriction is constitutional simply because it has not been challenged.

CONCURRENCE AND DISSENT: (Stevens, J.) The purchaser of the property at issue in this case purchased from another. Her predecessor in interest owned the property at the time the regulation was enacted. Accordingly, a taking occurred at that point and any compensation must be paid to the owner of the property at the time the regulation was enacted. Accordingly, the current owner of the property has no standing to bring the current claim.

DISSENT: (Ginsburg, J.) It is not clear from the record that the petitioner here ever received a final decision from the state regarding his application to build. If a petitioner in a takings action does not receive a final decision, the takings claim may not be ripe for judicial review. In addition, other justices are correct that a transfer of title will obviously affect a new owner's takings claim.

DISSENT: (Breyer, J.) Justice Ginsburg is correct that this takings claim is not ripe for adjudication. Accordingly, I dissent. However, I do agree with Justice O'Connor's statement that the transfer of ownership will not automatically bar a subsequent owner from challenging a land-use regulation.

▶ ANALYSIS

The Court here did away with the prior rule under *Lucas*, 505 U.S. 1003 (1992), and *Penn Central*, 438 U.S. 104 (1978), that a purchaser or successive title holder was deemed to have notice of an earlier-enacted restriction and was barred from bringing a takings claim. The Court also held that a state does not avoid the duty to compensate based on a "token interest." So long as a landowner is permitted to build a substantial residence on the parcel, then it is not deemed to constitute a deprivation of all economic value.

■▬■

Quicknotes

FIFTH AMENDMENT Provides that no person shall be compelled to serve as a witness against himself, or be subject to trial for the same offense twice, or be deprived of life, liberty, or property without due process of law.

Continued on next page.

INVERSE CONDEMNATION Taking of private property for public use so as to impair or decrease the value of property near or adjacent to, but not a part of, the property taken.

NOTICE Communication of information to a person by an authorized person or an otherwise proper source.

TAKING A governmental action that substantially deprives an owner of the use and enjoyment of his or her property, requiring compensation.

Tahoe-Sierra Preservation Council, Inc. v. Tahoe Regional Planning Agency

Landowners (P) v. Regional planning agency (D)

535 U.S. 302 (2002).

NATURE OF CASE: Appeal from reversal of judgment finding a per se taking of property.

FACT SUMMARY: Tahoe Regional Planning Agency (TRPA) (D) imposed two moratoria, totaling 32 months, on development in the Lake Tahoe Basin while formulating a comprehensive land-use plan for the area. Landowners (P) affected by the moratoria filed suit, claiming that TRPA's (D) actions constituted a taking of their property without just compensation in violation of the Takings Clause.

RULE OF LAW
A moratorium on development imposed during the process of devising a comprehensive land-use plan does not constitute a per se taking of property requiring compensation under the Takings Clause.

FACTS: Tahoe Regional Planning Agency (TRPA) (D) imposed two moratoria, one, from 1981 to 1983, and a more restrictive one, from 1983 to 1984, totaling 32 months, on development in the Lake Tahoe region while formulating a comprehensive land-use plan of environmentally sound growth for the area. During the moratoria, virtually all development was prohibited. Landowners (P) affected by the moratoria filed suit, claiming that TRPA's (D) actions constituted a taking of their property without just compensation in violation of the Takings Clause. The district court found a taking, but the court of appeals reversed. The United States Supreme Court granted review.

ISSUE: Does a moratorium on development imposed during the process of devising a comprehensive land-use plan constitute a per se taking of property requiring compensation under the Takings Clause?

HOLDING AND DECISION: (Stevens, J.) No. A moratorium on development imposed during the process of devising a comprehensive land-use plan does not constitute a per se taking of property requiring compensation under the Takings Clause. The attack on the moratoria is only facial. The landowners contend that the mere enactment of a temporary regulation that, while in effect, denies a property owner of all viable economic use of the property gives rise to an unqualified constitutional obligation to compensate for the value of the property's use during that period. The landowners want a categorical rule, but the Court's cases do not support such a rule. The answer to any given case depends on the particular circumstances of the case, and the circumstances in this case are best analyzed within the framework of *Penn Central Transp. Co. v.*

New York, 438 U.S. 104 (1978). The long-standing distinction between physical and regulatory takings makes it inappropriate to treat precedent from one as controlling on the other. The landowners (P) in this case rely on *First English Evangelical Lutheran Church of Glendale v. County of Los Angeles*, 482 U.S. 304 (1987) and *Lucas v. South Carolina Coastal Council*, 505 U.S. 1003 (1992)—both regulatory takings cases—to argue for a categorical rule that whenever the government imposes a deprivation of all economically viable use of property, no matter how brief, it effects a taking. In *First English*, the Court addressed the separate remedial question of how compensation is measured once a regulatory taking is established, but not the different and prior question whether the temporary regulation was in fact a taking. Nor is *Lucas* dispositive of the question presented. Its categorical rule—requiring compensation when a regulation permanently deprives an owner of "all economically beneficial uses" of his land—does not answer the question whether a regulation prohibiting any economic use of land for 32 months must be compensated. The landowners (P) attempt to bring this case under the rule in *Lucas* by focusing exclusively on the property during the moratoria is unavailing. This Court has consistently rejected such an approach to the "denominator" question. To sever a 32-month segment from the remainder of each fee simple estate and then ask whether that segment has been taken in its entirety would ignore *Penn Central's* admonition to focus on "the parcel as a whole." Both dimensions of a real property interest—the metes and bounds describing its geographic dimensions and the term of years describing its temporal aspect—must be considered when viewing the interest in its entirety. A permanent deprivation of all use is a taking of the parcel as a whole, but a temporary restriction causing a diminution in value is not, for the property will recover value when the prohibition is lifted. *Lucas* was carved out for the "extraordinary case" in which a regulation permanently deprives property of all use; the default rule remains that a fact specific inquiry is required in the regulatory taking context. Nevertheless, the Court will consider the landowners' (P) argument that the interest in protecting property owners from bearing public burdens "which, in all fairness and justice, should be borne by the public as a whole," justifies creating a new categorical rule. "Fairness and justice" will not be better served by a categorical rule that any deprivation of all economic use, no matter how brief, constitutes a compensable taking. That rule would apply to numerous

Continued on next page.

normal delays—in obtaining building permits, variances, zoning changes, etc.—and would require changes in practices that have long been considered permissible exercises of the police power. Such an important change in the law should be the product of legislative rulemaking, not adjudication. More importantly, the better approach to a temporary regulatory taking claim requires careful examination and weighing of all the relevant circumstances— only one of which is the length of the delay. A narrower rule excluding normal delays in processing permits, or covering only delays of more than a year, would have a less severe impact on prevailing practices, but would still impose serious constraints on the planning process. Moratoria are an essential tool of successful development. The interest in informed decision-making counsels against adopting a per se rule that would treat such interim measures as takings—regardless of the planners' good faith, the landowners' reasonable expectations, or the moratorium's actual impact on property values. The financial constraints of compensating property owners during a moratorium may force officials to rush through the planning process or abandon the practice altogether. And the interest in protecting the decisional process is even stronger when an agency is developing a regional plan than when it is considering a permit for a single parcel. Here, TRPA obtained the benefit of comments and criticisms from interested parties during its deliberations, but a categorical rule tied to the deliberations' length would likely create added pressure on decision makers to quickly resolve land-use questions, disadvantaging landowners and interest groups less organized or familiar with the planning process. Moreover, with a temporary development ban, there is less risk that individual landowners will be singled out to bear a special burden that should be shared by the public as a whole. It may be true that a moratorium lasting more than one year should be viewed with special skepticism, but the district court found that the instant delay was not unreasonable. The restriction's duration is one factor for a court to consider in appraising regulatory takings claims, but with respect to that factor, the temptation to adopt per se rules in either direction must be resisted. Affirmed.

DISSENT: (Rehnquist, C.J.) The relevant time frame here is not, as the majority indicates, 32 months, but rather it is six years because the 1984 Regional Plan that was implemented after the moratoria were lifted also denied landowners (P) all use of their property until 1987, thus extending the period from 1981 to 1987. Neither the takings clause nor the Court's precedent, supports a distinction between "temporary" and "permanent" prohibitions. Such a distinction is tenuous—here, the "temporary" prohibition lasted six years, whereas the "permanent" prohibition in *Lucas* lasted only two years. Using this distinction, the government only has to label its prohibition "temporary" in order avoid compensation. Such a designation would not preclude the government from repeatedly extending the "temporary" prohibition into a long-term ban on all development. Even if a practical distinction between temporary

and permanent deprivations were plausible, to treat the two differently in terms of takings law would be at odds with the justification for the *Lucas* rule. The *Lucas* rule is derived from the fact that a total deprivation of use is, from the landowner's point of view, the equivalent of a physical appropriation. Because the rationale for the *Lucas* rule applies just as strongly in this case, the "temporary" denial of all viable use of land for six years is a taking. The majority is concerned that applying *Lucas* here would compel a finding that many traditional, short-term, land-use planning devices are takings. However, the Court has recognized that property rights are enjoyed under an implied limitation. When a regulation merely delays a final land use decision, there are other background principles of state property law that prevent the delay from being deemed a taking, as in the case of normal delays in obtaining building permits, changes in zoning ordinances, variances, and the like. Thus, the short-term delays attendant to zoning and permit regimes are a longstanding feature of state property law and part of a landowner's reasonable investment-backed expectations. But a moratorium prohibiting all economic use for a period of six years is not one of the longstanding, implied limitations of state property law. As is the case with most governmental action that furthers the public interest, here the preservation of Lake Tahoe should be borne by the public at large and not just by a few landowners, and the moratoria constitute a taking that requires compensation.

▶ *ANALYSIS*

With this case, the majority of the Court seems to have adopted the approach recommended by Justice O'Connor's concurring opinion in *Palazzolo v. Rhode Island*, 533 U.S. 606 (2001)—namely, an ad hoc approach that evaluates the circumstances of each case using the *Penn Central* framework—and rejected a categorical rule for all regulatory takings cases. The majority also seemed to resolve the "denominator" issue that had hitherto been unsettled in takings jurisprudence.

Quicknotes

CONDEMNATION The taking of private property for public use so long as just compensation is paid therefor.

LAND-USE PLAN General plan for real estate, including local zoning ordinances or real estate development scheme.

MORATORIUM Suspension of legal remedies or proceedings.

REGULATARY TAKING A governmental action that substantially deprives an owner of the use and enjoyment of his property; where the application of a law or regulation deprives the owner of economically viable use of his property, requiring compensation.

Stop the Beach Renourishment, Inc. v. Florida Department of Environmental Protection

Beachfront property owners (P) v. State (D)

560 U.S. 702 (2010).

NATURE OF CASE: Appeal from the determination by the state's highest that legislation to restore and maintain beaches, a process that modifies private property boundary lines, did not constitute a judicial taking or violate the due process clause.

FACT SUMMARY: Florida adopted legislation to restore and maintain beaches. With the proposed increase in the width of the beaches, a new boundary line would be created, altering the common-law boundary rights of beachfront property owners. After unsuccessfully changing the State's (D) administrative agency's determinations, Stop the Beach (a nonprofit group, hereinafter "Plaintiffs") (P) sought an appeal and rehearing, which were also denied. The Plaintiffs (P) appealed, arguing that the state supreme court's decision constituted a judicial taking or violated their rights to due process.

RULE OF LAW
(1) In upholding the state's legislation to restore beaches, a process that modifies private property boundary lines, the court's decision does not constitute a judicial taking or violate the due process clause.
(2) Beachfront property owners do not have a right of accretion superior to the state's right to fill in reclaimed land.

FACTS: The State (D) holds in trust for the public the land permanently submerged beneath navigable waters and the foreshore (the land between the low-tide line and the mean high-water line). Thus, the mean high-water line is the ordinary boundary between private beachfront, or littoral property, and state-owned land. At the center of this case is the right to accretions and relictions. Accretions are additions of alluvions (sand, sediment, or other deposits) to waterfront land; relictions are lands once covered by water that become dry when the water recedes). In Florida, at common law, the beachfront or littoral owner automatically takes title to dry land added to his property; but formerly submerged land that has become dry by avulsion continues to belong to the State.

Florida's Beach and Shore Preservation Act establishes procedures for beach restoration and nourishment projects designed to deposit sand on eroded beaches (restoration) and to maintain the deposited sand (nourishment). Once a beach restoration is determined to be undertaken the State's (D) Board of Trustees of the Internal Improvement Trust Fund (Board) sets what is called "an erosion control line," in reference to the existing mean high-water line. Once the

erosion-control new line is recorded, the common law ceases to apply. Thus, when accretion moves the mean high-water line seaward, the property of beachfront landowners is not extended to that line, but remains bounded by the permanent erosion-control line.

Residents of several jurisdictions sought permits to restore 6.9 miles of beach eroded by several hurricanes that would add about 75 feet of dry sand seaward of the mean high-water line (to be denominated the erosion-control line). Plaintiffs' (P) members, Stop the Beach Renourishment, Inc., a nonprofit corporation formed by owners of beachfront property bordering the project, brought suit against the "State" (D) when the State's Department of Environmental Protection (D) approved the permit. The District Court of Appeal for the First District concluded that the State's (D) order had eliminated the Plaintiffs' (D) littoral rights (1) to receive accretions to their properties and (2) to have their property's contact with the water remain intact. Deciding that this would be an unconstitutional "taking" and would require an additional administrative requirement to be met, the court set aside the order, remanded the proceeding, and certified to the Florida Supreme Court the question whether the Beach and Shore Preservation Act (the Act) unconstitutionally deprived the Plaintiffs (P) of littoral rights without just compensation. The Florida Supreme Court answered in the negative and quashed the remand, concluding that the Plaintiffs (P) did not have a right to the property supposedly taken. The request for a rehearing on the grounds that the decision effected a taking of the Plaintiffs' (P) littoral rights contrary to the Fifth and Fourteenths was denied. The United States Supreme Court then granted certiorari.

ISSUE:
(1) In upholding Florida legislation to restore beaches, a process that modifies private property boundary lines, did the Florida court's decision constitute a judicial taking or violate the due process clause?
(2) Do beachfront property owners have a right of accretion superior to the state's right to fill in reclaimed land?

HOLDING AND DECISION: (Scalia, J.)
(1) No. In upholding Florida legislation to restore beaches, a process that modifies private property boundary lines, the Florida court's decision did not constitute a judicial taking or violate the due process clause. The Takings Clause ("nor shall private property be taken for public

Continued on next page.

use, without just compensation," United States Constitution, Amendment 5) applies as fully to the taking of a landowner's riparian rights as it does to the taking of an estate in land. Moreover, though the classic taking is a transfer of property to the state or to another private party by eminent domain, the Takings Clause applies to other state actions that achieve the same thing. Thus, when the government uses its own property in such a way that it destroys private property, it has taken that property. Similarly, our doctrine of regulatory takings aims to identify regulatory actions that are functionally equivalent to the classic taking. Thus, it is a taking when a state regulation forces a property owner to submit to a permanent physical occupation, or deprives him of all economically beneficial use of his property. *Lucas* v. *South Carolina Coastal Council*, 505 U.S. 1003 (1992). Finally, states effect a taking if they re-characterize as public property what was previously private property. The Takings Clause (unlike, for instance, the Ex Post Facto Clauses) is not addressed to the action of a specific branch or branches. It is concerned simply with the act, and not with the governmental actor. There is no textual justification for saying that the existence or the scope of a state's power to expropriate private property without just compensation varies according to the branch of government effecting the expropriation. Nor does common sense recommend such a principle. It would be absurd to allow a state to do by judicial decree what the Takings Clause forbids it to do by legislative fiat. In sum, the Takings Clause bars the state from taking private property without paying for it, no matter which branch is the instrument of the taking. To be sure, the manner of state action may matter. Condemnation by eminent domain, for example, is always a taking, while a legislative, executive, or judicial restriction of property use may or may not be, depending on its nature and extent. But the particular state actor is irrelevant. If a legislature or a court declares that what was once an established right of private property no longer exists, it has taken that property, no less than if the State (D) had physically appropriated it or destroyed its value by regulation. Plaintiffs (P) put forward a number of arguments that contradict, to a greater or lesser degree, the principle that the existence of a taking does not depend upon the branch of government that effects it. First, in a case claiming a judicial taking they would add to the normal takings inquiry a requirement that the court's decision have no "fair and substantial basis." To assure that there is no "evasion" of judicial authority to review federal questions, courts have insisted that the nonfederal ground of decision have "fair support." A test designed to determine whether there has been an evasion is not obviously appropriate for determining whether there has been a taking of property. But if it is to be extended there it must mean that there is a "fair and substantial basis" for believing that Plaintiffs (P) did not have a property

right to future accretions which the Act would take away. This is no different from the requirement that Plaintiffs (P) must prove the elimination of an established property right. Next, Plaintiffs (P) argue that federal courts lack the knowledge of state law required to decide whether a judicial decision that purports merely to clarify property rights has instead taken them. But federal courts must often decide what state property rights exist in nontakings contexts. A constitutional provision that forbids the uncompensated taking of property is quite simply insusceptible of enforcement by federal courts unless they have the power to decide what property rights exist under state law. Plaintiffs (P) also warn against depriving common-law judging of needed flexibility. That argument has little appeal when directed against the enforcement of a constitutional guarantee adopted in an era when, courts had no power to "change" the common law. But in any case, courts have no peculiar need of flexibility. It is no more essential that judges be free to overrule prior cases that establish property entitlements than that state legislators be free to revise pre-existing statutes that confer property entitlements, or agency heads pre-existing regulations that do so. And insofar as courts merely clarify and elaborate property entitlements that were previously unclear, they cannot be said to have taken an established property right. For its part, Plaintiffs (P) propose an unpredictability test, arguing that a judicial taking consists of a decision that "'constitutes a sudden change in state law, unpredictable in terms of relevant precedents.'" The focus of Plaintiffs' (P) test is misdirected. What counts is not whether there is precedent for the allegedly confiscatory decision, but whether the property right allegedly taken was established. A "predictability of change" test would cover both too much and too little. Too much, because a judicial property decision need not be predictable, so long as it does not declare that what had been private property under established law no longer is. A decision that clarifies property entitlements (or the lack thereof), which were previously unclear, might be difficult to predict but it does not eliminate established property rights. And the predictability test covers too little, because a judicial elimination of established private-property rights that is foreshadowed by dicta or even by holdings years in advance is nonetheless a taking. Plaintiffs' (P) argue that the state supreme court took two of the property rights of the Plaintiffs (P) by declaring that those rights did not exist: the right to accretions and the right to have littoral property touch the water. There is no taking unless Plaintiffs (P) can show that, before the state supreme court's decision, littoral-property owners had rights to future accretions and contact with the water superior to the State's (D) right to fill in its sub-

Continued on next page.

merged land. Though some may think the question close, the showing cannot be made. Two core principles of state property law intersect in this case. First, the State (D) as owner of the submerged land adjacent to littoral property has the right to fill that land, so long as it does not interfere with the rights of the public and the rights of littoral landowners. Second, if an avulsion exposes land seaward of littoral property that had previously been submerged, that land belongs to the State (D) even if it interrupts the littoral owner's contact with the water.

(2) No. Beachfront property owners do not have a right of accretion superior to the state's right to fill in reclaimed land. The issue here is whether there is an exception to this rule when the State (D) is the cause of the avulsion. Prior law suggests there is not. Thus, state law has allowed the State (D) to fill in its own seabed, and the resulting sudden exposure of previously submerged land was treated like an avulsion for purposes of ownership. The right to accretions was therefore subordinate to the State's (D) right to fill. The state supreme court decision is consistent with these background principles of state property law. It did not abolish the Plaintiffs' (P) right to future accretions, but merely held that the right was not implicated by the beach-restoration project, because the doctrine of avulsion applied. Plaintiffs (P) also contend that the State (D) took their littoral right to have their property continually maintain contact with the water. Plaintiffs (P) argue instead that they have a separate right for the boundary of their property to be always the mean high-water line. The state supreme court states that "there is no independent right of contact with the water" but it "exists to preserve the upland owner's core littoral right of access to the water." Because the state supreme court's decision did not contravene the established property rights of Plaintiffs (P), the State (D) has not violated the Fifth and Fourteenth Amendments. Because the Florida Supreme Court's decision did not contravene the established property rights of Plaintiffs (P), Florida has not violated the Fifth and Fourteenth Amendments. The judgment of the Florida Supreme Court is therefore affirmed.

CONCURRENCE: (Kennedy, J.) The analysis of the principles that control ownership of the land in question, and of the rights of Plaintiffs (P) as adjacent owners, is correct. This case does not require a determination whether, or when, a judicial decision determining the rights of property owners can violate the Takings Clause of the Fifth Amendment. This separate question notes certain difficulties that should be considered before accepting the theory that a judicial decision that eliminates an established property right constitutes a violation.

If a judicial decision, as opposed to an act of the executive or the legislature, eliminates an established property right, the judgment could be set aside as a deprivation of property without due process of law. The Due Process Clause, in both its substantive and procedural aspects, is a central limitation upon the exercise of judicial power. When courts act without direction from the executive or legislature, they may not have the power to eliminate established property rights by judicial decision. Courts, unlike the executive or legislature, are not designed to make policy decisions about "the need for, and likely effectiveness of, regulatory actions." The Court would be on strong footing in ruling that a judicial decision that eliminates or substantially changes established property rights, which are a legitimate expectation of the owner, is "arbitrary or irrational" under the Due Process Clause.

CONCURRENCE: (Breyer, J.) There is no unconstitutional taking of property occurred in this case. Parts of the plurality unnecessarily address question of constitutional law that are better left for another day.

▶ ANALYSIS

The Court's plurality opinion held that the adjacent beachfront property owners could not show they had rights to the future exposed land and contact with the water superior to the State's (D) right to fill in submerged land. The State's (D) right to modify Plaintiffs' (P) boundaries was consistent with the doctrine of avulsion. It did not, however, view the Plaintiffs' rights to future accretions to be forbidden. This was a key determination before deciding whether the Florida Supreme Court effectuated a taking without just compensation in violation of the Fifth and Fourteenth Amendments.

━■━■

Quicknotes

TAKING A governmental action that substantially deprives an owner of the use and enjoyment of his property, requiring compensation.

TAKINGS CLAUSE Provision of the Fifth Amendment to the United States Constitution prohibiting the government from taking private property for public use without providing just compensation therefor.

━■━■

Nollan v. California Coastal Commission

Beachfront property owner (P) v. State (D)

483 U.S. 825 (1987).

NATURE OF CASE: Review of court order upholding conditional land-use permit.

FACT SUMMARY: The California Coastal Commission (D) conditioned a building permit on the owners' granting of a public beach access easement.

🏛 RULE OF LAW
A state may not condition a property use permit on an act not addressing the problem caused by the permitted use.

FACTS: The Nollans (P) owned certain beachfront property. They applied for a permit to build a residence upon it. The California Coastal Commission (D), finding that such a use would impede public viewing of the beach, conditioned the permit upon the Nollans' (P) granting of a public easement permitting lateral movement along the Nollans' (P) property to adjacent public beaches. The Nollans (P) challenged this as a deprivation of property rights without due process. The trial court agreed and enjoined the condition. The court of appeal reversed. The United States Supreme Court accepted review.

ISSUE: May a state condition a property use permit on an act not addressing the problem caused by the permitted use?

HOLDING AND DECISION: (Scalia, J.) No. A state may not condition a property use permit on an act not addressing the problem caused by the permitted use. A land-use regulation does not effect a taking if it substantially advances legitimate state interests and does not deny an owner economically viable use of his land. Thus, when a state finds a public interest and does not leave the owner with useless property, no taking occurs when a land use is prohibited. However, this constitutional propriety disappears when the condition substituted for outright prohibition fails to further the end advanced as the justification for the prohibition. When this occurs, the prohibition no longer becomes a vehicle for advancing a state interest, but rather a manner of extorting a property right without paying just compensation. Here, the recognized public interest was preventing the blockage of the beach from public view. The condition, providing an easement for lateral public access along the beach, does nothing to alleviate this perceived problem. The conditional use, therefore, fails to advance a state interest and therefore constitutes a taking. Reversed.

▶ ANALYSIS

The Court was far from clear as to what sort of nexus must exist between a condition and the interest advanced by the original prohibition. At one point, the opinion notes that a taking will occur if there is "utterly" no connection, which implies only a slight relationship as being necessary. On the other hand, language in the opinion speaks of a "substantial relationship" as being necessary.

Quicknotes

DUE PROCESS CLAUSE Clauses found in the Fifth and Fourteenth Amendments to the United States Constitution, providing that no person shall be deprived of "life, liberty, or property, without due process of law."

JUST COMPENSATION The right guaranteed by the Fifth Amendment to the United States Constitution of a person, when his property is taken for public use by the state, to receive adequate compensation in order to restore him to the position he enjoyed prior to the appropriation.

LAND-USE PERMIT Permit to utilize or develop property for a particular use described therein.

NEXUS Presence; contact.

PROHIBITION Law or statute that prohibits certain activity.

PROPERTY RIGHTS A legal right in specified personal or real property.

PUBLIC EASEMENT The right to utilize a portion of another's real property for a specific use that is reserved to the public.

PUBLIC INTEREST Something in which the public has either a monetary or legal interest.

TAKING A governmental action that substantially deprives an owner of the use and enjoyment of his or her property, requiring compensation.

Dolan v. City of Tigard

Beachfront property owner (P) v. City (D)

512 U.S. 374 (1994).

NATURE OF CASE: Review of order upholding conditions imposed on a building permit.

FACT SUMMARY: The City of Tigard (D) conditioned approval of Dolan's (P) application for a building permit on dedication of a part of her property for a floodplain easement and pedestrian/bicycle path.

> ## 🏛 RULE OF LAW
> A city may condition a land-use permit upon dedication of the land to a public use if such dedication is roughly proportional to the impact upon the community caused by the proposed land use.

FACTS: Dolan (P) operated a retail establishment in Tigard, Oregon (the City) (D). She applied for a building permit that would have approximately doubled the size of the store. The local planning commission conditioned approval of the permit on Dolan (P) dedicating a portion of the property, which fronted a 100-year floodplain, as a public easement for a floodplain and a bikeway. The dedicated portion of her property would have equaled about 15 percent thereof. The stated rationale for the condition imposed by the commission was that the easement would address concerns of increased traffic congestion due to the larger store, and increased flood hazard due to the increase in impermeable surface. After the city council approved the conditions, Dolan (P) challenged the dedication requirement as an uncompensated taking of her property under the Fifth Amendment. The trial court found in favor of the City (D), and the Oregon Supreme Court affirmed. The United States Supreme Court granted review.

ISSUE: May a city condition a land-use permit upon dedication of the land to public use if such dedication is roughly proportional to the impact upon the community caused by the proposed land use?

HOLDING AND DECISION: (Rehnquist, C.J.) Yes. A city may condition a land-use permit upon dedication of the land to public use if such dedication is roughly proportional to the impact upon the community caused by the proposed land use. The Fifth and Fourteenth Amendments mandate that, if government takes private property, just compensation must be paid. This rule conflicts with the right of local government to properly regulate use of property within its jurisdiction, and litigation on this issue usually deals with where legitimate regulation ends and taking occurs. This Court has held that a land-use permit cannot be conditioned on a giving up of property rights having no relation to the owner's proposed use. What must be answered in this case is the level of relation needed between the proposed owner's development and the city's mandated dedication that will sustain Fifth Amendment scrutiny. Some states require only a generalized statement as to the connection to survive due process concerns, a standard this Court considers too lax. Others require an exacting, particularized nexus between the development and the conditions imposed thereon, which this Court considers too stringent a standard. Rather, this Court believes that the best test to balance the competing interest is one that requires a "rough proportionality" between the burden caused on the community by the development and the condition placed on the owner. Using that standard here, the alleged burdens cited by the commission were (1) increased flooding hazard due to increased impermeable surface, and (2) increased traffic. The condition imposed, dedication of about 15 percent of Dolan's (P) land for a floodplain and bike path, bears little relation to the concerns supposedly being addressed. This being so the condition imposed was in violation of the Fifth and Fourteenth Amendments. Reversed and remanded.

▶ ANALYSIS

For most of the Twentieth Century, federal courts had been extremely deferential to governments when use regulations were challenged. The Takings Clause seemed to be something of a constitutional dead letter. Then, the case *Nollan v. California Coastal Commission*, 483 U.S. 825 (1987), suddenly turned matters around, in that a landowner was able to prevail over a governmental regulatory body. The present case seems to portend a continuation of that trend.

■■■

Quicknotes

DEDICATION Conveyance of land to the public by a private owner.

EASEMENT The right to utilize a portion of another's real property for a specific use.

FIFTH AMENDMENT Provides that no person shall be compelled to serve as a witness against himself, or be subject to trial for the same offense twice, or be deprived of life, liberty, or property without due process of law.

JUST COMPENSATION The right guaranteed by the Fifth Amendment to the United States Constitution of a person, when his property is taken for public use by the state, to receive adequate compensation in order to restore him to the position he enjoyed prior to the appropriation.

LAND-USE PERMIT Permit to utilize or develop property for a particular use described therein.

PUBLIC USE Basis for governmental taking of property pursuant to its power of eminent domain so that property taken may be utilized for the benefit of the public at large.

TAKING A governmental action that substantially deprives an owner of the use and enjoyment of his or her property, requiring compensation.

■≡■

Koontz v. St. Johns River Water Management District

Landowner (P) v. State agency (D)

133 S.Ct. 2586 (2013).

NATURE OF CASE: Appeal from state supreme court decision holding that state agency's order requiring landowner to pay for improvements to wet lands not attached to landowner's property was not unlawful.

FACT SUMMARY: Koontz (P) sought to develop a portion of wetlands he owned to build an office building. To mitigate the environment impact, St. Johns River Water Management District ("the District") (D) allegedly ordered him to convey several acres of his undeveloped property to the state as a conservation easement. In addition, the District (D) allegedly required Koontz (P) to hire contractors and fund repairs to District-owned wetlands several miles away.

🏛 RULE OF LAW
Under the unconstitutional conditions doctrine, a government agency may condition the approval of a permit on the landowner's dedication of property to the public only if there is a nexus or rough proportionality between the property the government agency demands and the social costs of the permit applicant's development plans.

FACTS: Koontz (P) sought to develop a portion of wetlands he owned to build an office building. Specifically, he planned on developing 3.7 acres of property. He offered an additional, contiguous eleven acres to the state as a conservation easement to mitigate the environmental impact. The St. Johns River Water Management District ("the District") (D) allegedly ordered him to decrease the size of the development and convey fourteen acres to the state as the conservation easement. In addition, the District (D) allegedly required Koontz (P) to hire contractors and fund repairs to District-owned wetlands several miles away. Koontz (P) believed the demands were excessive and brought suit in a Florida state court against the District (D). The suit alleged the District's (D) demands constituted a taking without just compensation pursuant to the particular Florida statute. He did not file a Fifth Amendment takings claim. A state trial court found the District's (D) demands that Koontz (P) fund repairs to other District-owned wetlands lacked a nexus and rough proportionality to the environmental impact of Koontz's (P) proposed development. Eventually, the Florida Supreme Court reversed. The United States Supreme Court granted Koontz's (P) petition for further review.

ISSUE: Under the unconstitutional conditions doctrine, may a government agency condition the approval of a permit on the landowner's dedication of property to the public only if there is a nexus or rough proportionality

between the property the government agency demands and the social costs of the permit applicant's development plans?

HOLDING AND DECISION: (Alito, J.) Yes. Under the unconstitutional conditions doctrine, a government agency may condition the approval of a permit on the landowner's dedication of property to the public only if there is a nexus or rough proportionality between the property the government agency demands and the social costs of the permit applicant's development plans. The doctrine protects landowners' Fifth Amendment right to just compensation for property the government takes during a permitting process. The rationale for the doctrine is that permit applicants, in need of various building and environmental permits to proceed, are vulnerable to governmental coercion. The permit is likely worth more than the uninhabitable land the government seeks to take. By forcing a landowner to deed over a certain portion of land for conservation purposes, the government may force a landowner to give up land voluntarily than normally would require just compensation under the Fifth Amendment. Accordingly, while governments may order landowners to remedy or mitigate the environmental impacts of their projects, a government may not leverage its ability to grant a permit to pursue other governmental interests that lack a nexus to the environmental impacts of the project in question. That is the case here. Allegedly forcing Koontz (P) to fund repairs for wetlands unrelated to his project does not bear a nexus to the impacts of his particular project. The Florida Supreme Court did not analyze this case using these principles. Accordingly, the matter is reversed and remanded for the state courts to determine if the District (D) actually made the demand to Koontz (P) to repair the unrelated wetlands. Reversed and remanded.

DISSENT: (Kagan, J.) The majority has mischaracterized the actions of the District (D) in this case. If the District (D) ordered Koontz (P) to repair the unrelated wetlands, that is a monetary obligation, not the taking of real property. Accordingly, the unconstitutional conditions doctrine does not apply. This Court has already decided that the Fifth Amendment does not apply when the government requires a private entity to make a monetary contribution as opposed to taking real property. The fear is that this decision may prohibit municipalities from applying various land use fees that have been common for decades.

Continued on next page.

▶ *ANALYSIS*

Taxes and fees upon land are not considered takings. The minority argued the District's (D) actions were more of a permissible tax or fee upon the landowner and were independent of the permitting process. The majority's analysis focused on the District's (D) actions as a whole, finding that its' alleged order that Koontz (P) turn over additional lands and repair others constituted an unconstitutional condition in the permitting process.

■━■

Quicknotes

TAKINGS CLAUSE Provision of the Fifth Amendment to the United States Constitution prohibiting the government from taking private property for public use without providing just compensation therefor.

■━■

Glossary

Common Latin Words and Phrases Encountered in the Law

A FORTIORI: Because one fact exists or has been proven, therefore a second fact that is related to the first fact must also exist.

A PRIORI: From the cause to the effect. A term of logic used to denote that when one generally accepted truth is shown to be a cause, another particular effect must necessarily follow.

AB INITIO: From the beginning; a condition which has existed throughout, as in a marriage which was void ab initio.

ACTUS REUS: The wrongful act; in criminal law, such action sufficient to trigger criminal liability.

AD VALOREM: According to value; an ad valorem tax is imposed upon an item located within the taxing jurisdiction calculated by the value of such item.

AMICUS CURIAE: Friend of the court. Its most common usage takes the form of an amicus curiae brief, filed by a person who is not a party to an action but is nonetheless allowed to offer an argument supporting his legal interests.

ARGUENDO: In arguing. A statement, possibly hypothetical, made for the purpose of argument, is one made arguendo.

BILL QUIA TIMET: A bill to quiet title (establish ownership) to real property.

BONA FIDE: True, honest, or genuine. May refer to a person's legal position based on good faith or lacking notice of fraud (such as a bona fide purchaser for value) or to the authenticity of a particular document (such as a bona fide last will and testament).

CAUSA MORTIS: With approaching death in mind. A gift causa mortis is a gift given by a party who feels certain that death is imminent.

CAVEAT EMPTOR: Let the buyer beware. This maxim is reflected in the rule of law that a buyer purchases at his own risk because it is his responsibility to examine, judge, test, and otherwise inspect what he is buying.

CERTIORARI: A writ of review. Petitions for review of a case by the United States Supreme Court are most often done by means of a writ of certiorari.

CONTRA: On the other hand. Opposite. Contrary to.

CORAM NOBIS: Before us; writs of error directed to the court that originally rendered the judgment.

CORAM VOBIS: Before you; writs of error directed by an appellate court to a lower court to correct a factual error.

CORPUS DELICTI: The body of the crime; the requisite elements of a crime amounting to objective proof that a crime has been committed.

CUM TESTAMENTO ANNEXO, ADMINISTRATOR (ADMINISTRATOR C.T.A.): With will annexed; an administrator c.t.a. settles an estate pursuant to a will in which he is not appointed.

DE BONIS NON, ADMINISTRATOR (ADMINISTRATOR D.B.N.): Of goods not administered; an administrator d.b.n. settles a partially settled estate.

DE FACTO: In fact; in reality; actually. Existing in fact but not officially approved or engendered.

DE JURE: By right; lawful. Describes a condition that is legitimate "as a matter of law," in contrast to the term "de facto," which connotes something existing in fact but not legally sanctioned or authorized. For example, de facto segregation refers to segregation brought about by housing patterns, etc., whereas de jure segregation refers to segregation created by law.

DE MINIMIS: Of minimal importance; insignificant; a trifle; not worth bothering about.

DE NOVO: Anew; a second time; afresh. A trial de novo is a new trial held at the appellate level as if the case originated there and the trial at a lower level had not taken place.

DICTA: Generally used as an abbreviated form of obiter dicta, a term describing those portions of a judicial opinion incidental or not necessary to resolution of the specific question before the court. Such nonessential statements and remarks are not considered to be binding precedent.

DUCES TECUM: Refers to a particular type of writ or subpoena requesting a party or organization to produce certain documents in their possession.

EN BANC: Full bench. Where a court sits with all justices present rather than the usual quorum.

EX PARTE: For one side or one party only. An ex parte proceeding is one undertaken for the benefit of only one party, without notice to, or an appearance by, an adverse party.

EX POST FACTO: After the fact. An ex post facto law is a law that retroactively changes the consequences of a prior act.

EX REL.: Abbreviated form of the term "ex relatione," meaning upon relation or information. When the state brings an action in which it has no interest against an individual at the instigation of one who has a private interest in the matter.

FORUM NON CONVENIENS: Inconvenient forum. Although a court may have jurisdiction over the case, the action should be tried in a more conveniently located court, one to which parties and witnesses may more easily travel, for example.

GUARDIAN AD LITEM: A guardian of an infant as to litigation, appointed to represent the infant and pursue his/her rights.

HABEAS CORPUS: You have the body. The modern writ of habeas corpus is a writ directing that a person (body) being detained (such as a prisoner) be brought before the court so that the legality of his detention can be judicially ascertained.

IN CAMERA: In private, in chambers. When a hearing is held before a judge in his chambers or when all spectators are excluded from the courtroom.

IN FORMA PAUPERIS: In the manner of a pauper. A party who proceeds in forma pauperis because of his poverty is one who is allowed to bring suit without liability for costs.

INFRA: Below, under. A word referring the reader to a later part of a book. (The opposite of supra.)

IN LOCO PARENTIS: In the place of a parent.

IN PARI DELICTO: Equally wrong; a court of equity will not grant requested relief to an applicant who is in pari delicto, or as much at fault in the transactions giving rise to the controversy as is the opponent of the applicant.

IN PARI MATERIA: On like subject matter or upon the same matter. Statutes relating to the same person or things are said to be in pari materia. It is a general rule of statutory construction that such statutes should be construed together, i.e., looked at as if they together constituted one law.

IN PERSONAM: Against the person. Jurisdiction over the person of an individual.

IN RE: In the matter of. Used to designate a proceeding involving an estate or other property.

IN REM: A term that signifies an action against the res, or thing. An action in rem is basically one that is taken directly against property, as distinguished from an action in personam, i.e., against the person.

INTER ALIA: Among other things. Used to show that the whole of a statement, pleading, list, statute, etc., has not been set forth in its entirety.

INTER PARTES: Between the parties. May refer to contracts, conveyances or other transactions having legal significance.

INTER VIVOS: Between the living. An inter vivos gift is a gift made by a living grantor, as distinguished from bequests contained in a will, which pass upon the death of the testator.

IPSO FACTO: By the mere fact itself.

JUS: Law or the entire body of law.

LEX LOCI: The law of the place; the notion that the rights of parties to a legal proceeding are governed by the law of the place where those rights arose.

MALUM IN SE: Evil or wrong in and of itself; inherently wrong. This term describes an act that is wrong by its very nature, as opposed to one which would not be wrong but for the fact that there is a specific legal prohibition against it (malum prohibitum).

MALUM PROHIBITUM: Wrong because prohibited, but not inherently evil. Used to describe something that is wrong because it is expressly forbidden by law but that is not in and of itself evil, e.g., speeding.

MANDAMUS: We command. A writ directing an official to take a certain action.

MENS REA: A guilty mind; a criminal intent. A term used to signify the mental state that accompanies a crime or other prohibited act. Some crimes require only a general mens rea (general intent to do the prohibited act), but others, like assault with intent to murder, require the existence of a specific mens rea.

MODUS OPERANDI: Method of operating; generally refers to the manner or style of a criminal in committing crimes, admissible in appropriate cases as evidence of the identity of a defendant.

NEXUS: A connection to.

NISI PRIUS: A court of first impression. A nisi prius court is one where issues of fact are tried before a judge or jury.

N.O.V. (NON OBSTANTE VEREDICTO): Notwithstanding the verdict. A judgment n.o.v. is a judgment given in favor of one party despite the fact that a verdict was returned in favor of the other party, the justification being that the verdict either had no reasonable support in fact or was contrary to law.

NUNC PRO TUNC: Now for then. This phrase refers to actions that may be taken and will then have full retroactive effect.

PENDENTE LITE: Pending the suit; pending litigation under way.

PER CAPITA: By head; beneficiaries of an estate, if they take in equal shares, take per capita.

PER CURIAM: By the court; signifies an opinion ostensibly written "by the whole court" and with no identified author.

PER SE: By itself, in itself; inherently.

PER STIRPES: By representation. Used primarily in the law of wills to describe the method of distribution where a person, generally because of death, is unable to take that which is left to him by the will of another, and therefore his heirs divide such property between them rather than take under the will individually.

PRIMA FACIE: On its face, at first sight. A prima facie case is one that is sufficient on its face, meaning that the evidence supporting it is adequate to establish the case until contradicted or overcome by other evidence.

PRO TANTO: For so much; as far as it goes. Often used in eminent domain cases when a property owner receives partial payment for his land without prejudice to his right to bring suit for the full amount he claims his land to be worth.

QUANTUM MERUIT: As much as he deserves. Refers to recovery based on the doctrine of unjust enrichment in those cases in which a party has rendered valuable services or furnished materials that were accepted and enjoyed by another under circumstances that would reasonably notify the recipient that the rendering party expected to be paid. In essence, the law implies a contract to pay the reasonable value of the services or materials furnished.

QUASI: Almost like; as if; nearly. This term is essentially used to signify that one subject or thing is almost analogous to another but that material differences between them do exist. For example, a quasi-criminal proceeding is one that is not strictly criminal but shares enough of the same characteristics to require some of the same safeguards (e.g., procedural due process must be followed in a parole hearing).

QUID PRO QUO: Something for something. In contract law, the consideration, something of value, passed between the parties to render the contract binding.

RES GESTAE: Things done; in evidence law, this principle justifies the admission of a statement that would otherwise be hearsay when it is made so closely to the event in question as to be said to be a part of it, or with such spontaneity as not to have the possibility of falsehood.

RES IPSA LOQUITUR: The thing speaks for itself. This doctrine gives rise to a rebuttable presumption of negligence when the instrumentality causing the injury was within the exclusive control of the defendant, and the injury was one that does not normally occur unless a person has been negligent.

RES JUDICATA: A matter adjudged. Doctrine which provides that once a court of competent jurisdiction has rendered a final judgment or decree on the merits, that judgment or decree is conclusive upon the parties to the case and prevents them from engaging in any other litigation on the points and issues determined therein.

RESPONDEAT SUPERIOR: Let the master reply. This doctrine holds the master liable for the wrongful acts of his servant (or the principal for his agent) in those cases in which the servant (or agent) was acting within the scope of his authority at the time of the injury.

STARE DECISIS: To stand by or adhere to that which has been decided. The common law doctrine of stare decisis attempts to give security and certainty to the law by following the policy that once a principle of law as applicable to a certain set of facts has been set forth in a decision, it forms a precedent which will subsequently be followed, even though a different decision might be made were it the first time the question had arisen. Of course, stare decisis is not an inviolable principle and is departed from in instances where there is good cause (e.g., considerations of public policy led the Supreme Court to disregard prior decisions sanctioning segregation).

SUPRA: Above. A word referring a reader to an earlier part of a book.

ULTRA VIRES: Beyond the power. This phrase is most commonly used to refer to actions taken by a corporation that are beyond the power or legal authority of the corporation.

Addendum of French Derivatives

IN PAIS: Not pursuant to legal proceedings.

CHATTEL: Tangible personal property.

CY PRES: Doctrine permitting courts to apply trust funds to purposes not expressed in the trust but necessary to carry out the settlor's intent.

PER AUTRE VIE: For another's life; during another's life. In property law, an estate may be granted that will terminate upon the death of someone other than the grantee.

PROFIT A PRENDRE: A license to remove minerals or other produce from land.

VOIR DIRE: Process of questioning jurors as to their predispositions about the case or parties to a proceeding in order to identify those jurors displaying bias or prejudice.

Casenote® Legal Briefs

Administrative Law	Breyer, Stewart, Sunstein, Vermeule & Herz
Administrative Law	Cass, Diver, Beermann & Freeman
Administrative Law	Funk, Shapiro & Weaver
Administrative Law	Mashaw, Merrill & Shane
Administrative Law	Strauss, Rakoff, Farina & Metzger (Gellhorn & Byse)
Agency & Partnership	Hynes & Loewenstein
Antitrust	Pitofsky, Goldschmid & Wood
Antitrust	Sullivan, Hovenkamp & Schelanski
Bankruptcy	Warren, Bussel & Skeel
Business Organizations	Allen, Kraakman & Subramanian
Business Organizations	Bauman, Weiss & Palmiter
Business Organizations	Hamilton, Macey & Moll
Business Organizations	Klein, Ramseyer & Bainbridge
Business Organizations	O'Kelley & Thompson
Business Organizations	Smiddy & Cunningham
Civil Procedure	Field, Kaplan & Clermont
Civil Procedure	Freer & Perdue
Civil Procedure	Friedenthal, Miller, Sexton & Hershkoff
Civil Procedure	Hazard, Tait, Fletcher & Bundy
Civil Procedure	Marcus, Redish, Sherman & Pfander
Civil Procedure	Subrin, Minow, Brodin & Main
Civil Procedure	Yeazell
Commercial Law	LoPucki, Warren, Keating & Mann
Commercial Law	Warren & Walt
Commercial Law	Whaley & McJohn
Community Property	Bird
Community Property	Blumberg
Conflicts	Brilmayer, Goldsmith & O'Connor
Conflicts	Currie, Kay, Kramer & Roosevelt
Constitutional Law	Brest, Levinson, Balkin & Amar
Constitutional Law	Chemerinsky
Constitutional Law	Choper, Fallon, Kamisar & Shiffrin (Lockhart)
Constitutional Law	Farber, Eskridge & Frickey
Constitutional Law	Rotunda
Constitutional Law	Stone, Seidman, Sunstein, Tushnet & Karlan
Constitutional Law	Sullivan & Gunther
Constitutional Law	Varat, Amar & Cohen
Contracts	Ayres & Klass
Contracts	Barnett
Contracts	Blum & Bushaw
Contracts	Burton
Contracts	Calamari, Perillo & Bender
Contracts	Crandall & Whaley
Contracts	Dawson, Harvey, Henderson & Baird
Contracts	Farnsworth, Sanger, Cohen, Brooks & Garvin
Contracts	Fuller & Eisenberg
Contracts	Knapp, Crystal & Prince
Copyright	Cohen, Loren, Okediji & O'Rourke
Copyright	Gorman, Ginsburg & Reese
Copyright, Patent, and Trademark	Goldstein & Reese
Criminal Law	Bonnie, Coughlin, Jeffries & Low
Criminal Law	Boyce, Dripps & Perkins
Criminal Law	Dressler & Garvey
Criminal Law	Kadish, Schulhofer, Steiker & Barkow
Criminal Law	Kaplan, Weisberg & Binder
Criminal Procedure	Allen, Stuntz, Hoffman, Livingston & Leipold
Criminal Procedure	Chemerinsky & Levenson
Criminal Procedure	Dressler & Thomas
Criminal Procedure	Kamisar, LaFave, Israel, King, Kerr & Primus
Criminal Procedure	Saltzburg & Capra
Debtors and Creditors	Warren & Westbrook
Employment Discrimination	Friedman
Employment Discrimination	Zimmer, Sullivan & White
Employment Law	Rothstein & Liebman
Environmental Law	Percival, Schroeder, Miller & Leape
Environmental Law	Plater, Abrams, Goldfarb, Graham, Heinzerling & Wirth
Estates and Trusts	Sterk, Leslie & Dobris
Evidence	Broun, Mosteller & Giannelli
Evidence	Fisher
Evidence	Mueller & Kirkpatrick
Evidence	Park & Friedman
Family Law	Areen, Spindelman & Tsoukala
Family Law	Ellman, Kurtz, Weithorn, Bix, Czapanskiy & Eichner
Family Law	Harris, Carbone & Teitelbaum
Family Law	Wadlington, O'Brien & Wilson
Family Law	Weisberg & Appleton
Federal Courts	Fallon, Meltzer & Shapiro (Hart & Wechsler)
Federal Courts	Low, Jeffries & Bradley
Health Law	Furrow, Greaney, Johnson, Jost & Schwartz
Immigration Law	Aleinikoff, Martin, Motomura & Fullerton
Immigration Law	Legomsky & Rodriguez
Insurance Law	Abraham
Intellectual Property	Merges, Menell & Lemley
International Business Transactions	Folsom, Gordon, Spanogle & Fitzgerald
International Law	Carter & Weiner
International Law	Damrosch, Henkin, Murphy & Smit
International Law	Dunoff, Ratner & Wippman
Labor Law	Cox, Bok, Gorman & Finkin
Land Use	Callies, Freilich & Roberts
Oil & Gas	Lowe, Anderson, Smith & Pierce
Patent Law	Adelman, Rader & Thomas
Products Liability	Owen, Montgomery & Davis
Professional Responsibility	Gillers
Professional Responsibility	Hazard, Koniak, Cramton, Cohen & Wendel
Professional Responsibility	Martyn & Fox
Property	Casner, Leach, French, Korngold & VanderVelde
Property	Cribbet, Findley, Smith & Dzienkowski
Property	Donahue, Kauper & Martin
Property	Dukeminier, Krier, Alexander, Schill & Strahilevitz
Property	Haar & Liebman
Property	Kurtz, Hovenkamp & Brown
Property	Nelson, Stoebuck & Whitman
Property	Rabin, Kwall, Kwall & Arnold
Property	Singer, Berger, Davidson, & Peñalver
Real Estate	Korngold & Goldstein
Real Estate Transactions	Nelson, Whitman, Burkhart & Freyermuth
Remedies	Laycock
Remedies	Shoben, Tabb & Janutis
Securities Regulation	Coffee & Sale
Securities Regulation	Cox, Hillman & Langevoort
Sports Law	Weiler, Roberts, Abrams & Ross
Taxation (Corporate)	Lind, Schwartz, Lathrope & Rosenberg
Taxation (Individual)	Bankman, Shaviro & Stark
Taxation (Individual)	Burke & Friel
Taxation (Individual)	Freeland, Lathrope, Lind & Stephens
Torts	Dobbs, Hayden & Bublick
Torts	Epstein & Sharkey
Torts	Franklin, Rabin & Green
Torts	Goldberg, Sebok & Zipursky
Torts	Henderson, Pearson & Kysar
Torts	Schwartz, Kelly & Partlett (Prosser)
Trademark	Ginsburg, Litman & Kevlin
Wills, Trusts & Estates	Dukeminier & Sitkoff
Wills, Trusts & Estates	Scoles, Halbach, Roberts & Begleiter